Lost Oasis

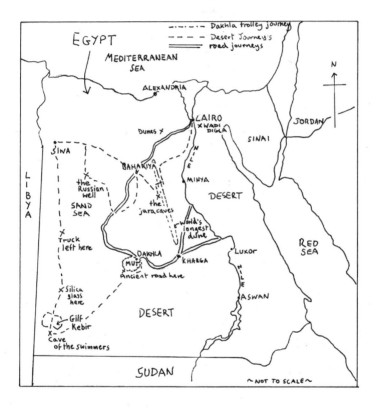

Lost Oasis

In Search of Paradise

ROBERT TWIGGER

Weidenfeld & Nicolson
LONDON

First published in hardback in Great Britain in 2007 by
Weidenfeld & Nicolson
an imprint of the Orion Publishing Group Ltd
Orion House, 5 Upper St Martin's Lane,
London WC2H 9EA

1 3 5 7 9 10 8 6 4 2

A CIP catalogue record for this book is available
from the British Library.

ISBN: 978 0 297 84812 7

Typeset by Input Data Services Ltd, Frome

Printed and bound in Great Britain by Mackays of Chatham plc
Chatham, Kent

The Orion Publishing Group's policy is to use papers that are natural,
renewable and recyclable and made from wood grown in sustainable
forests. The logging and manufacturing processes are expected to
conform to the environmental regulations of the country of origin.

Every effort has been made to fulfil requirements with regard to
reproducing copyright material. The author and publisher will be
glad to rectify any omissions at the earliest opportunity.

CONTENTS

Plate Section Captions

PLATES

I went in search of paradise and this is what I found

I would like to thank all those who helped me in the making of this book. Some names I cannot mention but among those I can are: Abdelhamid Abouyoussef, Hosam Mostafa, Richard Head, Mahmoud Mohareb, Richard Netherwood, Dr Maryam's Pharmacy, Dave Morrison, Mike Welland, Arita Baaijens, Shaheer Youstos, Ahmed Mestakawi, Wak Kani, Fawzia Fadel, Jean and Tony Twigger, Zarzora expedition company, Ian Preece, Stephanie Cabot, Natasha Fairweather, and all my usual partners in crime. Also Richard Mohun and Claudia Filsinger-Mohun.

For anyone interested in learning the craft of desert exploration please check my website theexplorerschool.com

To Helena

One

THE CONTAINER NOT THE CONTENT

I

The ignominious, ever-present need for money. What bill broke us? What expense broke my wife's nerve? I was like someone dragging their feet in a game or a conversation, hoping for it to end. At last she cracked and said, 'Let's move to Egypt.' So we did.

She left, and I remained to cram our life of the last five years into a twenty-foot-long container on an old airfield in the Oxfordshire countryside. The first time I drove out there, having investigated and rejected other more expensive forms of storage, I was strangely excited. The airfield was like a deserted, weed-strewn racetrack around rows of big Nissen huts. These had stored green goddesses, the army firetrucks used during the firemen's strike. Now they were used by myriad small businesses: a forklift and a guy and a van that turned up throughout the day to take shrink-wrapped goods away. I drove around the perimeter road looking for speed bumps but there were only two; this meant I could drive quite fast to my container, which was stacked on top of another container and reachable via a wide metal stair and gangway. I was inordinately proud of this container and the airfield-turned-business-park – no 'park' was the wrong word; it conjured up images of company cars and mown lawns and flags outside glass-fronted buildings. The airfield was more of a marginal business zone, a place for dodginess and hiding things in containers and hooped hangars with massive gleaming padlocks. Ringed by a security fence with an amiable old guard on the electric barrier, this place felt like somewhere I ought to have found years ago; it felt like a real zone of possibility. I fantasized about renting one of the mini-hangars that were each as big as three basketball pitches. I knew of course that it was too late, which made the fantasizing easier. I was selling up and leaving and had no need of a hangar to start something in. Yet I felt keenly that merely owning or renting one of these hangars (cheap at £150 a week, I discovered) could be the start of something new and exciting.

I was particularly happy with the twenty-four-hour access I could have to my container. I would visit late at night after the pubs had shut (not that I was going to pubs much, but I was always up at that time) or early in the morning when no one else was on the roads except milk floats and Belgian lorries. The pain of packing up the house and all its contents was alleviated, a little, by the magic of having a container I could visit at all hours.

But the pain of packing up still took its toll. Somehow it is beyond the scope of this book, but I definitely began to lose my bearings. I became sad and hopeless, close to tears, though deep repressive instincts made the relief of crying impossible. I thought about those sadness-inducing chemicals that crying voids from your body, the unhappiness poisons you store up year after year, and I wanted to be rid of them; but I couldn't. I became angry with my family and the world – why was I stuck trying to pack up a house when I should be in Egypt writing a book about the desert?

I learnt that I was psychologically far frailer than I had imagined. Alone, without support, I began to lose my way. Days went by and all I would achieve would be to discover the cost of hiring a skip. Indecisiveness ruled. Plus I was desperate to get my deposit back on the expensive house we had rented as our home for the last five years. Money again. This time I couldn't afford to walk away. I had known a short period of relative wealth but now I was always bumping up against a shortage of funds. It was not a great feeling but I was used to it. But we were at the limit now, and Egypt would save us – plus I could write a book there, which would be cheaper than keeping a house in England and making expensive research trips abroad.

As soon as my wife had suggested Egypt as the solution to our financial worries my immediate thought was that I would write a book about the desert. At that moment it felt like a dream come true, one that I can map precisely from an early reading of Earle Stanley Gardner's *Hunting the Desert Whale*, via Geoffrey Moorhouse's *The Fearful Void* and the James Stewart movie *Flight of the Phoenix*; a dream that became realer with my first visit to Egypt, twelve years ago, to a Bedouin camp near El Alamein. I stayed at the El Alamein resthouse on the site of the battle and had terrible dreams all night of steel, screams, thunder and fire. The desert here was hard underfoot, good for tanks; some vegetation – tamarisk, spinosa, saltbush and a cluster of date palms by the road. I could see the moonlight reflected off this desert as I walked across it to the sea, which was guarded by a tin shack full of sleepy soldiers.

The Bedouins lived between the sea and the resthouse. They showed me their hunting falcons when they saw my eagle-head ring, which I wore at the time as a mild protest against being a high-school teacher in Japan. I felt at home with them and their communal pot of food, from which we all ate with our hands. The oldest was a wily old man who wanted some money for the food, but when I gave him two Egyptian pounds, which was about a dollar, he was obviously disappointed. But this was when I knew the Bedouin were my kind of people – his son and daughter-in-law and other sundry relatives all burst out laughing. Instead of rounding on the foreigner they saw the funny side of Grandad's great scheme gone wrong. These were desert people and I wanted to know them better, live where they lived, know the secrets of their desert existence.

On another trip I met a rootless American who lived in Alexandria and rode his big BMW bike into the desert. The hugeness of the Sahara is more apparent when you are on the edge of it in a big city. You think of the city as the biggest thing around and then your perceptions get upturned when you see the desert as it stretches without road or dwelling or anything (I was still hazy then about the exact contents of the desert) for one, two, three thousand miles – as far as the tropical heart of Africa, another world from the sunny Mediterranean of Alexandria. This American, in his purple T-shirt, drinking spritzers at the Spitfire bar in Alex, made me see that the hugeness of the desert could be accessed by a private individual – as long as he had a motorbike, of course. Up until then I had considered all deserts the preserve of armies and explorers with sponsorship from Shell and BP.

A few years later, in Cairo on holiday, now married to Samia, I attended a slide show given by a Frenchman living and working in Cairo as a teacher at the lycée. Eric was full of irrepressible verbal energy: he could talk all night, which he did, over hundreds and hundreds of slides of his two trips to the White Desert and the Sinai. He drove a battered Lada Niva which he'd bought in Egypt for £1,500 (then he'd hired another to be safe in the desert). This slide show was the inadvertent cause of my wife losing one of her oldest friends, since I insisted we stay until the very very last slide, which was after 2 a.m. The friend who had invited us in the first place was exceedingly bored, especially as she didn't understand French. But I needed to ask Eric lots of questions about Lada Nivas, and water, and getting bogged in sand, etc. At the end when I asked him these questions he answered at great length, which further delayed our departure. For this reason Samia's friend took against me (she was relying on us for a lift) and the relationship never recovered. So already a certain ruthlessness had entered my passion to get out into the desert.

Then I bought an out-of-date Haynes workshop manual for the Toyota Land Cruiser 1968–80. It was reduced in a bookshop sale to 50p, and I couldn't resist the exploded diagrams of the military-looking FJ40 Jeep, the big simple engines and double gearboxes. Deserts brought me back to a childhood love of cars that had long been dormant, crushed under an ecologically informed series of anxieties that plagued my thirties. The car thing was further encouraged by reading Chris Scott's *Sahara Overland* handbook. This book is the last word, almost, on criss-crossing the Sahara by motorbike or car. It details the failings of Land-Rovers, the slack steering of Land Cruiser FJ61s, the ingenious brutal simplicity of the Niva's unitary shell construction. I read and reread this book, especially the section about cars. I had it by memory and the pages had a grey edge, like the page edges of a library copy of *Lady Chatterly's Lover*. The ostensible reason for this upsurge in interest, I now recall, was a novel I was writing, which metamorphosed later into something completely different but at the time involved three men starting a tour business using a knackered Land Cruiser with a trailer (there was a dead body in the trailer). It was a measure of my ignorance that I had no idea how impossible it is to tow a trailer through sand (the strain breaks the linkage and you can't reverse, which is essential for getting out of soft stuff) and yet two years later I would find myself doing this in reality (trying to set up a business with a knackered Land Cruiser) which was before I knew I would be going to the desert, since it was before that fateful night pouring Samia a glass of cheap red wine when all of a sudden she said, 'Let's move to Egypt.' To be fair, she also added, 'To save money.' But I simply nodded. The chance to escape my tedious life and do something exciting and unanticipated was irresistible. Because I often veto my wife's suggestions she had little power to resist when, perhaps unexpectedly, I wholeheartedly backed this idea.

The next day I started researching interesting stories about the desert, found good material about lost oases, threw in more research I had done for my novel, and when the publishers said maybe we were set to go.

I couldn't rid myself of the notion that there must be special significance attaching to having written a novel that I was now about to start living. Did that mean that novel-writing was a substitute for life? As good as life? Or that life was as fictional and ideational as novel-writing? Or did it mean that I was destined to be involved with deserts – and that if it didn't happen in the visible world it would happen in the invisible world of my mind? Already the compulsion to 'get out into the desert' (which is how I always put it to myself) was so strong it felt palpable. I was as keen and excited as someone looking forward to a date with a new lover. Whenever I thought about the desert, this urge to get out there came over me. It was especially hard to explain to others, since I didn't really know much about the desert except that there was precious little in it. It was a passion for nothingness – or so I assumed.

Around this time, late at night, I saw on TV the film of *The English Patient*. At first I thought it was corny nonsense; then, when I saw the tiny yellow biplane flying over the vastness of the dunes, I felt some deep truth had been revealed. A truth not just for hopeless romantics but for level-headed folk too. Strangely the book did not appeal so much, perhaps because by then I knew that the real-life English Patient, Laszlo Almasy, was not a womanizer, like the Ralph Fiennes character, but a homosexual fascist who founded the Hungarian Boy Scout movement.

Despite this unappealing background I soon discovered that Almasy (1895–1951) had pioneered desert exploration in Egypt and Sudan in the 1920s and 30s. A Hungarian aristocrat, he had also been a World War I fighter ace, had achieved several gliding and big-game hunting records and had spirited spies into Cairo right under the nose of the British during World War II; on a humbler scale he had studied car maintenance in Eastbourne, where he also went to school for a while. Shortly before his death King Farouk appointed him first director of the Cairo Desert Institute.

I ordered from Abebooks a German edition of Almasy's *Unknown Sahara*. I don't read German, especially in gothic script, but the photographs made it worth getting. Much later, I found a translation and it became my favourite book about the Egyptian Sahara. Looking at the photographs, turning the yellowing pages, I felt sand was about to drain out of the spine. Long, thin and suave-looking, Almasy is always smoking, even when he's map-reading or driving. Like many desert explorers of the 1930s he favoured long shorts and long socks – the Boy Scout influence, perhaps. He looked too thin and wimpy to be a man of action but he undoubtedly was. His cars were rudimentary and always overladen. In one photograph a tiny vehicle, piled high with gear, ascends an endless expanse of white sand. Some of the desert shots, in faded black and white, looked like the Antarctic or the surface of the moon.

I read, in a book of literary blunders, that it was a sign of Ondaatje's masterful style that you do not question the scene where the English Patient buries his De Havilland biplane and comes back ten years later and digs it up and flies away. This is considered, in literary circles, to be an impossibility, yet in 1992 a Long Range Desert Group 30cwt Chevrolet was found east of the Gilf Kebir, an area Almasy explored, and not far from the fictional aeroplane-burying scene. The truck, lost in 1941, was refuelled and its tyres reinflated, and it was then driven to El Alamein Military Museum. In the desert rust comes slowly, a thin golden glaze of a rust, especially on quality steel. Even cheap Shell 'benzine' tins, fifty years old, have the surface browning a can gets in wetter climates after a month or so. Under the sand there is even less rusting, and the dryness enables paper, wood and rubber to be preserved as if new. Petrol would evaporate over time, but not if it was in sealed aviation-fuel bottles or cans. The impossible was, as Ondaatje imagined, possible – but only in the desert.

Reading about Almasy I discovered his English counterpart,

Major Ralph Bagnold. In desert terms Almasy was Amundsen and Bagnold was Scott – sort of. Certainly desert enthusiasts divide into Bagnold or Almasy fans: if you like one you tend to dismiss the other.

Bagnold (1896–1990) was just as strange and multi-talented as Almasy. In his autobiography he relates with relish his early enthusiasm for building drains out of Plasticine, complete with working toilets. A master mechanic, he was an army engineer and then a member of the Signals Corps. Stationed in Egypt in the 1920s he climbed 'about sixty pyramids' before he got bored and started to explore the desert in a Model T Ford. Like his rival Almasy, he led many expeditions, looking for the lost oasis of Zerzura.

During World War II he started the Long Range Desert Group, a special-forces unit that carried the SAS into battle. I read about the LRDG and even searched for their old HQ in Maadi, near to my mother-in-law's flat, but owing to massive 1960s reconstruction I never found it. Heroic though the LRDG were, I could never get that interested in their doings. Bagnold only interested me when he was seaching for the lost oasis.

My reading intensified. It did not get much wider, or only accidentally, when I chanced upon a new book. Mostly it just got deeper. Endless rereading of Scott's handbook, where I almost always found things I had overlooked. I memorized the disadvantages of a 9 x 16 tyre on the half-shafts of a Land-Rover Series 3 (snaps 'em regularly), the myth of early-morning 'crust' on the dunes, the tendency for a Unimog 'to be a bit of a dog on the piste'. Scott's laconic, reserved yet humorous style appealed to me, as did the allusion in his chapter and section headings. 'Defenders in the Desert' was obviously 'Riders on the storm'; 'Mysteries of the Southern Piste' suggested to me the avant-garde Yugoslav film *WR Mysteries of the Organism* – I was giving Scott far more attention than his workaday handbook demanded. In short, I was becoming obsessed.

*

Scott had a website to promote his books and the tours he operated. He also sold old maps of the Sahara. I bought a 1913 'Zerzura' map, copied or taken from the *Geographical Journal*. The map was compiled by the traveller and writer William Joseph Harding King for an article entitled 'The Libyan Desert From Native Information'. All I cared about at this stage was that the map was the only one available that had the magic word 'Zerzura' printed on it. Zerzura was the name for the lost oasis searched for by Harding King and a dozen other twentieth-century explorers including Bagnold and Almasy. It is no exaggeration to say that the search for Zerzura drove the exploration of the eastern Sahara, the Libyan desert, as it was called – though half of it's in Egypt.

Zerzura had never been found. I fantasized about finding it myself at the same time as knowing it wasn't there. *But just imagine if it was.* A TV producer told me you could tell from looking at satellite images, but I wasn't convinced. What if it was inside a canyon with overhanging cliffs, as I had written in my novel? The water would be invisible.

Though it was getting out into the desert that drove my imagination, I knew that the search for Zerzura would be a way of organizing my obsession, of explaining it to others. The historical information involved fabulous tales of white stone gates carved with birds, sleeping kings and queens guarding treasure, flocks of birds over the oasis and three verdant valleys. All this was in a fifteenth-century treasure-hunting manual appropriately called *The Book of Treasures*, or in some translations, *The Book of Pearls*. In Arabic literature the pearl is a metaphor for wisdom, so I suspected that the lavish accounts of lost treasure might also serve a meta-phorical purpose. It might really be a handbook for seeking enlightenment, or very possibly both. I was getting used to that in Egypt. Don't always assume things only have one function.

The more I read and reread Scott's manual on desert expedi-tioning, the more expensive and complicated it appeared to be. You needed a vehicle, and Scott leaves you in little doubt that a Toyota Land Cruiser HJ61, if you get one with a non-rusty chassis, is the thing to have. It's a discontinued turbo diesel available in Europe but not England, as is his other strong recommendation, the Land Cruiser HJZ75, an even more spartan and utilitarian vehicle, favoured as an outback exploration tool by mining companies and other organizations with deep-desert interests.

'Deep desert' was another phrase I had acquired a liking and a use for. There was desert, which could be visited by ordinary people pootling along black asphalt; and there was deep desert – which only special vehicles, expensive special vehicles, could reach.

I had not even considered using camels, though in the Egyptian desert there is some reason for this. Water is so scarce that the official exploration of the place had to wait until motor cars were sufficiently advanced to make long journeys carrying all their fuel and water. The only camel expeditions skirted the giant waterless land-mass of the Gilf Kebir, an area the size of Switzerland. Only with the car expeditions of the 1920s and 30s could it be reached. And it was in the Gilf that Almasy claimed he found Zerzura, or three valleys with vegetation that might once have supported a community. Then and there the distant Gilf achieved mythical status, a promised land I promised myself I had to visit.

Both Bagnold and Almasy found desert-exploring expensive. Both had private incomes, though Almasy quickly blew his and relied on wealthy patrons and adventurous tourists to fund his desert trips. The nasty paradox was that I was escaping England to save money and yet embarking at the same time on a project I could barely afford. There had to be a cheaper way.

There was only one surviving member of the so-called Zerzura Club, a 1930s dining society composed of people who had searched for the lost oasis. This was Rupert Harding Newman, a former brigadier in the Tank Regiment and scrum-half for the army rugby XV, ninety-five years old and, though a little deaf, still with all his faculties. Unfortunately, because he lived so far north it took me two days to drive there and I perhaps foolishly broke my journey in Edinburgh, where I engaged in a lengthy whisky-drinking session with a friend of mine who lives there, which left me in poor condition for continuing the journey north the next day. To cut a long story short I was an hour late for the interview with Brigadier Harding Newman and he wasn't happy, though to his credit he quickly softened and told me to forget it. He was keen to drive me to the local hotel for a drink and I should have said yes immediately, instead I insisted on interviewing him, with a tape recorder, which made him a little stiff. His wife was present too, so although the experience was interesting in a historical sense I didn't really break through the layers of politeness and apology I had helped erect around myself after the debacle of arriving late.

Rupert was a short man, white-haired and moustached. In the hall of his large house he showed me a portrait of a Civil War ancestor – 'young Newman' – who was smiling and wearing armour. The house was on a farm, far north of Inverness; he had only lived there for about ten years, the move from the south of England prompted, I guessed, by the need to conserve money. He waved his hand about him as we passed through the large rooms: 'This place costs me a fortune to run.' I made a mental note: avoid expensive houses when you are entering the latter part of your tenth decade. His wife had better hearing and was younger, I guessed. I suspected he really wanted to get down to the hotel bar to get away from all these family surroundings, his big mug of tea and later his whisky and soda which he had every day at the same time. Three sugars in the tea, a brimming pint cup, and a biscuit too. A man of regular habits. Whenever I meet elderly people who seem to be doing OK, I ask myself what tips for living a long life can they pass on. In Harding Newman's case I would guess doing all that sport in his youth must have helped. Then there were his regular habits, and

11

that was about it. As for having a big house in Scotland, that seemed to be a negative influence if anything. Though he did like the long drives south, which he broke at a Travelodge near Carlisle.

Oh, and he was a big fan of organic honey, which he ate every day. Maybe honey is the secret.

The Travelodge, which he recommended heartily as a good place to take a break, came as an utter incongruity. Here was a man who had driven over dunes alongside Bagnold. Who had worn a dinner jacket in Wadi Halfa while seated next to Laszlo Almasy, the real English Patient. Who had helped found the most successful special-forces unit of World War II. And who was human after all and proving it by recommending a crap chain hotel on the M6.

Move with the times: another long-life tip.

'What was he like – Almasy, I mean?' I asked.

Rupert looked me straight in the eye and said, 'Perfectly nice chap.'

He was not so complimentary about everyone. Of Hugh Boustead, one of his fellow explorers, he said, 'Awful man. Full of himself. Didn't help. Useless, in fact.'

There was a death on that expedition – Colonel Strutt, one of the expedition sponsors, who fell from the running-board of the car and fatally punctured a lung, as his much younger wife drove in pursuit of a leopard they were chasing. 'She was a terrible driver,' said Rupert. 'Didn't know her limits.'

He loved cars, I could tell that. He was very proud of having his advanced driving test even at the advanced age of ninety-five. Bagnold loved cars too, as did Almasy, though Almasy is much less nerdy than Bagnold. This is where I sensed I parted company with those motorhead explorers. Cars are, despite my intense interest in Toyota Land Cruisers, one of the major despoilers of the planet. Cars are crap, intellectually speaking. We all use them, but it would be better if we didn't. Whenever I thought about making a car expedition I was excited about the place, about getting there, but disquieted, bored, even scared of the car side. Scared because cars invite breakdowns and extra costs and accidents. Cars divide desert explorers and I think in the end I will end up saying goodbye to cars and hello to something slower. I suspect that travel is measured in days' travelling rather than distance covered. Less is more. But all that would come later. Then and there I was right in with the car crowd.

Harding Newman was a tech-head, even at ninety-five. He complained that he had been unable to find a certain kind of rubber washer anywhere in Scotland to repair his soda siphon (he was proud of making all his soda himself). When I offered to join in the search he waved me friendlily away. I had missed the point, which was: you can't get the spare parts any more.

He was a likeable, simple, friendly and helpful man. Perhaps a bit shy. He told me he still got the *Geographical Journal*, that great publication that records almost all the exploration of the last two centuries, but with a wry grin he added, 'Can't understand the articles these days though.'

Neither did I. In Bagnold and Kennedy Shaw and Newbold's articles the meaning is clear. Tech-words, statistics and boring information intended to show off to peers are kept to a minimum. These days the *Geographical Journal* is not about exploration, it is about scientific research done in remote places. The writing lacks any literary merit – really, the computer-generated spam I receive from Viagra companies has more spark to it. The jargon is rife, a sure sign that things have gone deeply wrong somewhere. The decline of the *Geographical Journal* from something valued and interesting to all into a kind of score card between dull PhD types trying to 'advance' their careers is something overlooked as a major trend of our time. I suspect the kind of refreshing information once recorded at the *Geographical Journal* can now be found at confluence.org, the amateur website dedicated to visiting all the whole-integer intersections of latitude and longitude lines. The old institutions are dying and Harding Newman could only be ironic about it. Because, of course, his gang were part of them. That was why, in the end, I preferred

Almasy to Bagnold and co. Almasy comes over as truly modern. He had no blind attachment to empire, white men (Baggers and Newman never travelled with natives: draw your own conclusions), rules, playing the game, half-baked boring 'science' that denied mystery and wonder to the desert. Almasy's love of the desert and the transcendental nature of the place was obvious on every page of Unknown Sahara. His desire to spend three days alone at Bir Messaha was ridiculed by the British explorers – yet it seemed an obvious and interesting test to me. Baggers and crew were part of the exterminating effort to make the world boring, conformist, mapped and 'known'. They were explorers, but with no poetry in their souls. Bagnold's *Libyan Sands* has its defenders, but personally I found the book opaque and constrictive. It is more about cars than sand. And the laughable subtitle 'Travels in a Dead Land' couldn't be further from the truth.

Needless to say, Harding Newman had the highest opinion of Bagnold: 'He was probably the most intelligent man I ever met. Bagnold could lecture on anything; anything you mentioned, he knew about.'

He agreed that Bagnold's only negative trait was his impatience to be on the move: 'On on Baggers', they called him.

Libyan Sands is a strange travel book. The travellers meet very few people. They converse very little. There are no adventures, no incidents beyond bent axles and worn cogs. It is a record of exploration, but exploration at a remove, propelled by the speeding car, the ever faithful Model T and A Fords. In the twentieth century, for exploration to have any meaning it must involve people and not machines. But I'd learn all this much later.

Bagnold believed that the desert was boring and travelling at 40mph speeded it up enough to make it interesting. This seemed wrong even as I read it, but then I didn't really know.

By the end of my second interview with Rupert Harding Newman I thought him a lovable person and probably an excellent grandfather. He told me to choose a piece of silica glass from two sackfuls he'd collected in 1935. 'We took every bit we could find,' he said apologetically; 'I doubt if there's any left now.' Silica glass only occurs in a few places in the world, and nowhere is it as clear as the natural glass of the Sahara, caused by a meteorite impact, the *Geographical Journal* believes. Other explanations include a nuclear test by Atlanteans in 20,000 BC – take your pick. Silica glass looks like glass you find on the beach, sand-blasted and, when chipped, sharp and jewel-bright. In fact it is now known that Tutankhamun's chest jewel was made of silica glass, which is very mysterious as the area it occurs in is a small one of about thirty square kilometres in the Great Sand Sea, three hundred kilometres from the oases of Egypt and far from any known camel route. I treasured the gift and decided that, whatever it took, when I got to Egypt I would go and see if there was any still left out there in the dunes.

In Egypt, every middle-class family has servants. It's like Europe in the nineteenth century. Even 'poor' people who live with their mother-in-law and used their mother-in-law's car, like I would be doing, could have servants, since the monthly wage for a driver was about £38 – the cost of a full tank of petrol in Blighty; and a full tank of petrol, I now thought with calm ease, would only set me back £3.80.

I did not struggle with the concept of domestic servants: that was a luxury we could afford in the mighty West. In Egypt, with soaring unemployment and a hungry population, it would have been unjust and stingy *not* to have had servants. Besides, I was looking forward to my finely pressed shirt (with or without a starched collar) every day, or twice a day; I could pull them on and off like Gatsby in his dressing room. I had to admit part of the attraction of living in Egypt was (a) never having to do the ironing again, ever, and (b) always having perfect, uncreased shirts and trousers to wear.

There were other, more subtle, experiences I sought to have. A Syrian friend studying in Oxford explained it to me. He was blind and perhaps that increased his determination to study, which was immense, aided by computer programs that converted internet pages into speech and a university service that provided tapes of all the texts he needed. But despite this he still couldn't enjoy living in England. 'I don't feel like I'm anybody here. It's hard to explain. In Damascus I can go into the shop next door, buy some cigarettes, maybe the shopkeeper doesn't know me, but the way he serves me, even if my clothes are poor, gives me some sort of attention, a human sort of attention you don't get in England. It's as if everyone here is afraid of the person in front of them, as if they are a problem to get rid of. I even tried going to pubs but it didn't work out ...'

I wondered how an English pub bore would deal with a super-intelligent blind Syrian with an interest in nineteenth-century French drama. It was a hard image to sustain. In the Middle East people might want to rip you off, mislead you, lie to you and deceive you, but they'll do it in a human way. It isn't even about being caring or charitable – there's plenty of that in the West, and we are certainly streets ahead when it comes to having a sense of public good; what it's about is a micro-thing that, I think, boils down to 'I've got time for you.'

In the modern post-industrial West we've created an extra-ordinary situation where almost everyone feels they have too little time. Like the Arabic joke: a man is furiously painting a door, and when asked why he's hurrying he says, 'I've only got a little paint left. If I don't hurry it might run out before I've finished the door.'

I was the same. And I had my excuses, my very good excuses, just like everyone else. Too little time to give others the attention they crave. So they don't give it back.

And in Egypt attention could always lead to a higher level of involvement. A chance encounter in the East is a zone of immense possibility. You sit next to someone on a bus and they turn out to have a family hotel on the Red Sea that needs an English-language brochure in return for unlimited nights of residence. Or the guy who cleans your shoes knows someone who has a nice line in dodgy satellite cards. Or your

Arabic-teacher offers to design your website. Any interaction could turn into a business partnership to rival Goldman & Sachs or Fortnum & Mason, or maybe not. At the very least there will be a social dimension, but even that isn't guaranteed in the West. How many dinner parties had I been to where the barely disguised hostility could only be avoided by excessive and stultifying drinking?

In short, alienated writer seeks refuge from harsh realities of the Western world.

Egypt would save me. I could be free there. I sensed that the existential pressure to perform and conform to standards I thought arbitrary and bogus would be less. Egypt was, in my imagination (and the experience of half a dozen brief trips), a wild, un-PC haven for dodginess, rule-breaking, humanity. The *system*, as I conceived it, was flawed and disregarded there, people still had the edge over the prisons we contrive to make life easier for all of us.

It seemed appropriate that when I landed and was picked up from the airport by Haney, my brother in law, who a few short years before had been an unrepentant playboy and was now most improbably a judge, the streets were lined with policemen – with their backs to the traffic. Thousands of them. Turning their back on us as we drove by.

'Why aren't they looking?' I asked.

'Someone too important just passed by,' explained Haney. 'They aren't looking out of respect.'

'Maybe it's for me, maybe this is my welcome home,' I quipped, full of the joy of having started a new life elsewhere.

I was in for a rude awakening.

Two

MY FIRST BIRTHDAY PARTY

My mother-in-law found me a small two-bedroom apartment to work in, the rent only £20 a week. I started immediately, trying to catch up on all the time I'd spent not filling the container. This work apartment was a five-minute walk from her – our – place, which was on the fifth and final floor of an older building shaded by two tall acacia trees. The plan was to move out as soon as we found somewhere suitable.

Day and night my mother-in-law's building was looked after by the caretaker, or *bawab*, Magoob. Magoob lived with his wife and two daughters in two sheds at the bottom of the building with a few chickens in a wire-netting run. Whenever he saw me he cast his eyes downward. He was from the south of the country, what they call an Upper Egyptian, proud, with none of the sly Cairene's constant worming to get the upper hand. He knew his place and stayed there, guarded it, he was a guard after all, guarding our building against intruders, washing down the wide stone steps, stealing small paving slabs from a state road project so that we wouldn't have to walk across five metres of dirt from the road to the steps. I always greeted Magoob, even though he tried to look else-where; but that felt right – no jockeying with Magoob.

We had a home and the kids had a school. I always disliked school, but there I was, putting my children through the same old mill. I had flirted with the idea of home education, but after reading several books on the subject I suspected I would make a lousy home educator. Samia was also strongly against it. The Victorians home-educated their kids, I moaned without conviction. The Brontës were home-educated – look what that produced. Jorge Luis Borges wasn't even allowed out of the house until he was nine years old (admittedly his parents owned a pretty big house), and he turned out OK. But all along I knew my kids would be going to school. The bottom line with home education is: if you aren't prepared to do it yourself don't expect your wife to want to do it for you. Samia was adamant: 'Just because you're fucked up doesn't mean you can fuck up your kids. They like school.' Deep down I was scared I might be wrong; plus I had had the benefits of school and university, which I now chose to denigrate and yet every person I'd met who had been denied such things had always envied me. My kids would attend school. If they hated it they could reject it all at twenty-one – only sixteen more years. Shit, sixteen more years, and in Egypt I'd be paying for it too. Even free schools in Egypt, with their seventy-plus class sizes and endemic corruption (teachers bribed to obtain extra lessons and better grades), weren't free any more. That meant a private school, preferably an international school rather than one whose main language was Arabic. There were French, German, American and British schools. In order to offset the extremity of my decision to relocate to the Third World, we chose the British inspired Cairo English College. C.E.C. It also had an excellent repu-tation, and the headmaster and his wife were very welcoming.

Due to container-filling etc., my kids were already attending C.E.C. when I arrived in Egypt. The school was manned by highly qualified British teachers in a purpose-built concrete shell right on the edge of the desert. It was a fifteen-minute drive through light traffic (by Cairo standards) from my wife's mother's house in Maadi, a suburb south of the centre. Light traffic by Cairo standards: it always kept moving, but the fumes were bad and the driver, Mohamed, was so intimidating I wasn't always in the mood to confront him over his window-open driving style. Sometimes I forced myself to make him wind up his window, hoping that persistence would encourage him to always have the window up when I got in the car, but Mohamed, with his troll face and big gaunt frame bent over the steering wheel, had no intention of abandoning a lifetime of open-air motoring.

The car was modest – my mother-in-law's Honda Civic – but having a driver felt posh. At first. Then I realized everyone who could afford £38 a month, which even in Egypt is a lot of people, had one. In any case I was glad I wasn't driving. This was the first paradox of my chosen paradise: I was scared of the traffic. There was too much of it moving too fast in random spurts of knackered vibrating exhaust fumes following indecipherable trajectories around roundabouts, sometimes the wrong way. Mohamed drove with consummate heavy-footed confidence. His preferred position was right up the arse of the next car in front. He used horn and lights to signal his impatience, displeasure and lordliness over all other vehicles. We often got into neck-and-neck races with monster 4x4s driven by mothers of other kids at the school. Despite the massive disparity in engine size we always won, even if it meant boxing the startled mum into a slow-moving traffic obstruction like two donkey carts coming the wrong way towards us. Mohamed gave way to no one, gave absolutely no quarter, and relished making loud blasts of the horn right outside the school at anyone with the temerity to hold us up for even a second. The part of me that wasn't fearful of the mad speed at which he drove derived covert satisfaction from the utter disrespect he showed the more expensive vehicles driven by 90 per cent of the parents at the school.

This was another shock to me. Foreign workers in Egypt, if American or British, receive a monster Toyota or Jeep as part of their salary package. These cars were always painted either silver or gold and they would be lined up outside the school when we arrived, making it look like a luxury car dealer's forecourt. I was frankly envious, though I hid my envy with derision and tacit support for Mohamed's antisocial driving skills. All the parents had drivers, but some preferred to drive themselves. These were the ones Mohamed mainly picked on, especially as they debouched their little ones in front of the school gates. We even received complaints, but I never reprimanded Mohamed; in his sturdy aggression I saw my own thwarted social progress, for it was obvious from day two or three that I had landed in an arena of vicious snobbery and petty-minded bourgeois conventionality of the very worst kind.

It became obvious after about one and a half conversations with mums wearing shades and jodhpurs after their morning ride at the club that not working for a faceless international business with a dubious track record of human and environmental service was a serious handicap. In my cocooned naïvety I had imagined that all people who worked for such global monstrosities did so under duress, just for the money, the chance to travel, etc. But these people were actually proud of being cogs in the great wheels of global resource depletion. Writing was definitely a suspect occupation, one up from the dole, but only just. Being married to an Egyptian made me doubly suspect because although the foreigners enjoyed all the benefits of salaries far higher than most locals earned, they kept entirely to themselves and were rude to and dismissive of Egyptians. This depressed Samia but she put on a brave front. It made me angry at my powerlessness to receive the kind of attention my ego craved. Why hadn't we moved to France, where being an *écrivain* is everyone's envy? Merde. I'd been introduced to drunken sailors in a Breton port by my French publisher and been toasted in cider for just being a writer. *Merde.*

So my kids were in school and every day I was going to school with them, sharing some quality time with my offspring, though often we drove in silence with my son looking intently out of the window and me reading the newspaper. In England I had walked my son to school (my daughter had been too young then) and the mile-long walk had been enjoyable, a good start to the day, keeping us both fit.

21

Sometimes I ran home, just to up the fitness element of the experience. Now all that was gone, thrown away when I canned England as my place of residence. Now, we were driven everywhere and the only exercise my kids were getting was running from the car to the elevator doors, competing to be the first one to push the button.

Before moving to Egypt I had dropped my son off at his Oxford school without talking to anyone, just giving a cheery wave to the mother of his best friend (the best friend we had now forced him to leave for ever). But here, at this school devoted to passing on a British style of education, the playground was as social as a cocktail party every morning of the week – an exclusive party hosted by, and for, the wives of petroleum executives. The Petroleum Wives even had their own club, which I had seen advertised in the English-language freebie magazines often sponsored by Christian churches eager to gain support in a predominantly Muslim country. The Petroleum Wives were, on average, older and more equine-looking, rougher around the edges, than the equivalents I had only glanced at in passing at my son's old primary school. I made some effort to banish such negative thinking with generous reflections on the qualities of the teachers, who were all, it seemed to me, excellent and dedicated and the very opposite of stuck-up and snobbish. But the parents, that was a different matter.

It was obvious the Petroleum Wives were living the kind of life they dreamed of having in England but couldn't afford (private school, big car, servants, horse-riding, membership of a country club). Because they had suddenly upgraded they felt they had to act differently. It seemed to me that they were very inferior people – this based solely on observing the way they walked, parked their monster 4x4s and talked to the teachers about their kids, their innocent little kids who daily grew more repulsive.

Before I formed all these hate-filled opinions however I was invited to a birthday party, or rather my son was, but birthday parties were always attended by parents and were actually an

22

extension of their own social lives. Petroleum people had no life except the job and the school and they therefore inflated harmless school-based activities into events where they could show off to each other. Now I must be more precise about this showing off. It wasn't so much individual one-upmanship as group one-upmanship. It was as if they were saying, 'Look, I go riding in the morning *too*, I'm a member of the club *too*,' the club being in this case a hypothetical club, rather in the way members of VIP airline lounges kind of preen themselves on entering even though everyone watching is also a member. It's a joint preening rather than the stark exhibitionism of driving a Rolls-Royce through a deprived neighbourhood. And I wasn't a member.

I attended the birthday, however, full of high hopes and with a spring in my tread. And, strangely, while watching the clowns in front of the bouncy castle and summoning a beer from the waiter – these birthdays being also about showing how you can afford staff, entertainment and bouncy castles, i.e. belong to the club – I met Richard Head, who I very quickly realized shared my interest in the desert. Richard worked for a petroleum company as the head of health and safety and his wife was a teacher at the school, not a Petroleum Wife. He was forty but looked about twenty-eight. Slim and athletic, he liked to go mountain-biking in the nearby desert and had ridden a motorbike all the way to the Gilf Kebir. We had read all the same books and immediately he lent me some more. I told my wife what a stroke of luck it was meeting someone like that at the first birthday party I had attended, despite me effectively gate-crashing a party that our son had not especially enjoyed (he spent quite a lot of the time hiding in the bouncy castle).

Richard lived in a big villa on Road 9. Most of the roads in Maadi have numbers. We lived on Road 100, which few petroleum people knew. The numbers of importance spread out from 9 to about 20 and then from 210 to 250: these were the key places to live, where the villas were biggest, the roads quietest and emptiest since they all had off-street parking for their monster 4x4s. Richard had a Prado himself, which is a less monstrous version of a Land Cruiser than a 100 Series, but he didn't pretend it was his own – he was straightforward about being given it by the petroleum company he worked for as one more sweetener for working in Egypt. The sweeteners worked because most of the petroleum people enjoyed living in Egypt. They liked the lifestyle. Richard did too, but he also liked the desert. He was a nice guy, easy to talk to and he gave me two pieces of good advice. The first was: just get out into the desert any way you can. Take a tour if necessary to see what it's like. The second was: if you don't know what you want you can't expect to control people who work for you. Especially in Egypt.

Richard had lots of stone tools, both neolithic and palaeo-lithic, that he'd found on his various desert trips, but he had no silica glass. I brought round my piece of glass and we both handled it reverently. Unlike the Petroleum Wives, Richard knew its iconic status. He wanted to hear about my meeting with Rupert Harding Newman. We made keen, amiable plans to get out there and see if there was still any glass left in the Great Sand Sea.

Three

CLUBLAND

I needed to be fit if I wanted to be a desert explorer, so I joined the Maadi Sporting and Social Club. Everyone took the question of clubs seriously.

In Egypt all the nice pieces of public space have been privatized. Poor people have to make do with laying out picnic blankets on the worn grass of traffic islands or along the heaving edge of the Nile, a strip of verdure and banyan trees deeply littered with cigarette butts but at least free. A 'public' park, paid for by the Aga Khan, was recently completed along the eastern edge of the city but though it was leafy and well laid out it wasn't free and my son's football was confiscated at the turnstile. Unfortunately despite my pleas that he was unable to kick a ball far enough for it to land in a flowerbed the ball was firmly retained for later collection. Once inside the park we were restricted to a fraction of its extensive grounds. A minister was visiting with his entourage and that meant most of the park was off limits to the ordinary users. Would the minister's ball have been confiscated? I asked my wife. I saw that in Egypt something 'public' is assumed to be the private property of whichever government department it is administered by. To get something better than a lay-by or a piece of pavement on a bridge over the Nile (a favourite spot for hard-up courting couples), I'd need to go private and join a club.

I'd always liked the idea of clubs, but my experience had

25

all been vicarious, using clubs for which friends paid the membership fees. When I first starting coming to Cairo it was possible to climb over the fence of the Gezira Club or pay the guard E£10 and you were in. But the previous decade had been hard on those who enjoyed lax security, plus Samia hated climbing fences while wearing a dress. We'd have to pay up and join.

In England I knew people who were members of gentlemen's clubs that now admitted ladies, but these were austere bastions of privilege without kiddies' playgrounds, cashpoints and places where you could get government forms registered in a fraction of the time it took at a 'public' office. Egyptian clubs offered all these facilities, together with tree-lined walkways, outdoor restaurants, swimming pools and croquet lawns. Samia's mother had been a doctor in the air force and we'd gone a few times to an air force club, though I was under strict orders to not speak English as all military facilities are off limits to foreigners. This was a trying restriction. I was determined to join one of the three main clubs that accepted non-Egyptians, all started by the British before the war, each one serving a different segment of the middle-class population. The best and biggest was the Gezira, with its two-mile riding track and exclusive position on the Nile island of Zemalek. In better times Samia's family had been members, but long ago they had sold their life membership. The Heliopolis Club was also attractive, but crowded and far away.

The obvious choice was the Maadi Sporting and Social Club. By joining this I also got to be a member of the Maadi Yacht Club, which had a clubhouse on the Nile and several rowing eights which, the very season I joined, finally rotted away. They lay gently decomposing in the boathouse, along with several dinghies and rowing boats, waiting for repairs that would never happen. There was a tiny marina with a few motor craft and sailing yachts but I never once saw a boat being used.

The club was really just another place to drink tea, smoke

shisha and watch the Nile kingfishers plunge from on high, splash and return, fluttering upwards with tiny silvery fish in their beaks. It was also a good place to watch the fisher-families rowing with their ungainly log-like oars, up and down in front of the rich club members, throwing out their nets and hauling them in, often empty. The fishermen would raft their boats together at night and eat supper with a Tilley lamp flickering on the deck. They lived, ate, worked and slept on these boats, and now a few even had small outboard motors (used only when going against the current, oars were still used while actually fishing) so they must have made some money. I once looked down into the surprisingly clear water at the edge of the Nile and saw a great shoal of small fish called *bolti*, none longer than six inches, all resting in the warm shallows. The fisher-folk's kids were always swimming and larking about in the river. It looked clean enough. Recently a new sewer pipe has been completed that empties Cairo's waste twenty miles out into the desert, so the Nile is no longer the toilet of fifteen million people.

The Maadi Sporting and Social Club had extensive grounds, a running track, a gym, two swimming pools and several outdoor areas for sitting around drinking Turkish coffee. But it was the croquet lawn that sold the place to me. I'm not even sure why, since croquet is a game I actually have little interest in. I knew I would probably never play and neither did I ever see anyone else playing, though Samia told me she did, once. Not that it was *easy* to play, as the lawn-maintenance crew were engaged in the Sisyphean task of perpetual rolling. I joined the club because of the muted glamour of that lawn, a zone of possibility with all the over-tones of empire and *English Patient* romance.

The Maadi Sporting and Social Club had other old-world attractions, for example the changing-room attendant, a small, ratty-faced man who would grind out his cigarette and salute me. For this act of obeisance, which was most welcome after the daily lack of attention at the school, I paid him 10 or 20p per day. I varied the amount so that he would not get

27

complacent. At first he not only saluted but also brought a grubby piece of carpet out of his office for me to stand on while I was getting changed, but though I liked the higher level of service the carpet signified it was too unappetizing to risk actually standing on in bare feet. He would also switch on the lights for the shower for me, and even once produced a bar of soap, but as I didn't use it he took it away. The man would bow obsequiously as I handed over the crumpled paper money tip and I would leave the club feeling good. But in a pattern that I would later recognize in many Egyptian relationships, the level of service began to decline when the regularity of the tip became assured. He stopped bringing out the carpet, and then the lights remained off. He still saluted but then one day he just saluted from his sitting position reading a newspaper outside the changing rooms. In an attempt to reincentivize him I reduced the tip to a miserly 5p. The carpet made a brief reappearance but he never stood again.

Despite my considerable involvement with the saluting attendant I did also manage some lacklustre running around the lovely tree-lined track. I also used the weights machines, housed in a shed and guarded by another attendant who took great pleasure in throwing out any men who stayed after 9 a.m. on Tuesdays and Thursdays, which were women-only days in the gym. There was only ever one woman who came specifically to train at that time; all the other women came during the mixed training times. The woman was large and veiled, with a grumpy, frog-like face. Despite the veil's religious intention of covering up distracting beauty, it very often served the opposite purpose of concealing veritable ugliness.

It was outside the Maadi that Mohamed and I had our first confrontation. I discovered that if I shaved and wore a pressed shirt and a tie, Mohamed would drive the short distance from where he had parked to the front of the building to pick me up. If I was unshaven and not wearing a tie he would flash the car headlights to summon me to the vehicle. I duly did this on a number of occasions, thinking, What the hell, it's just as quick for me to walk to the car as it is for him to start it up and drive over. Then one day, when I was unshaven and not wearing a tie, he parked the car not outside the club but across a busy, even dangerous, road. With blinding clarity it struck me that if I didn't oppose Mohamed, in the way I had to oppose my young son when he desired to watch endless TV and eat entire packets of biscuits, I would pretty soon be serving him, not him me, and I would be paying for it to boot (though admittedly not very much). This was a shocking and uncomfortable realization. Mohamed had been, so far, a careful (if aggressive) driver who was always on time. I thought he was on my side. He was about fifty-three: too old, surely, for silly mind games. My mother-in-law was always very strict with him. She never walked to the car and she certainly never got dropped off with a busy road to fight against before reaching her destination. I didn't yet know how to behave in such situations in Egypt so I got very angry. I had tolerated his wild driving, his control of the electric window button so that we winged over the flyover being buffeted with polluted wind, his refusal to hand me my brief-case until I had first opened the door when we parked. I had tolerated his light-flashing summons but outside the Maadi Sporting and Social Club he went too far. I blew my top. I berated him for hogging the electric window button, for failing to call me Mister Robert, which he'd done for a week but now he simply grunted. I was so full of pent-up frustrations I went one further: from now on he had to address me as ... as ... 'captain', which I thought, in Anglo-Egyptian, was a term of respect. He complied, but was there a hint of amusement in the way he held open the door and said, 'OK, captain. Very good captain'? Sadly, I'd made a cultural gaffe of tremendous proportions. 'Captain' was a derisive term used for summoning young boys in the street, Samia laughingly told me. It was like asking the butler to call you 'laddie'. No wonder the bastard told Magoob and Hanya, a wizened little old man who lived in the electricity box in front of our

29

building and polished cars and opened doors for a small consideration. But Mohamed, after he'd had his fun, could not tolerate serving such a poor buffoon for long. Stretching his face into a grotesque and unfamiliar smile of submission he touchingly suggested he simply call me 'mister' instead. I quickly agreed and we entered into a new and uneasy but satisfactory phase of the master–servant struggle. I understood now why my mother-in-law berated Mohamed unjustly every few weeks or so; if she didn't, he'd stop doing things the way she wanted them done. It seemed so wasteful. I was deeply wedded to the idea of the contract: you say what you want, you pay for it and it gets done. But in Egypt the feudal model is nearer in history. People work for money, but not solely for money. They want a masterful master, not someone just like them whose only distinction is having money. Hence the better service when you dress well and act in a snotty manner. Extreme assertiveness, sadly, is a useful public behaviour in Egypt.

Being a regular at the Maadi Sporting and Social Club, I soon discovered its drawbacks. The staff were lazy and uncooperative. The women were mainly veiled, which I didn't mind until I noticed there were fewer veiled women in the Gezira Club. The other gym users were all elderly men, friendly but on the verge of some serious ailment they had left too late to remedy. At least there was no one pumping iron competitively, no one strutting their biceps and mirror-flexing their lats and abs. Mostly there was a little lacklustre pedalling and lifting interspersed with long ruminative conversations lying side by side at full stretch on the leg-press machines. Indeed, on popular days, the elderly gents would draw up the various pieces of equipment with seats attached and gather round for a full discussion of heart problems and varicose veins. No, the gym was fine, as was the pool, despite the fact that pigeons nested in the changing rooms. At least I was a member of a club that was recognized throughout the city as a benchmark of respectability. I even started manoeuvring for a named locker, the final sign of club acceptance.

Some strange transformation was going on. All that latent conventionality I'd suppressed for years in England was breaking out in Cairo. I was going straight and enjoying it.

My dress sense, now that I was wearing superbly pressed shirts, was also undergoing a change. I began to hanker after a hand-made suit, which, I was assured, would only cost £30 sterling. I spent several days handling cloth under the ingratiating eye of a downtown tailor. Above the till was a huge red leather-bound Koran in a kind of niche, and the tailor, or rather the boss of the shop, had a double *zabeeba*, which confirmed his desire to appear religious. The *zabeeba*, literally 'raisin', is a mysteriously obtained circular dark mark on the forehead of men who wish to demonstrate their religious devotion. Those with *zabeebas* were too humble ever to explain how they obtained them. Those without never seemed to know. It was obvious that a certain amount of rubbing whilst one had one's head down on the prayer rug was the cause, though this is never observable at public places of worship. The *zabeeba* requires private dedication to the task and they were flowering all over Cairo, mostly amongst government workers, clerks, shopkeepers and police officers. Ten years ago they were comparatively rare, but like veils for women they have spread like fungus spore – indeed, some even look like fungoid growths, raised, a little scabby, the result of hours of rubbing one's forehead against a dirty, grit-laden rug. There was almost certainly a quick route to getting a *zabeeba* but I was quickly learning that when it came to religion one could not afford to be anything other than grave in one's enquiries. The merest suggestion that you were implying hypocrisy met with a stony glare and haughty silence. It was like the increasing volume of the call to prayer – everyone complained at the mega-decibel noise, always getting louder, and the multi-hour sermons on Fridays, also broadcast at top volume, but no one dared to complain. I felt like someone in early-Victorian England observing the slide from eighteenth-century freedom to prudery and religious domination.

The tailoring boss showed me many beautiful fabrics but I

settled on a loud Prince of Wales check in a lovely smooth wool. I sketched out the precise style of peg-topped trousers drawn in at the ankle, reminiscent, I privately thought, of Steve McQueen in *The Thomas Crown Affair*. The surprising part was the way they fitted the jacket. After I'd specified four buttons and a precise width of lapel I was led into a darkened room, more like a small warehouse, with racks full of jackets in the same beige polyester. The *zabeeba*ed tailor smiled munificently. Here, he assured me, was every single suit size ever encountered. Whenever a new customer of a peculiarly odd and eye-arresting form entered the shop they would run up a second jacket in cheap cloth as a record of his size. Over the years they had amassed a storehouse of human variety, from the commonplace to the startlingly abnormal. Jaws from the Bond films or the Incredible Hulk could have found a polyester three-piece in that place. One rack was devoted to the unusually tall. Another had the childlike dimensions of a midget or dwarf. With a practised eye I was directed to the most worn section, aimed at the merely average. I was suspicious at first. I had hoped for something less mechanized and frankly more reminiscent of Savile Row, but, as Samia put it, 'What do you expect for thirty quid?' My suspicions evaporated as I tried six or seven similar jackets, all of which fitted; they differed only, fractionally, in sleeve length. Jacket no. 56 was perfect.

'We have every size possible,' the shopkeeper boasted.

'How many?' I asked.

'One hundred and thirty-seven. There are only a hundred and thirty-seven men in the world,' he joked, 'and we can dress all of them.'

I had one fitting for the trousers, and when the suit came, though it was unspeakably ostentatious, it was exactly my size. Including the cloth it cost less than a tank of premium unleaded petrol in England.

Petrol. It was never far from my mind. My wife had a cousin who owned a gas station so I could probably buy it for even less than the 10p a litre usually charged. Diesel was even cheaper – recently there'd been a public outcry when it went up from 4p to 6p a litre. Though Egypt has only small oil reserves it was fuelling its economic expansion on cheap gas from the Gulf, zero taxes, maximum pollution, and roads groaning with ancient knackered trucks and cars – which were all incredibly expensive. Importing second-hand cars was virtually impossible, and new cars had 200 per cent duty slapped on top. Even Egyptian-assembled Hyundais could be sold five years later for almost their original price. Cheap spares and even cheaper labour ensured that once you had a car, keeping it running wasn't that expensive. Perhaps there's a lesson here for the build-'em-and-trash-'em nations of the richer parts of the world. In Egypt you don't so much buy a car as the right to improve and maintain one. This was doubly true of the Toyota Land Cruiser, favoured by all Bedouin as the modern ship of the desert.

It seemed absurd that I employed a driver and didn't have a car. Though the family Honda Civic was nominally always available, in practice my mother-in-law needed it for the short drive (about a five-minute walk) to the local *bourse* where she gambled each day on the riotous Cairo stock market; then there were trips to visit her many friends and relations and of course the regular appropriations by my brother-in-law whenever his expensive Beamer sustained another injury to its undercarriage. Bought at the tail-end of his career as a playboy, the BMW was a tuned and lowered sport model imported from Munich, and every time he took a speed bump too fast, which was always, another piece of metal sheared off. Speed bumps are everywhere in Cairo, never signposted, mostly hidden amidst road debris and invisible dips in the tarmac, always monstrously high, like small hills with the deep scour marks of a thousand sundered sumps. Even Mohamed was respectful of certain key bumps that could only be taken at an angle without bottoming out amidst a shower of sparks.

Sometimes I rode the subway, which was French-built, roomier than the London tube, surprisingly extensive and efficient, and you could go anywhere for 5p. Big municipal buses, some the remnant of a stock of old school buses donated by Jimmy Carter in the 1970s, were also dirt cheap, as were the ubiquitous microbuses that often drove along with their bonnets raised to facilitate engine cooling in the worst summer traffic jams. But, in my Prince of Wales four-button suit with Steve McQueen trousers, I felt a trifle overdressed for such proletarian modes of transport. Mostly I took taxis, beaten black and white Ladas with front seats sometimes held in by rope and a non-functioning meter sitting in a purely symbolic role next to the driver. The price you ended up paying was related to psychological, not geographical, notions of how near or far something was.

Quite soon I developed a nose for precisely how far 'near' was, or how much I could stretch the definition of 'slightly further'. This was essential to avoid the 100 per cent surcharge usually meted out to foreigners. Knowing the 'true' price, there was no need for the hasty barter session on the pavement as recommended in most travel guides. On arrival I learnt to fold the money into a tightwad's tight wad the size of a postage stamp, which I slid into the taxi driver's palm, having first worked out which bit of wire operated the door handle. Torn between unravelling the package (biggest denominations on the outside of course) and pursuing me into the street for the tourist supertax, the driver always grumpily relented. This was the key: if you got no cheery 'Goodbye, mister' or even '*Masallama*,' then you knew you'd paid the right amount. There is, however, a significant exception – the non-greedy, honest taxi driver, of which there is a sizeable number in Cairo. That's why it's sometimes prudent to ask the price at the end of the ride (having had a good chance to psychically appraise the likely honesty of the driver, the way he chats or doesn't, the people he chooses not to run over or threaten, the presence or non-presence of Korans or plastic flowers, a hundred subtle signs) because the honest driver will charge you exactly the going rate for Egyptian nationals and may even say goodbye with a cheery wave. If

I liked the driver I would mentally decide what I would pay him as the drive proceeded. If he got hopelessly lost or drove madly then I would drop the price – but all Cairene taxi drivers have a psychic ability to know what your initial decision was so that, when it comes to wrangle time, if you proffer less than that amount they will mysteriously have only enough change to leave you paying the unspoken initial quantity you had in mind. How do they know? They just know.

Mohamed ferried me from the school to the club and then to the writing apartment, or 'office', as I called it. I wanted to impress upon him that though I lacked a car and a home of my own I too worked for a living. My Arabic was poor but improving, though not fast enough. I found a place that cut hair but due to a slight misunderstanding I ended up having a full facial that took an hour and a half. I was at sea in a foreign country and my routine – school, club, office, home – was something I could cling to. The cost of joining the club, renting the 'office' and paying Mohamed was all very little compared to the everyday costs of living in England.

I was working, I had my routine, but things weren't quite right. I wasn't getting any closer to the desert.

Through all this upheaval – taking my family to another continent (Africa too, that made it sound further than Egypt), running my finances into the ground through choosing a poorly remunerated career path, forcing such changes on my family, taking away the playroom and bedroom and garden my kids had known since birth and replacing them all with a single small room in my mother-in-law's flat that she had decorated with semi-relief Disney characters – surely I'd have to have very good reason to do such a crazy thing? There had to be something of greater magnitude pulling me on, forcing such changes when my family were perfectly happy? I had taken my wife's fear about money and run with it. I'd used that as my grand alibi for escape, but secretly I had other plans. I had my plans of the desert waiting in the wings, ready to be used at any time. And now I was out there I could go any time. Nobody and nothing was stopping me.

I even got to see the desert every day when I took the kids to their school, which was built right on the edge of it, with quarries and concrete factories on either side. This sort of desert I was familiar with: the margin, the edge where it comes into contact with roads and cities or the sea. I had grown used to the likeness this sort of desert bears to a building site – even down to the heaps of sand and stones, as if someone has been clearing up (probably somebody has, or else sometimes the desert really does form piles of sand naturally). This kind of desert has lots of tyre tracks from turning trucks or people eager to go a little way in, but not too far. Lots of rubbish, too – plastic water bottles with their healthy blue tint, broken glass catching the sun, shreds of tyre with the white inner core exposed, rusty exhaust systems and scrubby little bushes growing out of micro-sand dunes.

I had observed the margins and thought at first that they looked as they did because of their proximity to the catastrophe of road- or city-building, but this was only half the story. The desert gets messed up really quickly. What falls there stays. Orange peel flung from a speeding truck cab dries out into something dark brown, hard as a walnut shell, still there sixty years on; a banana skin becomes something resembling a gourd; dung gets eaten, it's true, but the desert is short of the sort of scavengers and micro-organisms that allow woods and grassland to swallow garbage and abuse. It's a fragile surface, despite that surface being stone sometimes. What falls stays, and when one sees that one moves on: no point stopping somewhere that looks like the municipal tip.

Soon after I moved to Cairo we passed through the Eastern Desert on our way to the Red Sea coast. It was rocky desert and cut with wadis, dry ravines. There were camels carrying men and goods there in the early 1990s; nowadays the Bedouin still graze camels but they use trucks for moving about.

But rocky deserts were not what I had in mind. To me the desert was about sand. Flat sand or sand in dunes, I didn't really mind as long as it was sand. Actually I preferred the idea of flat sand, endless to the horizon, even less to look at. The desert was about the void, the zero point, shrinking yourself and your concerns in the immensity and emptiness of it all. The desert was about a definite psychological need for vastness in the face of human confusion, brain fatigue. Mind-bothered Western man can take drugs, alter his lifestyle, turn off the television, pierce his body or run a marathon, it all amounts to just so much therapy to keep him loping along the same track towards the inevitable finishing post. I saw the desert as a huge right turn, a different path, another way out of what everyone was into, the money, goods and attention conflicts of the current century. The desert cured the malaise, not just the symptoms. Somehow the vastness of the desert signalled the infinite present, nowness, headspace, instant immortality.

But I needed sand. A few years before, I'd been driven out to Wadi Rayan, which is the nearest dune-filled photogenic desert to Cairo. I'd not been disappointed. The sand was white and hot, the sun dazzling. I'd climbed a crumbling *yardang*, an eroded mud mountain, and looked across the flat sand plain to see other hills and even pyramids in the distance. It's observed by everyone who visits the Egyptian desert that *yardangs*, also called mud lions, bear an uncanny resemblance to the Sphinx, and many of the flat-faced hills in the desert approach the geometrical simplicity of pyramids. The harsh contrast of sun and shade further emphasizes their pyramidal nature. Both *yardangs* and pyramidal hills are a feature of the Western Desert, not the Eastern, which is the rockier. If the original pharaonic culture originated out of the Western Desert it made sense that all their iconic objects should mimic the natural environment they came from. Pyramids and sphinxes came out of the desert. I liked that. Everything comes out of the desert and everything will return there.

At Wadi Rayan I walked from the car, which was parked on the extreme black of the asphalt, across the white sand towards a small shale hillock. Halfway there I got lost, despite the distance being so short, about a kilometre, no more. When I say lost, I mean I suffered that momentary vertigo, that involuntary rush of heartbeat and breath when you lose your bearings somewhere where losing your bearings is important. All I did was lose sight of the car, my mother-in-law's green Honda, Mohamed lounging next to it one minute and now gone, no sound of an engine in that soundless place. When the wind is low the desert is especially quiet. It almost turns your ears inside-out it's so quiet. Noise, especially when you live somewhere constantly noisy like Cairo (it's a gripe of filmmakers that Cairo is bad for filming because of the constant hum, whatever time of early morning you try to film you can never be rid of that deep city resonance, sixteen million people, the biggest city in Africa, just humming, humans making a noise like a giant hive; it was the reason I heard *The English Patient* wasn't filmed in Egypt, the Cairo hum, always there, ruining any direct sound recording) you get so used to noise that when it's not there you feel your body starting to expand, as if gravity is weaker, as if the lack of noise is causing your body parts, no, your very cells, to fly apart. Its almost unbearable, just for a moment, before you get a grip and relabel it 'relaxing' or 'absence of tension', but the first few minutes when it hits you it's terrifying, you begin to doubt that you'll hold together. It feels as if without noise we will perish and expand, with the pressure off we'll be like astronauts in punctured suits. I'm sure the reason many people do odd things the first moment they get into real desert is a desire to be rid of this uncanny silence. I've seen people sprint up steep dunes (common one, this), bellow and yodel, unzip and take a piss within inches of another person, knock rocks together, restart a car engine to check an unlikely fault, turn on or turn up the tape player in the car. My first thought was that Mohamed had gone off to pray, which is what he did at all times of the day and early night when waiting by the car for orders. But there were no mosques (or even people) in Wadi Rayan. He's just driven off, I thought. It was a hot day in spring, merciless sun at noon and thirty degrees in the shade, and no place for hanging around.

I thought his leaving highly unlikely but the evidence was there and that's when I experienced the peculiar nature of desert fear, which is different from other kinds of wilderness fear I'd experienced in the past. In the Canadian wilderness, where I had travelled the previous three summers, the fear of being alone was present and sharpened by the knowledge that bears were about, but even so you knew you could survive. Water and food were all around. In the desert there was no water, and the absence of water made the game different and interesting; it raised the stakes, just as climbing without a rope raises the stakes. It was then that I saw there were two deserts, at the very least. The first is the one you visit with others, adequately prepared; and the second is the one that will be the death of you unless you are lucky. Knowing this felt good. And, being calmer, I kept walking and saw the car, hidden in one of the almost imperceptible dips you encounter in the desert. The harsh midday light annihilates shade and perspective and makes the gently undulating sand look flat when it isn't. As I walked hurriedly back, following my meandering tracks, the car rose like a two-dimensional theatre set coming up from the stage floor. Mohammed waved from a distance. I waved back.

Now I was safe I could reflect on the intense burst of loneliness I'd felt, like the distilled essence of loneliness. Water, my essential friend, had been absent for only a few moments and that really shook me. Did I want to continue with this game? People who hate the desert – and there are plenty – must intuit this feeling before even visiting the place and, knowing it, leave well alone. But I was glad. It meant the desert, however man tamed it with cars and cool-boxes and GPS machines, still had teeth, was still a wild place where man went at his peril, had to have his wits about him. Man's instinct is to diminish the desert, reduce its dangers, build a town at the oasis and connect it by phone, rail, air and truck to the next oasis. I wanted to reduce its dangers too, but only so far. In the past you'd be limited by what was available – camels and leaky water skins. Desert dwellers, the Tebu, Bedouin and Tuareg, had all learnt to live with this fear. You would be judged irresponsible, by modern standards, if you wanted to recreate that danger, that balance of fear and possibility.

Despite a lot of this kind of thinking about the desert, in my first two months in Egypt I made very little progress in actually getting anywhere near the place. I had the excuse of writing, settling in, finding my feet, and all this took time, but increasingly I found the desert slipping away from me. It was as if Cairo and the fertile strip either side of the Nile were holding me back, penning me in, subtly keeping me from my aim. For some reason it all hinged around getting a suitable vehicle for desert exploration. Since reading and rereading Scott's *Sahara Overland* I had convinced myself that the only serious way to get out there was in a motorized contraption of some kind. Motorbikes had limited range, so that left a car or a truck.

The problem was that all cars in Egypt are between two and six times their real, i.e. rest-of-the-known-world, value. A knackered twenty-year-old 60 Series Land Cruiser costs £10–12,000 in Egypt. I couldn't afford that. Even a Lada Niva would set me back £2,500, and what with the school fees and the club fees and the hundred small expenses I had overlooked in the optimistic rush to escape England I was in no position to even contemplate getting a car. I'd be lucky to afford a pushbike, much less a motorcycle. It was time to get radical.

On the back of an envelope I doodled a long, thin six-wheeled trolley with mountain-bike wheels. In Canada I had towed a heavily laden canoe up a thousand miles of fast-running river. In the Arctic man-hauling had enjoyed a renaissance. Light sledges, heavily laden, were regularly towed to both the North and South Poles. Why couldn't I do the same in the desert? A sledge wouldn't work – sand offers too much resistance – but a trolley with enough wheel surface area to avoid it sinking in might just work. It was intensely exciting to be liberated from the tedious and complicated details of engines and transmissions and special tyres. If all else failed I would walk my way to the lost oasis, under my own steam.

My wife's Aunt Zaza lived in downtown Cairo in an area full of metalworking shops. She sent her driver, Yusef, out to find a place that would be able to manufacture my desert trolley. (Yusef had once been my mother-in-law's driver but she had sacked him after a regrettable incidence of insubordination. Yusef was a Nubian from Upper Egypt and a stickler for class division: at my wedding he had refused to eat because he felt it was wrong to eat at the same table as his employers. Only when I brought the food to him did he reluctantly eat. My mother-in-law had perhaps foolishly taken to discussing her life and concerns with him as he drove her around. In a moment of exasperation he had reprimanded her and been fired. Aunt Zaza had no such desire to discuss her problems and he now worked for her.)

Yusef was quite different from Mohamed, who was quintessentially Cairene in his approach, always looking for ways to get the upper hand, to assert himself and his own agenda. Yusef simply tried to do his best. We spent an afternoon searching the second-hand-wood shops of southern Cairo for a piece of plywood to make the base for the trolley. In a desire to save me money Yusef wouldn't hear of me buying a new piece of wood. The second-hand-wood dealers were a scummy lot, looking on with disdain as Yusef and I rummaged through piles of paint- and plaster-spattered wood to find one the exact size.

In the years since I'd known him Yusef had become more anxious and nervous. He had several children, one of whom was handicapped, and lived in Helwan, a town once famous for its clean air and TB cures but now a sink of industrial pollution. I sensed in his desperation to serve me, to find just the right piece of wood, all his anxiety to survive in the merciless, heaving metropolis. Wages had hardly increased in the last five years but inflation was unofficially running at 30 per cent. Instead of walking we almost ran from shop to shop, running to keep still in a city running away with itself. For some reason, though I had been loaned Yusef, I had not been loaned Aunt Zaza's car. Yusef was fully prepared for us to take a microbus but I said we could afford a taxi. We hired one with a long-bearded young driver who played the Koran at full blast as we drove through poor neighbourhoods with dust-caked roads, donkey carts, towering buildings and tiny alleyways running with overflowing sewage water. The taxi engine died several times and I was surprised we made it, long after night had fallen, to the metalworking shop that had received instructions to make the trolley axles and wheels.

The business was down an alleyway off Goumrayia Street in the downtown area. Welding sparks emitted from the open yard which was piled high with rusty lengths of steel. The boss sat on a wooden chair and invited me to sit with him. He had a big, ebullient body, a bulbous nose and a coat whose pockets were stuffed with banknotes. Like Yusef he spoke no English so I was reduced to diagrams, gestures and a six-week intensive Arabic course I'd taken three years earlier. The workers were all busy hammering, grinding and welding in the darkness under hissing Tilley lamps and a single glaring spotlight that was wired directly into a cable that poked out of the pavement. The racket was intensified by a petrol generator which supplied power to the welding and grinding gear. Their main business was making bicycle-powered rickshaws with a metal box at the front. I'd seen these around, selling everything from roast corncobs and chestnuts to sweets, and even piled high with sacks of cement.

We discussed wheels and the boss persuaded me I needed the ultra-heavy-duty moped-like wheels they put on the front of rickshaws. Then I was handed a piece of chalk to sketch out the dimensions on the flat concrete floor of the workshop. All the workers crowded round me and started muttering that I needed a *dongola*. The trolley would be disaster without a *dongola*. The boss shoved aside a bicycle-rickshaw man who'd brought his cart in for repair and showed me a simple luggage trolley behind it. The *dongola* was the steering mechanism.

The boss nodded sagely, making a steering gesture with his great scarred fists. 'You need *dongola*,' he said. '*Mafish dongola*. No *dongola*,' I replied. My trolley needed to be light and simple and the *dongola* was a heavy metal excrescence. The boss shrugged and gave rapid orders and the *dongola* team was disbanded. I was given tea and offered a *shisha* water-pipe while I waited.

The men worked at great speed with utter confidence. The boss shouted good-naturedly and pushed his men around, bullying and bossing to keep them at it. They did everything by eye, using the flat floor of the workshop to make sure the axle brackets were welded on at right-angles. A boy came back with four wheels shod with tyres made in China. Everything was bolted together. The trolley looked huge and quite unsuited to its task but I was happy. From drawing the design to having the completed vehicle had taken thirty-six hours and cost me £25. Such speed of execution would be inconceivable in England. Even if I never used the thing, it gave me a great surge of confidence. If all else failed I could walk, towing my life behind me. If all else failed I could walk.

Four

THE CAIRO DESERT EXPLORATION GROUP

Routine. I needed routine if I was going to survive in this heaving, chaotic city. With pathetic conviction I clung to my routine, but every day there was another drama or mini-disaster that consumed the household. My brother-in-law's BMW had finally conked out and he had appropriated the Honda, so we had to ferry the kids to school in taxis whose drivers didn't know the way. The maid stole a cardigan, which she returned. Then she stole $90 and was fired. The toilet squirter – a device like a shower hose that you used to blast your backside – exploded one night and silently filled the apartment with water. I awoke that morning, jumped out of bed and landed with a splash in six inches of water. My computer was standing in its case and was half submerged. My wife's computer charger was under water and probably destroyed. Using a hair dryer I rescued my laptop but the charger was shot. Magoob and his wife were summoned. 'Magoob! Magoob!' my mother-in-law bellowed from the balcony of our fifth-floor flat. Magoob had no phone and all times of the day and night you could hear residents bellowing for his assistance from their balconies. It would take me six months to master the exact combination of imperative and volume to be able to summon him myself.

Magoob spent the morning filling buckets of water and

pouring them into the bath and the loo. The whole rear part of the flat was under water. Books and clothes were saturated but everyone took it in their stride. I went out to find a new charger for Samia and in a computer shop not two hundred metres away I showed the broken box and asked without hope if they had another. The shop was in a basement complex of vaguely electronics-related shops. Mostly the shopkeepers sat alone with very few customers. One shop was where I always bought my refilled cartridges since no one sold new ones. The shop I had been directed to for the new charger was entirely empty except for a desk covered with broken computer bits, a soldering iron smoking in its stand and a multimeter of advanced age. The back of the shop had two plastic chairs and a huge pile of old computer screens, keyboards, cables and boxes. The shopkeeper took one look at the charger and without a word went to the pile and started rummaging around. As if pulling a snake from its lair he tugged on a cable end and pulled out a Toshiba laptop charger – exactly the one I needed. My wife was using her computer to do internet journalism every day and desperately needed to be up and running immediately. It seemed like a miracle that I'd solved things so easily. In England I'd have spent days trying to locate that now out-of-date piece of kit. Suddenly I saw Cairo as a miraculous place, but the shop-keeper had read my face. As I reached out for the charger he said, 'Three hundred pound.' Thirty English quid for some-thing worth almost nothing – except to me. I paid and learnt a double lesson: everything is possible in Cairo but the people are clairvoyant, so keep a poker face. It had been the same when I went searching for the piece of used plywood for the trolley – my need was obvious. I required lessons in hiding my intentions if I was to avoid paying through the nose.

A few days later we had another flood. The new maid used the loo by the front door that had been the private fiefdom of my father-in-law before he died. Possibly out of respect, but also necessity, no one now used that loo because it required a complicated series of manoeuvres to avoid the tank over-flowing. The maid flushed and the water kept coming. In desperation she opened the front door and swept gallons of water down the lift shaft, which erupted into the dangerous crackling of a massive short-circuit.

Without a routine I'd spend my life immersed in domestic crisis management. When it wasn't some part of the building that was breaking down there would be a family dispute that enveloped everyone. One cousin was suing the rest of the family over a will that involved forged signatures, a fatwa from the Grand Mufti and sundry other fantastic details. Aunt Zaza and my mother-in-law had fallen out over a mutual friend. My brother-in-law had returned the Honda but now the steering wheel vibrated like a pneumatic drill so my wife wouldn't talk to him. My routine would get me away from all of this. With the right routine I could finish the book that was overdue and finally get out into the desert to search for the lost oasis.

I had been doing more research into Zerzura, something that's always easier when you're closer to the location of your studies. In Egypt the name and the idea were almost commonplace. There was a Zerzara nightclub in the Marriott Hotel (I made a mental note to visit). There was a tour company that ran trips into the desert called Zarzora. There was a book by a local author that covered, with photos and workmanlike factual research, much of the subject I was inter-ested in. Zerzura, in any of its variant spellings, was old news. When I met an artist who lived on an island in the Nile he rolled his eyes and said, 'You're not doing that Zerzura thing too, are you?' I was.

But the clock was ticking. The season for desert travel was from October to March and we were already nearing the end of November. Every day in my ship's cabin of an 'office' I made lists of what I needed to do. The trolley had been dismantled and carried upstairs, where it sat in the gloom on the landing. Sometimes I jumped on it and wobbled it back and forth like riding a gigantic skateboard. The lists were full of good ideas but what I needed was people. You couldn't go out into the desert on your own.

Richard Head again came to my help. He told me about Shaheer, who ran an off-road supply company, and I paid him a visit at his shop in Heliopolis. Shaheer was cool, drove a bright red souped-up Jeep Wrangler and smoked English-tobacco roll-ups. He wore corduroy jackets and carried his papers in a leather satchel. He sold special maps, airbag jacks (like a mini bouncy castle, they could right a tipped-over car) and top German branded sandplates at E£2,000 a pair. His main trade was rebuilding Jeeps, but he was very unpushy on the subject. He told me about various other 4x4s that were for sale. He said he'd ask around for someone to act as my fixer. He recommended the Lost Oasis company if I wanted to do a deep-desert tour. He mentioned he only had one pair of German sandplates left and he wouldn't be getting any more until the next season.

I didn't have a car but I felt the need to own my own sandplates. Perhaps he read this with the same clairvoyance as the computer-charger salesman. Sandplates, in their present form, had been invented by Guy Prendergast, one of Bagnold's associates, who had gone out into the bazaars of Cairo in the 1920s and bought some old iron channels used for building dug-outs. Before that, chicken wire, canvas matting and grass had been used to stop vehicles sinking into soft sand. After the war pieces of steel and then aluminium PSP (perforated steel planking), a building material with holes in it that could be cut into convenient lengths, were adopted as the standard model for sandplates. Nowadays companies fabricated purpose-built sandplates that mimicked the style of PSP. A pair strapped to your roofrack was as vital to looking the part as jerry cans and sand tyres. In my febrile rush to get into the desert I needed talismans. Despite the expense I bought Shaheer's top German plates and stored them next to the trolley.

But I still needed people. In England I would join a club, but there was no longer a club for people searching for Zerzura.

So I started one. With a nod towards history I founded the Cairo Desert Exploration Group. Richard agreed to attend the first meeting, which was to happen at the Red Onion pub in Maadi, quite near to where I lived. I stuck up advertisements for the club in a supermarket and on the school noticeboard and placed small ads in the local English-language magazines. Now I was finally moving.

Shaheer told me a man called Ozman, who would be good as a fixer, might turn up to the first night of the club. I had mentioned a desultory wage, so I assumed Ozman might be a young man, possibly just out of college, but in the excitement of the approaching meeting I forgot all about him.

The Red Onion was a dark bar that also served food. The manager showed me to the largest table, which seated six. His name was Hisham and he agreed that if too many people arrived we could put more tables together. Richard said he might be a little late, so I sat there expectantly sipping my beer with several books with sand-dune pictures on their covers displayed so it would be obvious who I was.

After an hour alone and two beers I realized we would probably not have to put more tables together. The few customers I locked eyes with glanced away. No one looked remotely desertish. I gave up on the book I wasn't reading. In the corner of the bar stood an overweight man wearing a long coat, a large flat cap and a striped scarf wrapped once round his neck and dangling carelessly past his waist. It would have been impossible not to notice such an eccentrically dressed figure. He looked as if he was about to enter a 1970s motor treasure hunt, or had ransacked his wardrobe for a fancy-dress party where the object was to dress up like Lord Beaulieu. He kept coming in and going out again and finally after a long discussion with the manager he came over. There was sweat on his face and he was beaming. It was Ozman, dressed to kill, my first recruit to the Cairo Desert Exploration Group.

I liked him immediately, in his flat cap with a sort of bobble on top and his scarf, which looked like a home-knitted football supporter's scarf. I liked him, but I knew as soon as he proffered his card, which simply read OZMAN SAFARI, that he was eminently unsuitable for any job I might be able to offer. He was a decade or more older than me. He had a family to support. He was tubby and smoked heavily and when I mentioned the trolley there was a long moment of total incomprehension. But to his credit, when I sketched two stick figures harnessed to the wheeled sledge he managed a cheerful 'Like the ancient Egyptians. Building the pyramids.'

Weeks later, after the ignominious firing of Ozman, I'd reflect on all the things I perhaps should have done at the outset of our relationship, but then, as Richard pointed out, I didn't really know what I wanted. I was flailing, trying to start a new life and trying to leave it at the same time. Egypt was supposed to be my oasis and yet I was set on finding another somewhere out there in the desert.

Meanwhile, Ozman knew everyone in the desert tourism business in Egypt, had helped at the Pharaohs Rally and done several jobs in the car industry. He was sure he could find me the perfect desert car. Something in his insistent enthusiasm and confidence made me think, Well, even though I can't afford a bicycle it can't hurt to look at some cars, get some experience under my belt.

Richard arrived and we drank several more beers and hardly noticed that no one else had turned up. We toasted the Cairo Desert Exploration Group, which would surely go on to great things. Richard spoke about his motorcycle trip to the Gilf Kebir, all the Stone Age artefacts he'd found and the Shell petrol tin still in its paper wrapper he'd found at an old Long Range Desert Group airstrip. Sixty years old and still in its paper wrapper. The desert was like that: it slowed down time, halted ageing, preserved everything. We drank to the desert.

Despite my misgivings I arranged to get in touch with Ozman very soon. I started to mention money but he waved it away airily, almost as if it was the last thing on his mind. 'I can help you in every way,' he said. 'Anything you want, I can help you. I will teach you Arabic too, no problem, *mafish*

49

mushkella – see, I already taught you some!' When he rose to leave he took off his flat cap and bowed, showing a completely bald head. Then he quickly put it back on, as if he'd revealed too much.

Five

UNCLE MAHMOUD

The building had seen better days. Once there had been movie stars and famous singers living there. That was when the area around the old opera house was still a desirable place. Now the movie stars lived in villas in the suburbs while the city centre descended into chaotic decay. My wife used to point out where all the grand shops had been, now replaced by streets full of cheap imported goods. Uncle Mahmoud still lived in the building, the lower floors now dodgy import/export businesses, the doors always open with a couple of men sitting around an empty desk, a phone and an ashtray full of cigarette butts. On the corner of the building was a bicycle-repair shop that now had a profitable line in assembling and selling Chinese-made multi-gyms. Their fever-ish bolting spilled out into the entrance of the building, a vast, high-roofed atrium which was used during Ramadan for free suppers sponsored by rich businessmen to feed the poor. There was a wide flight of broken, grimy steps that led up to the lifts, which worked even if you didn't get the expanding door exactly shut. I was getting used to the open-elevator experience: our own lift had no door at all, and my son had taken to chiding me if I stood too close to the concrete sections of flooring shooting past. Actually, riding in open lifts is a good way to get a precise notion of how sturdily a building is built, the thickness of the floors, whether they seem to be rotting away or not. In Uncle Mahmoud's building rot was fairly well advanced.

On the fourth floor I stepped out of the lift and looked down, as I always did, on to the inner courtyard. Completely overshadowed by the many storeys above me, this piece of enclosed open space was more like a great chasm in the middle of the building. All the kitchens and bathrooms looked out on to the chasm, which also served as a kind of rubbish dump for the entire building. It was dark and stinky and at the bottom I glimpsed the cheerful decoration of orange peel scattered over the torn innards of an old mattress, damp black stickiness all around. The sewer pipes ran down the outside of the inside of the building, and around each leaking joint the corrosive effect of noxious waste was eating into the concrete.

Uncle Mahmoud was my favourite Egyptian uncle, and I had many, all inherited from my wife's extended family. He was one of my reasons for living in Egypt, or, rather, when I thought about the imaginary Egypt I loved, he was always part of it. He had also been my first Arabic teacher, and the best. Uncle Mahmoud was married to Zaza, who had been a looker in the 60s, wearing mini-skirts and dating fashion photographers. Now she moved heavily to answer the door and wore a scarf to cover her greying hair. She still had a striking face though, huge fierce eyes and an aquiline nose, and was capable of ridiculing any man with her startling line in obscenities. It is another surprising fact that the most demure and middle-class of Egyptian women can also be the most obscene, using gestures when words are insufficient or, as in my case, not fully understood. A cheery thumb's-up can never be the same when you've seen it twisted into a *baboous*, the exact meaning of which is 'Up your arse'. Not that she could shock Uncle Mahmoud, who was absolutely imperturbable and had a sense of humour that never deserted him even when his heart was slowing by the minute and panicked nurses were rushing him into theatre for an emergency pace-maker. When the hospital teaboy hesitated at the door Uncle

Mahmoud raised his head a fraction and quipped, 'You're too late for the tip, sonny.'

Uncle Mahmoud had been sick for as long as I'd known him but somehow he survived. He'd had a lot of training: imprisoned by the Israelis for a year in 1948; wounded while leading an infantry attack in 1956; years spent in both the Eastern and Western Deserts with the frontier guard. He'd retired as a general and gone on to be the administrative head in Aswan; when he finally retired he was running Cairo Airport. But unlike most men who reach high positions he had not a shred of pomposity or the pampered ego that tends to come with success. Uncle Mahmoud had instead the simple gift of inspiring extreme loyalty – 'love' might be a better word – in those who surrounded him. Every time we arrived at the airport there was the aged Haggar Abdu, a man who had worked for Uncle Mahmoud all his life, and despite being retired himself still hustled us through customs and baggage checks, limping along in his beautifully pressed light blue safari suit, haggling and bustling past officials, wielding his out-of-date security pass, eager to serve any friend of Uncle Mahmoud. Indeed Haggar's devotion to duty was so extreme that when my father arrived for a visit he kissed his hand, and when he visited the loo Haggar remained outside the cubicle, ready to hand over paper towels should the institutional toilet paper prove too insubstantial.

(The one enormous blot on Uncle Mahmoud's copybook was a result of his excessive generosity in helping others. A penniless carpenter who had worked for him had asked to borrow money to set up a furniture business. Mahmoud had helped him with finance, finding premises and obtaining permissions. The man had become very successful, quickly expanding his business and obtaining loans at the start of Sadat's open-door policy. Very soon he was a millionaire, but, not content with a fortune, he took up with Uncle Mahmoud's wife and finally absconded with a huge unpaid loan to Greece. Mahmoud then divorced his wife and married Zaza. Unable to return to Egypt, the carpenter squandered his money and was now growing old, bitterly regretting his inability to die in his own country.)

How can I describe Uncle Mahmoud's magical effect? He was always pleased to see you, absolutely genuinely pleased that you had come to visit. He never policed your reactions, he accepted all shows of affection without belittling them. When you left him, even if not much had been said, you felt cheerful and optimistic. He was never embarrassed, despite his ailments, including Parkinson's disease, which he simply ignored as if they were not there. I never heard him make one reference to his illness. I felt he had some secret to how to live as an old man. I compared him to my father-in-law, who had prided himself on being fit and spent considerable time supervising his special healthy diet. I remember seeing doddery Mahmoud sitting next to my wife's father, laughing and joking about all the soldiers they'd known who had died ridiculous deaths. The one who had loved to fly upside-down and had ploughed his plane into the underside of a well-known bridge he'd been attempting to fly under, the one who'd set an ambush and then walked into it and been blown up by his own mine. Mahmoud was genuinely laughing but I could see a fraction of concern eventually cross my father-in-law's face – he was thinking about his own death, whereas Mahmoud couldn't care less. In the week before he died my father-in-law spoke about the inevitability of failing memory and failing strength as one got older. I could feel him either giving up, or perhaps finally coming to terms with something he'd been trying to ignore. He had been an army doctor and then a successful consultant, a swimmer and weight lifter in his youth, and even in his early seventies ran for miles along the beach at Agamy on the Mediterranean. Seeing those two sitting together I had thought it sad that Uncle Mahmoud would probably die first, whereas my father-in-law with all his knowledge of diet and exercise would live to be a hundred. But Uncle Mahmoud was still alive and my father-in-law was dead two years now.

Mahmoud had no interest in money. He had enough and

he didn't care for more. He never let things bother him. At my wedding we had to visit a government office and unbeknown to me Zaza and Mahmoud had waited two hours before we arrived and then another hour while we were there. He was just as pleased to see me as ever. When a garrulous official perched himself against Mahmoud as he sat on a bench, Mahmoud made the slightest movement, the merest suggestion of *hauteur*, and the man immediately made space for him.

Not that there was anything outwardly commanding or even that impressive about Uncle Mahmoud. He was medium height, with the moustache and slightly hooded eyes, eyes spent too long outdoors giving orders, that military men the world over often develop. He was religious but did not pray now that he was ill. He went to the mosque on Fridays if there was someone to take him. If not he didn't go. He did not drink now, though he had in the past. He never spoke about religion. My father-in-law would criticize fun-damentalists but Uncle Mahmoud would make a wry joke instead. His secret of living seemed to be his readiness to leave this life with a smile.

When I started learning Arabic Uncle Mahmoud used to test me on my vocabulary. He had started literacy programmes when he'd been a junior officer and had the teacher's gift of knowing when to push and when to help the student. When I wanted to take a break and have a chat he wouldn't let up. 'You've got an urge to study right now so you should make the most of it,' he chided. Like all good teachers he got you to achieve much more than you thought you could.

Now that I was living in Cairo I visited Uncle Mahmoud to get his advice on how I should approach my desert project. Like most Egyptians he didn't see the attraction of the desert. 'Too many snakes,' he said. When I told him about the trolley however he saw the point of it immediately. 'It has to be extremely light,' was his only comment, comprehending the need to transport the thing to the desert in the first place as well as the obvious requirement for it not to sink into the first dune I came across. But for a man who'd spent years in the desert he was singularly unimpressed by the place. Perhaps it was all the mine clearance he'd had to do after World War II. 'Neither the Germans nor the British left proper mine maps. It was the Bedouin who made the maps for us by losing their hands and legs. Then they learnt to take them apart to make explosives to go fishing.' Perhaps he wanted to curtail my romantic reverence for Britain's role in the war. He told me to be careful rolling up my blanket in the morning because vipers sometimes crawled under to keep warm at night. Then he added that snakes were commonest near oases – the drier the desert, the fewer the snakes, and permanent camps were always more affected than those moving on every night.

But more than any specific advice, I treasured the way he treated my desire to get out there as entirely normal. It was just like my earlier desire to learn Arabic (which I had to get back, I kept telling myself): I had the urge so I ought to make the most of it. I felt I had to show him how I was progressing, a spur to action in itself. When I outlined all the difficulties in getting permissions he told me which offices to visit and in which ministry they were, but he told me as if he was expecting results. Why wasn't I out there already, he seemed to be implying. Why was I still hanging around Cairo? As I rode the grubby, cavernous lift down to the ground floor I made a decision. Instead of waiting around to make my own expedition I would go on somebody else's.

Six

WHAT IT TAKES TO BE A DESERT EXPLORER

Almasy, I discovered from further research, far from being a war criminal, had saved the lives of several Jews by helping them to escape the Nazi-sympathizing Hungarian police. Earlier, he had even offered his desert services to the British, who turned him down. That's when he went to work for Rommel.

Almasy was also alone among the Zerzura Club members in believing he had actually found the lost oasis. He placed it in the Gilf Kebir plateau, or rather in three wadis on the western side of the Gilf. Years later Bagnold agreed he had made a very good case. But cunning Bagnold also covered himself by announcing that Zerzura was a chimera, a necessary illusion to prompt men to explore. In a famous passage in *Libyan Sands* he wrote:

Zerzura will be there, still to be discovered. As time goes on it will become smaller, more delicate and specialized, but it will be there. Only when all difficulties of travel have been surmounted, when men can wander at will for indefinite periods over tracts of land on which life cannot normally exist, will Zerzura begin to decay.

My idea now was to test the various competitors for the

location of Zerzura and decide which was the most likely. Almasy's claim that the rain oases of the Gilf Kebir were the original location of Zerzura was backed by reasonable evidence, both Tebu tribal information and the animal remains he discovered. The British, apart from the venerable W. J. Harding King, mostly ignored local information. If I wanted to assess the merits of the Gilf as a location for Zerzura I needed to see the place.

So much for the alibi. I actually already knew what the three valleys of the Gilf looked like from photographs. I knew there would be a few stunted acacia trees and no water, except after recent rain. I could make up a good yarn like Almasy did, but what good would that do anyone? I needed to go beneath what Almasy *thought* he was looking for and see what he was *really* looking for. After the war, having solved the lost oasis question in his own mind, Almasy became equally obsessed with searching for the lost army of Cambyses, a quest he thought just as reasonable as hunting for Zerzura. Bagnold only started probing into the desert when he had climbed his 60 Nile pyramids. These were men with time on their hands and an itch that only the deep desert could scratch.

What did Almasy really find? Rock art. Caves and rock shelters full of art. The best-known was the Cave of the Swimmers. On the walls of the cave were pictures of diving, or swimming, men. Swimmers imply water. Oases are watery. Depicted in *The English Patient*, the Cave of the Swimmers achieves a mystical significance; in a way, it becomes Zerzura. The swimmers' cave was not visited for the actual film of *The English Patient* – too far away – instead they mocked up a replica in Tunisia.

I knew I would have to visit that cave. Strip out the fairy tale about lost oases and what you have left is evidence of previous dwellers: stone tools, rock art, caves. And in the previous year a new find had come to light – a new and even bigger cave had been discovered not thirty kilometres from Almasy's swimmers' cave. The new cave was being touted on the internet as the 'largest single site of rock art in Africa'. It had been discovered by an Italian paint millionaire called Bellini and an ex-Egyptian army officer, one Colonel Ahmed Ghali.

Ghali had his own expedition business taking tourists, scientists, oil companies and paint millionaires out into the more remote parts of the Sahara Desert. Having found the cave he kept its location a secret. If you wanted to see it you had to pay him to take you. Secrets for cash – it was that simple. The colonel's company was appropriately called Oasis Expedition. I paid my money to join a group of Italians going with him, and marvelled at how easy it was after all.

The day before we were due to leave, Michael Wafiq, the colonel's business partner, phoned and asked me why I wasn't at Bahariya Oasis. There had been a mistake over dates, half his fault, half mine, and they had left without me. I felt like I'd missed Christmas by oversleeping.

There was a solution, Michael said. I could take the notoriously uncomfortable night bus to Dahkla, the last oasis the expedition would pass through before heading off into deep desert. While the others slept in tents just off the desert road I would catch up and overtake them on the night bus, and we would meet the following lunchtime in Dakhla, a distance of about 850 kilometres from Cairo. There was no choice in the matter. I packed all my kit and met Michael at the bus station that afternoon.

Michael was in his mid-thirties, from an upper-class Egyptian family, and genuinely keen on the desert. But he wasn't *that* keen on sharing information. The desert was still a business to him. He didn't really want to be pals, despite being grateful for the book I gave him (though later he told me his dog ate it, which was not entirely convincing). I asked Michael at the bus-station café whether the expedition to the world's driest place was dry or not. He gave me a suddenly acute look.

'Ghali takes no alcohol but the Italians bring their own wine.'

'Oh good,' I said, relishing in anticipation a good bottle of

Chianti. Almasy had once driven from the Gilf Kebir to the Libyan oasis of Kufra to get water and had returned with a case of Chianti. The empties were supposed to be still out in the desert.

'Do you have any alcohol with you?' Michael added in a nonchalant way.

'Oh yes,' I said, 'a bottle of the finest Egyptian whisky. Old Horse – maybe you know the brand?'

Not surprisingly he didn't. I'd taken to drinking Old Horse as it was by far the cheapest powerful liquor available, £4.50 sterling. I liked the absolutely shameless way the Old Horse company printed 'Jonny Wakker export brand' on the label and honestly expected anyone to believe it. Old Horse was as rough as an old horse's hoof and about as tasty. Its deep amber colour was obviously the result of some noxious dye that imparted some of the authentic Old Horse taste, which was a little like cooking brandy mixed with TCP. But stuck in a sandstorm five hundred kilometres from civilization I'd be grateful for the stuff. And what with Ghali's reputation as a military stickler and the possibility that the sixteen Italians spoke no English, French or crap Arabic and might even hog all the Chianti to themselves, I needed all the support I could get.

'By the way,' Michael continued with a sort of twisted smile on his face, 'you haven't got a GPS, have you?'

'No,' I lied, sensing that this piece of kit might be disapproved of.

'Good,' he said. 'The colonel doesn't like people stealing his discoveries.'

'Anything else I can't do – I mean, anything else I should be careful about?'

Michael again twisted his smile into place. 'We don't like people taking away prehistoric artefacts.' Great. My prospective collection of stone axes and arrowheads just went pop. 'And Ghali only issues three cups of either tea or coffee a day.' That didn't sound too bad, even for a caffeine addict such as me. But the sudden appearance of rules was worrying.

I was going to the desert to escape rules, not find them.

Michael kindly waited until the bus arrived. It was operated by a company called Upper Egypt Buses Ltd and looked reasonable enough, apart from the sizeable hole in the coachwork just next to the rear door. I nodded in an ironic fashion towards the hole, through which I could see several men bedding down on the grimy-looking seats inside. Michael smiled and said, 'Put it this way: it won't be a journey you want to make twice.'

'Oh I like long bus journeys at night,' I said gamely. 'You know, you go to sleep and then you wake up and you've arrived.' We both looked at the bus with its blatant insomnia-inducing appearance. 'Even if you don't sleep,' I added, 'there are always the stops.'

'Ah yes, the stops,' said Michael mysteriously. 'Well, good luck. Meet the expedition at the Gorgeous restaurant in Mut. Everyone knows it.'

I climbed aboard the night bus and sat in an empty space behind two larking lads who had already identified themselves as also heading for Mut. Good, I'll just watch them, I thought. My greatest fear was falling asleep and waking up in Kharga, which was about two hundred kilometres further than where I wanted to be. But then it transpired my ticket had a seat number, in Arabic, which I read back to front (which is the right way to read letters but the wrong way to read numerals – I often made this mistake). The strange thing was, I thought, as a rather fussy man in spectacles evicted me from my seat, none of the seats actually had numbers on them. Oh there's one. And three rows back, another. It was like a tricky sudoku puzzle: use logic to fill in the gaps, but with the added psychological dimension of solving it without letting on you're lost. I could see 28 and 36, so where was 43? I really had no idea. By now the bus was full. Every passenger without exception was male. Many looked as if they had just finished doing dirty and dangerous work. Quite a few had several blue plastic laundry bags full of stuff. I was the only foreigner. And I was the only person not wearing a thick coat of some kind. I must have looked a little lost because a villainous-looking man with several missing teeth asked what number I was.

'Forty-three.'

'This is forty-three,' he said, and indicated the seat next to him, which was lucky as I could see no other vacant seats. (As a side note I should add that at about midnight I was resting my head against the seat in front when I uncovered the bent remains of the seat number, which was 45, and I was behind that so I was obviously in the wrong seat. This mystery was never solved.) There was a flicker of interest in me and where I might be going, started by a friendly bearded man two seats ahead of me. My destination, Mut, was repeated up and down the bus and the bearded man made a dismissive gesture with his hand that meant very clearly 'Far away'.

It was dark before the bus escaped the lights and traffic noise of Cairo. I had packed all my cold-weather gear (sweater and fleece and raincoat) in the locker at the side of the bus beneath a monstrous pile of luggage going to nearer destinations. All I wore was a thin shirt and a cotton moleskin jacket that I quickly turned up at the collar. Then I tucked it into my trousers, which I then tucked into my socks. Seat '43' was almost directly opposite the hole and a steady ice-cold draught soon had me shivering. I put my watch on the outside of my shirt cuff to further trap in warmth. I had heard it got colder in the desert at night than in the city but I had also read that this temperature drop is purely of a relative nature: it feels cold because it was so hot during the day. Bollocks. It *is* bloody cold at night in the desert. Like the 'scientific' explanation which diminishes the existence of a crust on the sand after a cold night, it sounds plausible until you experience it. The only exception is people who have done a lot of physical work during the day, either walking or setting up camp: they seem to feel the cold less. I sat in the icy wind and shivered. The villainous man dozed, wrapped in a thick blanket of coarse grey wool which was spotted with damp under his reddened nose, which was just poking out at the top.

He awoke immediately the bus stopped at the first roadside café. The place was open and barn-like, lit by fluorescent lights with a blue tint. I timidly ordered tea, and held the glass in both hands. Were we in the desert yet? All around looked pitch black and there was hardly any traffic. I supposed we must be. I thought about getting my warm clothes from the locker but then thought twice about digging in the dark through that mountain of huge laundry sacks and splitting cardboard boxes.

Back on the bus it was film time. A telly at the front was playing a film set in the 1940s, when the Egyptians were agitating for complete independence from Britain. The bad guy was an effeminate British officer who took sadistic pleasure in pistol-whipping pregnant Bedouin women, booting injured Arabs in their nether regions and even poisoning a well from which, it appeared, only children drank. This total bastard commanded faceless British soldiers whose idea of a good time was to bayonet a handicapped beggar and a few blind storytellers. I shrank down into my seat. As the only foreigner on the bus it was bad enough; imagine being the sole Arab on a greyhound going through North Dakota while a docudrama about Osama bin Laden is playing. I planned, if things got nasty, to deny my British ancestry and claim Irish descent. It was true I had an Irish great-great-grandmother, but this was scant justification for such cowardice. I knew Yanks sometimes went backpacking with Canadian flags sewn to their rucksacks. Being massacred because of assumed allegiance with a foreign policy has never appealed to me. But as the British abused and oppressed more and more of the Egyptian nation a periodic survey of my weary and half-interested fellow travellers revealed no obvious feeling of antagonism. These were oasis dwellers, farmers and workers who had more to worry about than buried resentments stirred up by inaccurate film-making. I hoped. Finally the officer overstretched himself and shot the leader of a group of peasants armed with mattocks and shovels. They quickly reduced him to a bloody pulp and the film ended.

What a relief. Exuding Irishness, I ordered another tea at the next stopping place and then waited my turn at the crowded urinals – all the tea from the last stop, not to mention the cold. Another hour and I saw the low, yellow-lit walls of a desert town through the window. This was Bahariya Oasis, but on the bus all the stops were named after villages, and there may be many villages within the ambit of an oasis. This made it a little confusing as my book with all the names of the oasis villages was in my pack in the bus locker.

I got off the bus and saw the sandy road: we had turned off from the main asphalt on to an unmade section. Several Land Cruiser 60 models patrolled about, just like the ones in Chris Scott's book. Bedouinmobiles. The roofs were all low, the buildings mud-walled. No other road traffic. Quiet. Stars in the sky when you got clear of the single streetlight. I had been excited, I remembered, when I had gone into the jungle for the first time, also the Canadian wilderness, but those places had none of the romance of the desert. Jungle and wilderness display all too soon the savage scars of nature, reminding you that man is of no account in such a place. Besides they are dirty, too, really muddy in the case of the jungle. Mud and romance don't go together unless you get off on WWI trench-warfare fantasies. The desert is different, I was learning. It is less, not more. It is the successive elimination of what we are used to. The jungle is more. There may be no cars and few people but there is a superabundance of everything else. Cities were also more, not less. I craved less.

I had quite forgotten the film by the time I reboarded the bus. As I tissue-plugged the ear that lay precisely in the jetstream created by the hole in the bus's side, I fondly hugged the secret knowledge to myself that the desert was my kind of place. I felt warmer already.

We ground on along the desert road, doing at least 100kmh I guessed from the wind noise past the hole. The going was smooth, there was hardly any traffic and we stopped at no checkpoints, which, illogically, were unmanned at night. Later, when I made the trip by day and in a private car, we were stopped for no little time going both into and out of each oasis.

By now the bus was emptying of its travellers and my villainous two-toothed companion had moved into a free seat opposite. I lay on the seat with my feet pulled up and my hands down my trousers, for warmth. I was past caring whether my fellow travellers thought I was up to something odd.

At five in the morning, the bus stopped. The villainous man leaned over and nodded his head: we had arrived at Mut. It was a bit like getting dropped off in the suburb of a French industrial town. There was a confluence of unnecessarily wide roads with high kerbs and obvious signs of municipal planting. But the place was quiet and empty. No cars at all. Good streetlights and new buildings set back from the road.

I started walking towards what I hoped was the Mebarez Hotel, which had been recommended by Michael. A lone microbus full of stacking chairs roared up behind me. 'Fain? Where?' the boy hanging out of the door called. I told them and the driver demanded E£20 to take me. For all I knew it was twenty kilometres back up the road. I agreed. No sooner had I perched myself on a toppling pile of plastic chairs than the microbus stopped again. Grins all round. A five-hundred-yard rip-off. I paid with poor grace and mentally changed the money into pounds sterling to make it seem trivial. I took the blankets off two beds and turned on the air conditioner to heat the room. I never switched it off.

At the Gorgeous restaurant the next day I grew nervous lest I had already missed the convoy. The misnamed Gorgeous was a long hut with tables outside at the edge of an empty two-lane highway. My impression of Mut as a new town was enhanced by the wide stretch of road I waited next to, yet

Dakhla Oasis, of which Mut was the centre, was mentioned by Herodotus. Mut was already old then. There are the remains of stone huts reckoned to be twelve thousand years old, making the place home to the oldest houses in Africa and maybe even the world. It seemed the right place to be starting my journey. Dakhla is also the source of most Zerzura legends.

The old centre of Mut was a mile or so away, but I did not explore. I sat outside reading old *National Geographic*s provided by Yusef Farid at his hut-like restaurant and quizzed him about the likely arrival time of Ghali. 'He is always here around twelve-thirty,' he said. At one-thirty he amended that to one-thirty. At two-thirty I was sure I had been left behind. What little traffic there had been was all lorries with sloping trailers and great vibrating snouts, and pick-ups laden with farm produce and workers. Men riding donkeys went along the hard shoulder.

Yusef Farid told me about an English backpacker called Paul who had slept at night on the restaurant floor and helped serve customers by day. Paul loved Mut so much he wanted to return and start a tour business with Yusef Farid. 'But Paul should become Muslim if he wants to stay in Mut,' cautioned Yusef, 'otherwise he will be lonely.' I did not know then that I would later have my own chance to assess Paul's state of mind. I did not yet know that coincidence is the organizing principle of the desert oases, rather than the side-effect it is in ordinary life.

Yusef had no other customers and nothing to do. He was quite happy whiling away the time with me. I like this place, I thought. Less worrying about time – less worry all round, except for me worrying that I've missed the expedition. 'Do not worry,' said Yusef, 'they always stop here for lunch. Always.' I looked over the wall of the restaurant and there was the desert. A small dune, and then some palm trees and then flatness off into the distance where you could just make out the lumpiness of more dunes. Hot now. Best to drink some water.

I had given considerable thought to the water requirements

of living in the desert. Summer or winter the LRDG ration was five pints per day per man, which included all cooking and cups of tea. Desert expert Nick Middleton had spent time with nomads in Niger who survived on two litres a day in forty-five-degree heat whereas he needed ten litres. 'But then you do see an awful lot of people there with kidney problems,' he remarked. Hassanein Bey, arguably the greatest of the Zerzura explorers, travelled with Bedouin who drank, in winter, a glass of water at dawn and another at dusk. To take any in between 'was considered an effeminacy'. This excluded the several powerful cups of Bedouin tea made each day with a handful of tea and a handful of sugar for each pint of tea. Chris Scott, when I had attended his lecture, had been blunt: 'You're not a Bedouin so don't expect to drink as little as they do.' This contradicted the experience of Wilfred Thesiger, whom I had met a few years before he died. In winter, riding camels, he'd drunk a pint of water a day. But maybe he had kidney stones too – I didn't ask, and now it was too late to find out.

A desire to emulate the past nudged me towards the low end of water consumption. There was definitely something wimpy about glugging back the H_2O while stone-faced nomads sucked on pebbles carried under their tongues to alleviate thirst. But a nasty experience I'd had in Indonesia suggested caution. Noonday beer-drinking, macho refusal to drink water and running a mile carrying a suitcase full of film stock on my shoulders had led to complete heat exhaustion. It wouldn't do to pass out in front of a bunch of Italians.

Heat death occurs when every last drop of water in your body has been expended in trying to cool you down. In a cold, humid climate, if you assiduously drink your own urine (biologically inert) you might expect to last a week. In the Sahara in summer you might manage two and a half days. Dehydration is massively hastened by the body's waste of water in sweat. A jackal can go a month without drinking: it has no sweat glands. A Barbary sheep never drinks: like the desert fox it gets all it needs from what it eats. Sweating is what makes humans particularly badly designed for arid climates, and I was heading for what was described as the 'most profoundly arid place on earth'. I liked that – the Atacama might get less rain but the Western Desert was more profoundly arid. This was a calculation based on the sheer absence of springs, wells and rivers, as well as lack of rainfall. In the Gilf Kebir you'd be three hundred kilometres from the nearest water – nowhere else in the Sahara is as far from life-giving moisture – and this had to be one of the reasons the lost oasis myths accumulated in this particular region. The less water you have, the more you fantasize about it.

In profoundly arid places, sweating can be fatal. Fat people are most at risk, followed by big people with a poor surface-to-volume ratio. Smaller, skinny people fare best, exactly the body type of the Goran, Tebu and Bidyat, the Saharan tribes whom even the Tuareg admire for their ability to survive with little water. Thin people cool down much more efficiently, do less work and therefore lose less water. One story has it that a Tebu, one of the black tribesmen who spread out from the Tibesti region, killed a goat and filled it with water. He ate the goat meat and drank the water as he walked. In ten days he arrived at his destination six hundred kilometres away.

There are other ways to remain cool when the temperature climbs above the red zone into the low forties. The Bedouin method is to insulate oneself from the heat. Instead of strip-ping off like a Desert Rat digging in at El Alamein, Bedouin are famously overdressed. Harding King, the first to tentatively name Zerzura on a map, wrote of Bedouin in high summer wearing woollen long-johns. But even the Bedu strip off when they do heavy physical work likely to make them sweat. If not, they remain covered up, following the principle of the cold box by having several wool (not cotton, a poor insulator) layers trapping in the cool air of the night for as long as possible. Especially if there is a hot wind blowing, insulation is the best way to remain cool.

In the far distance I could see dust being raised. The colonel was coming. Six Land Cruisers with boosted suspension, fully laden roofracks and natty sand-protecting vinyl stretched like a gartered sock over the bonnet make an impressive sight. I instantly knew, from my assiduous nighttime rereading of Scott, that the front two cruisers were 78 Series, the next three were 60 Series and the last a 43 Series pick-up. To anyone sad enough to want to spend time memorizing car data like a twelve-year-old skimming through his pack of Top Trumps, the above roll-call of vehicles was extremely impressive, a canny balance of reliability and load-carrying strength. To the rest of the human race it was six four-wheel-drives piled high with kit.

But the minutiae of Land Cruiser lore makes for a parable of our times. The inexorable drive towards more and more complicated and computer-assisted cars has been resisted by just one manufacturer – Toyota – but only in their comparatively unknown 70 Series Land Cruisers. You'll never see one of these on the High Street in Guildford. No *Hausfrau* in Connecticut would be seen in one at the mall. For a start, they fail most countries' rigorous emissions standards. Plus they're just too damn basic for the pampered populations of the northern hemisphere. On the diesel version the only thing that needs electricity is the clock. Wind-up windows, not electric, are standard. No silly door and seat-belt bleepers; in fact, if you're wearing a seat belt in a 70 Series you're in the wrong vehicle. 70 Series are designed for terrain that restricts your speed to sub-seat-belt-necessary speeds. Seat belts best protect you when you crash into something coming your way, but where the 70 Series go nothing is coming your way. Now that the Bedouin have largely given up their camels as a mode of transport (they are still kept for agricultural and cultural reasons), to own a 70 Series is the aim of every self-respecting nomad.

One can wax lyrical about camels and horses, and even elephants, but only a nerd goes on about cars. Yet there is something just a little awe-inspiring about the utter stark functionality of a 70 Series. Forget Land-Rover. Totally forget

Jeep. Those are complex cars for urban cowboys. The four-litre engine of the 70 Series is a completely repairable, mechanically simple fifty-year-old design. Spare parts are everywhere. The chassis has steel twice as thick as that of a Land-Rover.

Toyota have mucked about with their other Land Cruisers. The bloated 100 Series you see blocking the exit route at Sainsbury's is chock-full of electronics – reliable electronics, but when they go wrong you need a bloke with a laptop and a handful of silicon chips, not an unlettered nomad with a hammer and a rusty spanner. The earlier 80 Series has coil springs (harder to bodge than leaf springs) and a lot of electrical gadgets. You have to go back to the 60 Series, which stopped production in 1991, to get a car as simple and strong as the 70 Series. Which is why twenty-year-old 60 Series Land Cruisers in the oases still fetch £10,000 sterling even in a condition that would fetch about £700 in England. If you can't afford a 70 Series and you want to go out into the desert, probably to make money by driving tourists around, then you buy a 60 Series. I'd learnt as much from Shaheer, who had told me about one importer who brought in vehicles that were cut up to satisfy tax requirements (much less duty on spare parts, plus a car that old couldn't be imported anyway) and then secretly welded back together again, given false chassis numbers and sold on. Literally bent Toyotas plying the desert, and people in the oases were so desperate for them they paid up. Bahariya was the centre of the Land Cruiser market, and anyone who bought or sold Cruisers had a connection there. It was 350 kilometres out in the desert, and the world centre for one model of Japanese car.

I also liked the 60 and the 70 Series because they could be recycled. They might be cars, spewing filth and noise into the air, but at least there was no need to build any more of them. The Bedouin of Bahariya Oasis had done something the Green Party and ecologically minded Western democrats could only talk about – they'd taken a piece of Western technology and they'd found a way of using it more efficiently, by far, than we did. A 60 Series car in America was an interesting crock, or in a breaker's yard already. In Bahariya it was immortal. Unlike a Spitfire, which can only fly so many hours before it cracks apart, a 60 Series, if surrounded by limitless spares, can live for ever.

The Italians left the cars and waited impatiently while Yusef Farid built one long table for all of us to sit together (except the drivers, a surly-looking lot at first glance). I instantly recognized Colonel Ghali. He was tall, maybe six foot three, bulky but not fat, and wearing full camouflage jacket and trousers tucked neatly into Hi-Tec desert boots. He wore expensive aviator glasses with little leather anti-glare patches at each side. He had a smooth, massive, cherubic head, com-pletely bald, which was hidden by a camouflage baseball cap. There was something of Marlon Brando's Kurtz in that head, and the way he walked was very upright, board-straight: he was in the centre of things and he was in command.

I went up, expecting some *bonhomie* after my long journey and our successful rendezvous. It was hard to gauge his expres-sion behind the aviators, which, owing to the discrepancy in our heights I had to look up into, seeing my own wide-angle petitioning form staring back from a vanishing landscape. 'I made it,' I said.

He nodded, then turned to one of the drivers, a tubby lad with a wide moustache. 'Adil will take you. There is room in his car.'

'Er, Michael said that you would pay for the hotel I stayed in last night.' It sounded like lame begging.

'Your mistake, you pay,' he said with a bluntness that made me think, Oh shit, seventeen days with this bastard. What I have I let myself in for?

'Well I was given the wrong day, even if I was given the right date. It was half your mistake – well, your company's mistake – and half mine.'

He patted my arm and let out a barking laugh, the harsh laugh of someone who has left learning to laugh rather late in life. 'Go and get the bill and I'll pay you back,' he said.

It wasn't as if the bill, which was £6 sterling, was very much. It was a silly situation. As I paid and gathered my bags from the hotel with fat Adil waiting in the Land Cruiser outside I thought, Well, I'm obviously not going to give this to bill to the colonel, I've got some pride. Maybe that was what he expected. Oh shit, mind games already and we haven't even left the tarmac.

It was with muted enthusiasm therefore that I ate Yusef's meal and engaged in conversation with the Italian adventurers. They were not young, but they were keen and well informed. They came with an outfit called Kel 12, an Italian expedition company that could get you up Everest – if you had enough money. This was the trip of a lifetime for some of them. For others it was just one more notch, another experience to talk about when they got back to Milan. Several had been to Antarctica even, but just to feed the penguins, so to speak. Mainly they were couples, either childless or remarried at a later stage, spending their money on seeing the high-status parts of the world you couldn't normally get to. There was a heart doctor, retired, who looked like he might have heart trouble, and a surgeon called Franco, an irrepressible unshaven ladies' man of sixty-five who chain-smoked Marlboro Lights, his frail frame weighed down by his two Leica SLRs with monster lenses. Others had been consultants and academics with business connections. The only younger people were a couple, maybe late twenties, her a doctor, him a thin bearded computer expert who spoke shy but good Microsoft English.

Their minder from the expedition company was a round, short, cheerful Italian with a greying beard called Marino. I had to pay him for the beer I drank at the Gorgeous – the last beer for seventeen days, I quipped, and since everyone agreed I realized that none of them had secreted cans of lager along with the Chianti in their stylish kitbags – the Chianti I hoped was in their stylish kitbags. My Old Horse was in my day bag, better for avoiding breakages and snoopers. I also had my outlawed GPS and a sat-phone I had borrowed, which I also felt constrained to keep a secret.

Adil was driving one of the 60s, big and roomy like a giant station wagon. There was only me and a sparrow-like Italian called Massimo with him. We drove on down the thin, very black strip of road, which had limitless sand on either side. There were odd buildings in the sand that had a military flavour. Then there were no buildings and despite chatting to Massimo and Adil I was also observing myself entering the desert for the first time. It mostly looked messy and sunlit, sort of predictable. No palm trees. We passed two checkpoints and then, at a point I tried to memorize (slight incline behind, rows of low dunes on the right, conical hill away to the left), the cars pulled up in convoy fashion and the drivers jumped out and wedged each tyre valve open with a piece of match so that there was hissing all around. It was the only sound: mid-afternoon, sunny, quite hot, windless, the hissing of twenty-four tyres slowly deflating. This was it, the undeniably exciting moment when you leave behind the tarmac and head ... out there. My eyes narrowed as I scanned the wobbling horizon. The tyres are deflated so that they get a better grip on the sand. I knew all about the intricacies of tyres, how a tall thin tyre was better than a short fat one (when deflated the proportionate increase in contact with the ground is greater and offers less rolling resistance), how you sometimes had to go as low as 1 bar, 10 lbs/sq. in, to get any traction. The 1 bar club – an exclusive coterie of those who had been where the sand requires extreme measures.

Richard Burton maintained that there were always three starts to an expedition in Africa: the start, the long start and the real start. I had started in Cairo when I left my house. The long start took me to the oasis town of Mut. Now there was the real start, leaving the tarmac. There were no tracks to follow; I had learnt from Michael that Ghali always made a new route, even if the destination was somewhere he'd been before.

The sound of escaping air had never before been so redolent

of impending adventure. It was like setting sail across the ocean, leaving port after travelling down only rivers and canals. You forget how much of one's driving experience is following a track, a road, a predefined route laid out by someone else. Here you could drive anywhere, doughnut the desert into a pattern of personal Nazca lines, make your own road, be first. All that space. Just the thought of it expanded my mind.

Seven

THE COLONEL AND HIS FOX

My off-road driving experience was very limited, my off-road desert driving experience non-existent. But the desert here was hard and compacted, and, apart from the odd rock, afforded an easy passage. What was remarkable was that no one was telling us where to go. It was like setting sail on an ocean. Of course the authoritarian nature of the colonel made it hard to fully imbibe that sense of complete freedom, but it was there all right.

The flat sand soon ceased to amaze me. Now I wanted dunes, big wave-like ones. We passed some, but they were a long way off. Sometimes the car swayed and you felt its bulk wobble on the springs, the tyres yawing in the sand before Adil gunned the engine and set us straight again. We drove on, tyres hissing over the surface.

We drove in convoy fashion, linked by sputtering Arabic over the radio. When there was something to look at or an announcement the colonel would speak in French and then Marino, in the second car, would expand it into Italian. We quite soon came upon three low, shale-covered hills with a spreading patch of shade between them.

The colonel climbed out and stamped around, testing the sand. Then, using hand and arm gestures very reminiscent of the guys with table-tennis bats on aircraft carriers, he arranged the vehicles precisely into the shape of an E without the central bar. Inside the E a long table and folding chairs were set out, with a stove on a cook's table on one side.

We put up our tents with a modicum of incompetence. The colonel had a special way of putting them up, and everyone was nervous about doing it the wrong way. There was a lot of covert glancing across at other people's tents. No one wanted to put a peg wrong. Though I knew that hard-core desert explorers never used tents, I was glad of mine. It was somewhere to hide and slug whisky. No doubt I could have downed the whisky in front of everyone, but some obscure need for privacy, plus a reluctance to share with sixteen others, kept me behind zipped doors.

After convincing myself that my tent would pass muster and not be torn down during whatever 'inspection' the colonel had planned, I wandered with rock-climbing intent towards the first shale-covered hill. The colonel appeared out of his own orange tent (ours were white and of obvious lower status. I had also noticed his tent had been pitched by Ramadan, the kitchen boy). Sensing my urge to climb, the colonel announced that it was forbidden to climb the hills as the shale was dangerous. I nodded in cheerful acquiescence while at the same time thinking the kind of thoughts that, if unchecked, result in assassination and the formation of terrorist organizations. When we sat down to eat I noticed a walking stick with a metal tip at one end stuck into the ground at the head of the table. The stick had a curly wild-sheep's-horn handle. It was obviously the colonel's stick, and fixing it in the sand at the head of the table had an obvious meaning.

I nodded at the stick to Marino, who grinned. 'The sharp end is made from a captured Israeli bayonet.' Right. That figured.

But I abandoned this negative train of thought when the colonel staggered up to our now night-dark and wind-blown group carrying a huge slab of stone. I knew at once, from seeing something similar at Richard Head's house, that this was an ancient quern for grinding corn. Perhaps prehistoric, perhaps not, but certainly old. The interior was scoured out like a bowl after years of use. Such stones were still in use in the northern Sudan in the 1920s, according to explorer Douglas Newbold. The nomads would leave the grindstones along their route and simply carry corn, which could be ground up when needed. This stone could have been five thousand years or only a few centuries old, it was impossible to tell. But such quibbling was far from my mind as I gazed on this sizeable lump of booty. It was like the first time I'd seen a bear in the wilderness. How come such a big thing is allowed? Surely we've extinguished all the exciting stuff? I'd been brought up looking for flint shards on the South Downs and never finding one. I'd been brought up believing the world was all explored and dug up and recorded and now in a museum with cases that gave you tiny electric shocks when you touched them, enervated rather than excited by the experience. And here was genuine archaeological treasure. Immediately I suspected that the colonel had planted the stone on an earlier trip just so that we would be impressed, but I soon dismissed the idea. There had been no tracks leading to this place, and besides, it transpired it had been one of the drivers who'd stumbled across it while setting up the generator. This was the real thing. If I needed further reason to explain to myself my obsession with the desert I now had it: you could find treasure here.

I spent the meal at the conversational level just up from small-talk that you make when you are with a group you will see all day and every day for the next three weeks. You aren't brash, you tread a little carefully. It isn't like a weekend jaunt or even a week's, when you can remain stuffily silent hunched over the crossword the whole time; everyone sensed it was important that we all get on. I talked mainly to Geppo, a Milanese clothier, or ex-clothier – I guessed he was retired, but as he was sensitive to the connotations of the word he phrased it as 'The business was no longer competitive against Far Eastern imports.' He now styled himself as an expert in land snails. Even archaeologists had consulted him, he said. He told me some interesting facts about the way land snails can give all sorts of clues about what has happened and how. Snails leave behind their shells, which are more durable and less likely to be dispersed than bones. He painted such a rosy picture of the forensic utility of land snails that I found myself thinking, How come I have overlooked this very important field for so long? Snails are where it's at!

When Geppo had hooked me on to snails he turned adroitly away and engaged his wife in conversation. She was a leathery old hag with a big Nikon camera forever in a see-through plastic bag to protect it from dust. Her face, or the state of it, intrigued me. It was extremely dark brown, obviously the result of years of patient tanning. She might have been a little dark-skinned in the beginning, but the sun had turned her a kind of reddish chocolate colour. There had been a price to pay for being the most tanned bitch on the beach: the collapse of her epidermis into a miniature replica of a range of hills, like a relief map of the Lake District done in brown, her big blue fractious eyes were like lakes enfolded in the devastated skin. In her youth her catty snobbery would have been ignored because she was attractive; now, along with her ruined looks, it was just something you wanted to avoid.

Old Geppo, though, was still in great shape. He had one of those white beards, the Platonic ideal of the old sea-salt's beard, a clipped-back, utterly restrained version of Hemingway, neat as hell with no scraggly bits going down the neck, hair white too, all there, looking great against his perma-tan which looked merely healthy rather than overcooked.

There would be plenty of time to get to know the others. I had already taken against several of them, as I always do in such situations, usually for utterly trivial and imaginary reasons which sometimes harden into real enmity only to crack and soften, sometimes too late in the day when you realize they could have been your friend all along. I made only one resolution: do not go crazy. Every time I go on a trip that requires me to interact with others all day and every day for a long period of time (more than two weeks) I manage a single act of madness I later regret deeply.

My bouts of madness were neither very amusing nor very illuminating, unless you count threatening to brain an Indonesian performance artist with a broom handle as amusing. To be fair, the man had, for days, been taking samples of my sweat under the most trying circumstances during a jungle trip for his ongoing 'performance' entitled 'The White Man Sweats'.

Then there was the set-to with my old friend Ben after we disagreed over the correct way to extinguish a primus stove after it had just exploded over a fleece containing the address and telephone number of an attractive girl we had just met.

Or another one in the Canadian wilderness, over the utility of adding camomile tea to porridge in the absence of sugar and milk.

Bouts of madness. All over *nothing*. Only this time I was prepared. I had the Old Horse. I had a few cigars and a couple of novels. And I had a goal – see the cave, witness the marvel.

I deliberately used the utilitarian goal of 'getting desert info out of Ghali' as yet another reason not to blow it.

At dinner, the only confrontation occurred when Franco, the wheezing heart surgeon, produced his GPS. The colonel said they were not allowed, and Franco made a theatrical gesture of replacing it inside his coat pocket. There then followed a fairly conclusive exchange in which the colonel appealed to all of us in French, making a clear case for protecting his own discoveries while not exactly accusing Franco of intellectual property theft – is that what taking a GPS position is when you arrive under another's direction? I knew that fishermen and wreck divers were obsessive about the keeping secret of their 'numbers', and what was a waymark but the latitude and longitude of somewhere to aim for? If a seaman could be allowed to keep his treasures secret, so too could someone who sailed on the nearest equivalent to the sea, the desert. But it didn't quite seem the same. I had already intended to bag every position I could as soon as it was dark. I had cleverly pitched my tent right at the edge of the little cluster of domes, with easy access to a rock, behind which I could lock on to a friendly satellite.

I could see the logic in keeping the coordinates for the cave a secret. That was Ghali's treasure, the reason why the Italians signed up for the expedition. The biggest single site of rock art in Africa could only be turned into money if very few people knew where it was. But keeping us in the dark about where we were when we weren't anywhere special seemed like mere control-freakery.

As soon as I retired to my tent after the very palatable pasta stew with a side dish of ladies' fingers, I took out my little yellow GPS and, unzipping the tent door, peered out. All quiet. Good. I clambered out, shielding the GPS within the cover of my jacket, and padded across the now-cold sand in bare feet to the rock. I switched the machine on and it took an age to log on to the satellites. I read the numbers and scribbled them into a special notebook that I aimed to keep hidden, along with the GPS.

Back in the tent I unrolled a map that I'd been given by Richard Head and that, gauging roughly the intellectual climate of the trip, I judged it best not to reveal. The map, compiled in 1941 by and for the Long Range Desert Group, available as a download on the net or as a photocopy from Cambridge University or as a collector's item on eBay, was, strictly speaking, I knew, illegal for a foreigner to possess. Richard, who had lived long in the Middle East and was expert at getting his way, had obtained it from the Government Map Office using a combination of guile and company stationery. Also a few free pens and keyrings for the clerk's kids. The map was one of the last four in existence at the Map Office, a genuine 1941 print rather than the rubbish copies they also sell, which have considerable blurring on the inscriptions and details. The map is in English, with the later addition of Arabic place names. It is sixty years old but still regarded as one of the most useful maps to the area, despite being up to five hundred metres out in places. It contains concise and precise descriptions such as 'Two hills with stone circles on top' or

'Low dunes, poor going'. 'Map 10, Uweinat' was its name, and for anyone interested in Zerzura it was the only map you had to have.

Considering its age and complete availability as a copy worldwide it was hard to understand the reluctance of the Egyptian government to allow its sale. Unless you understand that information in the East is as precious a commodity as time is in the West. We give information away in the West too easily, since we can barely control its dissemination. It is felt that keeping things secret for no good reason is somehow a bad thing. But we don't give away time. Time is what we really sell, not information. When people talk about the information revolution they mean getting information faster, thus saving time. In the Middle East time is given away more generously. People give you the time of day, waste your time, generally treat time in a cavalier fashion. But information, even pretty crap, fifth-rate information, is hoarded like the innermost secrets of a pharaonic priest cult.

I plotted my illegally obtained GPS numbers against my illegally obtained map and saw that we were about three hundred kilometres from the Gilf Kebir. I made a faint cross in pencil, feeling just like Van der Poel, played by Anthony Quayle in *Ice Cold in Alex*, another desert inspiration and one of my five all-time favourite films. Quayle plays a Nazi spy who creeps off each night as John Mills and Sylvia Simms relax tensely around the campfire. He sets up his antenna and we realize his bulky knapsack is really a transmitter connected to Berlin. He pretends to the others that it contains a reserve supply of gin, a good enough cover since Mills is an alcoholic and reluctant to believe anything else. My knapsack was also bulky and containing contraband booze, and, even better – my sat-phone was like Quayle's Nazi radio; I could use it to broadcast my position, entered on my illegal map.

It was deeply satisfying to have this hidden dimension, to be playing at spies with nobody knowing. As long as nobody did know. Admittedly it was unlikely that the offences I'd committed would rate a firing squad, but still, I was eager to avoid reprimand and humiliation at the hands of the colonel.

I could see that he was in an unenviable position, psychologically. His professional training as a military intelligence officer probably heightened his sense of the power of information, yet at the same time he was now, as an expedition guide, in a profession that was about the dissemination of information, show and tell, the real story. It wasn't as if he were guiding ignoramuses out for a day trip from the oases. His whole market was the extremely well informed, who came precisely to increase their knowledge of the place. How much to tell? How much to keep mum about? What is the precise worth in euros over a five-year period of telling people they are taking a dump on a neolithic lakeside dwelling place?

In keeping with his generally tight hold on information the colonel wouldn't tell anyone what time reveille was the next morning. We were simply told to wait in our tents until Ramadan, a squat, bulky young chap who did all the washing-up, came round and roused us. I could feel a slight frisson of disapproval at not knowing the right time to be up. The Italians were all from the north and definitely not the type to want to lie in bed. Half of them probably had alarm clocks. Eventually, after half an hour of discussion, it transpired that breakfast would be at about seven. Even trivial information isn't free in Egypt.

I was up before Ramadan reached my tent. He was an odd chap and I tried to befriend him but he had only one master. I have an abiding image of Colonel Ghali, digging to free the car (more of that later) and shouting, 'Rama-daan!' – each name it seemed had an imperative form, just as Magoob became elongated into 'Ma-gooob' when you were shouting for him – and Ramadan came running like a small dog to its master, who had now finished digging and was brushing the sand off his trousers. The colonel kept him waiting before the one order: '*Maya*. Water,' and then Ramadan ran back to the pick-up he always rode in, grabbed a water bottle and ran back to the colonel's car, all in a noonday heat of about thirty degrees. But somehow, through an excess of zeal without desire for reward, Ramadan escaped the appearance of subservience. He was always busy, on top of a vehicle undoing knots, washing up, polishing the stove. In every group of Egyptians engaged on a job there is one who carries the baton of continuous work while the rest kind of drop in and out as required, spending time merely contemplating and discussing the work in progress. Ramadan was the silent one who always toils, the one who keeps the whole thing moving. I wondered if his presence was as necessary as the colonel's to the able running of our expedition.

Breakfast. Italians milling around the steel flasks of hot water. Teabags or instant, one tiny tin cup, handleless, at a time. Three a day not counting the one shot of espresso from the tight-girdled aluminium pot on the long folding trestle table where we all sit. Already a seating pattern: determined to break that. I sit next to tubby Adolfo, another former heart specialist who seems as timid and bulky as a peasant prised away from his home pastures. His wife clicks stones together in her palm; she's found two she thinks might be flint tools but one look and I know they aren't. I still don't believe such ordinary mortals as ourselves can find treasure.

The best bit so far: walking away this morning from camp in a general direction indicated by Ghali pointing his bayonet stick south-west. While they packed up camp and refuelled the cars in secret (I never once saw a vehicle being tanked up) we were allowed to walk as far as we could in the hour and a half or so it took them to finish. Almost everyone clustered around Marino, just like a popular tour guide. But they wandered too slowly for Massimo and me.

Massimo – skinny, bird-like and alert, no bleary pensioner specs for him – enjoyed hopping over rocks in the Dolomites, a pair of Zeiss binoculars round his neck for catching sight of eagles on the wing. He was ahead of me out on one flank, the shale hill behind him and in front of us a smooth rise of sand with nothing on it at all. A blank horizon, yellow, empty. No sound except my feet crunching through the sand. And yet there were things. Up ahead, a black dot. It seemed a big thing far away, but suddenly it was at my feet. First rule of the desert: it destroys perspective. There is nothing in the background to provide a comparison with any object you see, so it's impossible to maintain your sense of correct scale and distance. To counter this you need a suspension of decision, a willingness to tolerate an object as unknown not only in what it is but also how it is, its size and shape and distance from you. You need to suspend the need for certainty in the desert or you'll quickly come a cropper. Assume that rock is far away then bang!, you've driven into it.

The half-buried thing at my feet looked like a finely carved spearhead, so I assumed the sand was disguising its true nature, which was another piece of rogue rock lost amidst the dunes. But when I picked it up, I saw that it was without a shadow of a doubt a finely rendered neolithic spearhead. A quick look round. No one watching. Out of sight of the camp and all the Italians. I slipped the spearhead into my pocket where it lay heavily and hotly against my thigh. First bit of loot. Brilliant. I started scanning for more immediately. My own path started to waver towards the path Massimo was treading. He too had something in his hand. A broken length of flint, a flake with a finely chipped edge, without a shadow of a doubt a knife of some sort. He was grinning a wide-eyed, sparkling grin and I congratulated him heartily, reluctantly keeping my spearhead secret just in case he was a snitch. I noticed he kept his knife, which was a good sign. Perhaps he too was after all he could find. I formulated the second rule of the desert that morning: the desert is an endless beach without a sea. Desert walkers are beachcombers of the infinite. (Rule three was to come later: even the blankest piece of desert will reveal something.)

Back in the car, fat Adil went to put on the music but we said no. Not that jangly pop music from the bazaar, when all around was so much to see. We were flying along flat sand sheets, going 100kmh most of the time, hour after hour. Some hills that looked quite close stayed stubbornly far away for

hours, then suddenly we had flown past them. Mirages, the basic sort, stretched out like mirror pieces of chewing gum that snapped shut when you were on them. No music please. The sound of the wind outside the window, the endless, seemingly random progress. You could drive anywhere.

Then quite quickly we were in a canyon between old weathered hills. We waited for an hour. The pick-up had not appeared. When it did the story was quickly extracted. The thing had punctured a tyre and rolled sideways against a rock.

There was a lot of waiting around and more discussion than seemed necessary. I wondered if more information was being withheld. As we waited I wandered about over the hot grey lumpy volcanic rocks of the canyon. Adil brought me a stone that was flower-shaped, pinkish, as if with petals. 'Like a rose,' he said. I admired it and carried it for a while then ditched it when he wasn't looking. When I showed him my Stone Age spearhead I could tell he had no interest and could not see why it was better than his flower. Later, rather embarrassingly, he asked for his 'rose' back. I told him we'd been instructed not to take anything away from the desert.

As we waited for the damaged pick-up, Ghali probed ahead in his own immaculate 78 Series 'fox'. He had told me the Bedouin names for Land Cruisers – the 40 Series was a 'donkey's head', the 70, 75 and 78 were 'foxes'. The preternaturally ugly 55 Series was a 'tortoise' (or an 'old dog', I suggested, but he didn't get it). I had seen him the night before, brushing sand grains out of the cab of his vehicle with a small dust-brush and then using a paintbrush to get sand out from those crevices in the dashboard trim that most people give up on.

Now I could see him winding down the canyon on to small platforms of sand at successive levels, searching for a way through. At this point I had a low opinion of the man and thought he was simply lost. I was gearing up to oppose him, for no better reason than that he had been a little gruff with me. When we had what he called 'a briefing', which entailed a very basic (but still interesting, I reluctantly admitted) geography lesson involving him drawing a great map of the desert in the flat sand using again that damn bayonet-pointed stick, prised no doubt out of the hands of an Israeli he had just killed with his bare fists, I joined with Marino, in whom I also detected an antipathy to the colonel despite their nominal working together. We wandered off while the colonel kept up his lecture, both ignoring him. Some keen teachers invite opposition.

Then the snout of the fox came back and started down a different path, which even I could tell would soon dead-end. But he summoned us all to follow, which seemed to compound the potential folly, since reversing in the tight canyon would be impossible. We ground on downwards, going especially slowly over sharp exposed rocks with rows of knife-like flakes pointing upwards.

And then we were out of the canyon and back on the sand sheet again. I was so pleased that Ghali could actually do his job, was good at it in fact. It made me change my mind about him. I trusted him to make the right decisions now, even if he was a hard-ass with a bayonet-enhanced walking stick.

However, the complicated feelings the colonel engendered – resentment, admiration, a desire for his attention – did not affect my self-given spy mission. I found out that evening that the GPS worked if I just pointed it through the gap between the two zips securing the front flap. Lodged just behind the gap I could take my reading without leaving the tent, which was an improvement. I had also taken to swilling whisky into my water bottle (my son's school water bottle, fake army in a camouflage cover), adding some water and swigging it whilst wiggling my hot toes in the sand outside the front door of the tent. *Swigging* and no one else could tell, all busy putting up their tents. I watched the sun go down as I swigged and wiggled, now and then waving at people as they laboured gamely with mallets and tent pegs. I had decided against using all the pegs so my tent was up quickly, another small act of rebellion against Ghali's method.

The Method. He had a special way of doing everything. Take the mattresses. They were all numbered, to match the numbers of the tents. To pack them up they had to be folded a certain way or else they wouldn't fit in their canvas valise. And the tents, too, had to be packed in a certain way or else they defied all attempts to zip up the carry bag. I was shown how to do this by another of Ghali's faithful retainers, the seventy-year-old Mohamed. Of all of the drivers Mohamed looked the least schooled, the calmest and wisest, never thrown out of his good mood and certainly not suffering from feelings of foreigner-induced inferiority. He had frizzy grey hair and a peaky brown wrinkled face. Ever since Ghali had been a junior officer Mohamed had served him in some way. I had to admit to a grudging admiration for the loyalty the man commanded. But I doubted his pronouncements regarding tents. After a lot of folding and rolling, like making an apple strudel with force, I discovered there really was only one way to get that tent into its tight little bag and Ghali had found it.

It seems the others are picking up and keeping stone tools too. Show-and-ask: we run to Ghali or Marino and ask whether the thing is real or not. Then into the pocket and, later that night, wrapped in a growing sock at the bottom of the kitbag. If things keep on at this rate we'll more than make up for the weight of water drunk.

The water ration is needed and quickly consumed. Three litres, one before and after lunch, sometimes only a dribble for my whisky ration and then to bed with a dry mouth. Massimo tells me he is drinking about half a litre a day. The little runt, skinny and weightless as a sparrow, either he's lying or he's far better adapted to this waterless place than I. Ghali carries a bottle in a special vinyl holder behind his head as he drives. He reaches over, takes a swig and then drops it back into position. A system for everything. I am now riding in his car, since Massimo and I are always at the front of the walking party, and Ghali's always in the front of the convoy, so it's easiest for him to pick us up. There is already a certain amount of competition to be in Ghali's car. It's the cleanest and it's always in the lead, no tracks out in front.

There's also the computer to watch. His latest gadget, the laptop folds down from its natty securing in the cab roof to provide a moving chart plot of our progress against a series of sat-photos of where we are. At a click of the thigh-operated mouse (wireless), the colonel can flick to our position on the Russian maps, all faint brown contours and Cyrillic. It's a fantastic system, except that it doesn't work. Or rather it works some of the time but never when it's needed, when we're approaching a gap between hills and want to know if it's blocked with sand or not. Ghali spends every photo break, biscuit break, toilet break sitting and clicking in his cab. There is a stolid patience about the man. I can tell he is not computer-savvy yet he is going to master this thing, slowly, his way, bit by bit. You have to admire it.

But personally I hate the laptop. For one, when it's folded down, you can't see out of the front if you're sitting in the back of the car.

Oh, another system: in the colonel's car only he can operate the front seat. The lucky front passenger can disembark, whilst those behind must wait for release. This entails the colonel leaving his seat, getting out of the car, walking round, opening the door and operating two levers so that the front seat folds forwards then sideways out of the way. It's really very clever, in that it allows passage to even the fattest and most ungainly of pensioner expeditioners, but it has the singular drawback of having to be operated by the colonel. Surely he must realize the intense irritation at having to wait 2.8 seconds to be released from the back of a sweaty 4x4 simply because the seat is deemed *too complex* for you, a former heart surgeon/company president/tax lawyer, to operate. No doubt it was morally good that these people should be humbled by the colonel's seat. And in truth, it was complex, like scratching your stomach and patting your head at the same time, there was something counterintuitive about the order of releasing the various catches. Indeed, when Franco took the law into his own hands (and was reprimanded for it) and operated the seat-release mechanism himself he did bugger it up, jamming the thing between the radio and the handbrake, where it remained until everyone had pushed past and jammed it further. Now no one dared touch the thing. There was even a special way of securing it ready for the front man to take his place. You had to check it was correctly located then push down with a firm click-rewarded shove. Even that was a skill I took my time acquiring. There was something in the colonel's wait as you did it that unnerved you, made you fail, just to conform to his expectation that you would fail.

The difference between the West and the East: in the West we strive to remove the special trick to everything. In the East they not only learn to live with these tricks, they each strive to use them to their advantage.

The colonel's fox, with its strategic water bottle and special seat, was kitted out exactly as he wanted it. Behind was a four-hundred-litre fuel tank; in front, a special pouch on the dashboard for the tape box, the colonel's sunglasses case and the laptop manual, or rather the manual for the chart-plotting program. Boxes of tapes were fixed to the inside walls of the car. The colonel had lots of tapes, surprising stuff: chill-out mixes, world music, spaghetti western soundtracks and the Pointer Sisters' greatest hits. When he was concentrating he wouldn't allow music. Almost always if music was suggested he would refuse, pointing out his need to concentrate. It reminded me of long childhood journeys to Cornwall each summer when we'd ask Dad to tell us stories but he would only comply when the traffic was sufficiently sparse not to agitate him.

Then out of the blue he would suddenly ask for a tape and the music would be shockingly welcome.* There was something unexpected and extra about playing music as you

* Desert music – what to play. Eerie world music, chill-out tunes and Eric Satie work very well. Songs about being, or feeling, free. Sting's 'Desert Rose'. Highly rated is Art of Noise's 'Moments in Love', which a friend dubbed the greatest desert tape ever after thirteen continuous playings driving across the Jordan Desert from Aman to Baghdad.

drove through the desert. Some tunes were made trivial, others achieved a strange and unexpected grandeur, as if they were made for such an unlimited horizon. It took me back to a phase of listening I had forgotten, when the music you played was 'your music'; you owned it somehow and nobody else did. In the desert the music becomes the soundtrack to your own existential adventure, the rolling movie you feel you're starring in.

It was about the third day when we sighted the Gilf Kebir. That day I found an old Shell petrol can, over sixty years old with the side cut out. I speculated it was a stove left behind by one of Bagnold's expeditions – they had burnt wooden storage crates in such stoves. Later, in World War II, a more profligate way of brewing up was evolved by simply mixing up a soup of sand and petrol: the sand inhibits the blaze enough for it to work as a stove. The Germans never worked out something as simple and it is Anthony Quayle's ignorance of the brew-up system that gives him away as a spy in *Ice Cold in Alex*. I also found several more flint knives, palaeolithic, we now knew, from the single, rather rough edge, not double-edged and fine like the later neolithic tools. Everyone was at it now, picking over the ground looking for titbits.

The Gilf, when we saw it, was an unending line of cliffs in the distance. I was not surprised when it got no closer despite hours of driving. The air is so clear in the desert it distorts further the distorted sense of distance you already have. We were sixty miles away, though it looked as if we were about five. Sometimes it seemed as though the car was really standing still, like the reverse of being on a train at a station and thinking you're moving when really it's another train pulling out.

The fourth day saw a severe reprimand for Massimo, from which he never quite recovered. We were all in the cab, buttering the colonel up nicely, offering him sweeties – squares of Lindt chocolate, mints and pastilles – which he liked even when he was concentrating, and admiring the moving sat-photo image, when he began to talk of how the explorers like Almasy and Bagnold stole their information from native guides and never really credited them. 'If you look at Almasy's pictures there are always Bedouin or Nubians there. They told him about Aquaba Pass and the Cave of the Swimmers. They simply name them, that is all. And what's in a name?'

I was fiddling with the side window of the fox; it being a utilitarian vehicle, the window was the sliding sort. As if something had stung him on the neck the colonel turned to see what the gritty sliding noise was. 'Keep the window closed. It's too dusty,' he said, though we were the lead vehicle and there was no wind. Earlier there really had been dust and I could see a reason for keeping the window shut, but not now. I slid it shut, actually smiling to myself. I had predicted he would not let me even the tiny freedom of opening the window and now I didn't really mind. I understood the score. It was the colonel's vehicle and he needed absolute control of everything within it.

In fact the window-opening refusal emboldened me and I found myself forced to interrupt the colonel's rant against the European explorers' desire to rename things. 'But isn't that like you and the cave? You wanted it named the Ghali cave.'

I had hit a nerve, or at least a playback button. The colonel talked for a long time as we churned through the softer sand of Wadi Wissa, a short-cut across the southern tip of the Gilf.

After the colonel had told us some stories about his life as a border patrolman, a loquaciousness that came on him after his heated self-justification of naming stuff after yourself, he lapsed into his usual silence. Even I could tell he was now in a sort of phase where he might be regretting talking too much. But imbued with a new sense of camaraderie Massimo leant forward and said, with full confidence of getting what he wanted, 'Tell us, colonel, some more stories about your time in the desert.'

With a cold reserve that any Englishman would have been

proud of, the colonel snapped, 'I have to concentrate.'

Massimo's friendly grin died on his face as he retreated back from his eager craning. He never again asked Ghali a question on the trip.

The colonel didn't drink alcohol. Instead, just before dinner, Ramadan would appear with an ice-cold can of Birel and a glass. This had the Italians mesmerized. Birel is an alcohol-free malt drink, but the can looks very like a Stella Artois can weeping cold tears of condensation, evidence of (a) a fridge and (b) a secret stash. The Birel ritual was hastily explained by the colonel to the assembled company on day two: he had a little kidney trouble and his doctor had told him to drink malt drinks every day. I had tried the stuff myself: when cold, it was the best and most beer-like alcohol-free beer I'd ever tasted. It seemed a gross breach of campaign etiquette to be downing luxuries that were denied the rest of the team. I had to keep reminding myself that this was Egypt. I'd learnt with Mohamed that it was leadership your servants wanted, not equality. The Birel may have worked like that with the humble squad of drivers, but the fellow expeditioners probably felt, along with me, that it just wasn't quite right. Imagine Scott breaking out a half-bottle of Bolly while on his way to the pole and turning to Oates saying, 'And don't spill any while you pour,' then finishing the lot himself, claiming he needed it for his digestion. Or Edmund Hillary turning to Tenzing and eating an entire bar of Kendal Mint Cake without offering even a square to the loyal sherpa. At a pinch one could imagine it happening on board ship: Drake drinks his claret in his cabin while the sailors roll around clutching wooden tankards of grog. Maybe that was another reminder that desert travel was closer to the sea than to any other form of land exploration.

Any way you look at it, though, sipping an ice-cold soft drink while everyone else has a tin cup full of tepid water is hardly likely to win you friends.

*

92

It was a tip from the dying desert explorer Samir Lama that had sent Ghali in search of a new cave. He described a cave with many more pictures than Almasy's Cave of the Swimmers. There was also a photograph, not of the cave itself but of the surrounding cliffs, from a distance, so that you could recognize the entrance to the particular canyon it was situated in.

This was enough to spur Ghali into looking. He and his paint-millionaire sponsor would drive from likely spot to likely spot, looking initially for Lama's tyre tracks in the *serir*, the gravel-encrusted sand that holds tracks for a hundred years or more. The pebble-covered surface remains clear of sand, except in the lines gouged by vehicles, so these appear as yellow stripes. There are still such tracks in the Western Desert, left by Prince Kemal al Din's 1926 pioneering trip using Citroen-Kegresse half-tracks. Almasy left the unmistakable tracks of his tiny baby Ford – which later I would find. There are tracks, too, from World War II, left by the SAS and the Long Range Desert Group. And all over the Gilf are Lama's tracks and now, increasingly, Ghali's. It is only this half-soft, stone-studded surface that operates as a palimpsest, recording the history of the exploration as if it has just happened. Tracks are something we associate with impermanence, but these tracks stay for ever, mark the desert always, distorting our sense of past and present, running them together. Just as the desert distorts space, making it hard to judge distance, so it distorts time. The palaeolithic tools lie where they were worked on. You can find all the slivers cracked from one rock. In one account by explorer De Lancey Forth he found the discarded remains of stone tools on either side of a small dune but not under it, the inference being that the dune had not moved in five thousand years.

We assume that dunes move, but actually most do not. Creeping desertification occurs when an obstacle, man-made or not, is placed in the path of sand-carrying winds. This could be a road, vegetation, a line of fenceposts or a recent rockfall. Like the piece of grit in the oyster, this seeds the formation of a dune. Once a dune is built up it loses sand off one side and gains it on another but largely stays the same. The dune, mimicking such impermanent forms as the snow-drift or the ocean wave, turns out to be as much a piece of the landscape as a hill or a valley. Like the tracks, it remains, creating, by the very survival of something so fragile, a sense of immortality, of defying the natural ageing process. It is as if one suddenly found a mayfly that had lived for a thousand years. It achieves the status of time traveller, something from another dimension.

It was hot the day we arrived at the caves, the aim of all our wandering in the desert. Earlier we had found the bonnet of a 1940s Ford truck with the very fine sheen of rust that metal gets in the desert, not the chunky, devouring rust you see in wetter places. This rust is like a preservative and made me hopeful of finding a complete vehicle from the war. There are several dotted around, their location noted by LRDG enthusiasts, but I could tell the colonel, perhaps due to his military background, was uninterested in such recent junk. But we were different. Everyone took photos of the bonnet (wrongly assumed by some writers to have fallen off one of Almasy's cars). It was as if we were desperate for some sign of modern man. A week in the desert and already we were missing our world. The colonel rounded everyone up and said we had to make haste for the caves.

The cars had to be parked some distance from Ghali's cave. This was for two reasons, I believe. The first was that he didn't want his tracks leading like a giant arrow to the cave, which was up a steep slope of sand and invisible from ground level. The second was that walking to the cave rather than riding right up to it like a bunch of ill people being ferried through Heathrow on an electric trolley with a persistent beep somehow seemed more right, more in keeping with all the effort and money so far expended in getting here. It needed to be a little bit hard, a little bit physical, otherwise it wouldn't be a pilgrimage. For this is what it was. I understood that as soon as we had scrambled up the slope of sand against the boulder-strewn cliff.

These thousand-foot-high cliffs, up close, lose their mono-lithic quality and fissure into myriad rocky canyons spreading either side of abruptly sided rough stone hills. At the back of one such canyon, at the all-important secret GPS numbers up a slope that was not obviously the way to go, was the cave, a long overhanging lip protected by a wall of fallen rock making a kind of walk-through tube. All along the rock wall were pictures and handprints made by blowing paint over an outstretched hand. The handprints were everywhere, the pictures were everywhere. The overwhelming impression was one of extreme crowdedness, of a rough, chaotic creativity. The Italians spread out excitedly: the cave was long enough for each of the seventeen of us to have our own stretch of wall to investigate. There were noises of approval and satisfaction and cameras working overtime. The place was sucked dry again and again, it seemed. But a sort of worship was going on. I fantasized, from a superior position among the rocks looking down on the Italians at the cave face, that this was the start of a new religion, which like all the great monotheisms had started in the desert.

In this new religion, people suffered privation and con-siderable expense to look at paintings and carvings made thousands of years ago. But the months of anticipation followed by the four- or five-day journey were necessary for the correct appreciation of the paintings, which were mysterious (headless baboons, people with alien-shaped bodies, all those handprints like in a horror film) and very old. You knew they were old because the animals depicted had long ago left the desert – giraffes, monkeys, ostriches and crocodiles – and the one obvious desert beast, the camel, was nowhere drawn, since camels did not reach the Sahara until, it is thought, 500–400 BC. These pictures were at least five thousand years old, the work of a knowledgeable and highly skilled artist. Artists. There were paintings over paintings in that crowded place and in styles so different they had to be by different people. Not to mention the hands – many were very small; the majority in fact were smaller than my own, and I guessed they were women's or children's.

I was hot now and well into my second bottle of water. This religion had several flaws, I could see. It would only appeal to rich people. It was a highly élitist religion that required the back-up of technology: cars, sat-phones, plastic bottles of water. The next stage would have to be making these pilgrimages by the simplest means – camels or, better, on foot. Perhaps camels could make dumps of water in the desert and people, hordes of them, could set off in a reverential plod across the endless sands. All over the world the old and remote sites of rock art would provide a focus for renewal of the soul, a turning of one's back on the material, the unnecessary self-imposed trivia of life.

Meanwhile, even the keenest of the Italians had taken enough photographs. The pilgrims wanted lunch.

But for a few minutes, hundreds of kilometres from the rest of the world, there was a palpable sense of awe, of having done something intangible yet worthwhile. It started that moment they stopped the photography and just stared, just took in the absolute strangeness of the place. People looked at each other and knew. At that moment we were all of a piece, a team, a community, not driven that way by brainwashing and emotion but because of something better than ourselves. At that moment the barriers none of us wanted but all of us erected were down, just for a moment, long enough for a shy smile to go between us, long enough, not long enough.

I saw more paintings, across a sloping expanse of sand opposite the main cave. There were figures running down a small exposed piece of rock. I called the others over, full of excitement. But when Marino arrived I saw, with his more practised eyes, that these were just man-shaped drips of minerals, not pale paintings of men at all. 'Good joke!' he laughed, which let me off the hook of being an overenthusiastic berk.

But for a moment I'd been as sure and as excited as someone finding treasure.

By comparison the Cave of the Swimmers was a disappointment. The swimmers were small, some flaking off. There was carved graffiti in Arabic and English, from World War II: a signals captain had left his deep mark. The cave itself was very visible from the desert, right at the cliff-bottom. Perhaps Almasy had been led there by his guides, but I wouldn't have been surprised if he saw it while driving by looking for a pass into the Gilf Kebir.

That evening I sat for ages with the colonel in his cab and helped decipher the manual for the computer-map program. I watched the patient way the colonel was learning how to use his excessively complex-seeming computer tool. My function was to be a sounding board for his ideas and to look things up in the manual, which was in English. I felt useful and the colonel was grateful for the slight assistance I provided. It seemed strange to be out here in the middle of nowhere puzzling over Windows 2000 and the command-line function with the stars overhead as bright as I had ever seen them, nearer by their brightness, the original and infallible method of desert navigation.

The following day we were on the top of the high plateau. We bumped carefully over rocky expanses with tyres reinflated to avoid puncturing the sidewalls. We made a detour to see a plaque set in concrete right on the top of the cliff that looked all the way into Libya. This was placed by Ghali and Lama's wife earlier in the year, and here they scattered Lama's ashes into the constant breeze from the desert plain below. 'This was Lama's favourite viewpoint,' said the colonel. It was a bleak, wide, empty view over flat gravel-strewn sand as far as the eye could see. I knew it would be better at dawn or dusk. At midday there was no magic; the light flattens the desert into somewhere tiresomely devoid of interest. It looks a bit of a mess, as if caught halfway through the process of becoming something or having been something. The desert

97

is the purest example, if examples are needed, that beauty is purely a condition of the light and the thoughts that light stimulates. It serves to remind you that things serve the light, are almost an arbitrary ancillary to the light conditions, that the less stuff there is – and the desert is the most stripped-down of environments – the more magic the light can work. I thought of the Akhenaten friezes in the Cairo Museum, where each ray of light from the sun ends in an eye.

My first rock-art discovery. Off the beaten track, away from a low cliff-face engraved with cattle and giraffes, I found, high up in an awkward place, the lone depiction of a palm tree. Ibrahim, one of the drivers, who knew his way around the *gravures* in the Gilf, said he hadn't seen it before and that was enough for me. I'd made my discovery. I became a kind of instant expert as Massimo translated to the Italians my impromptu explanation that the palm was a sign of the oasis and an indication that the people who made these carvings had travelled as far as the oases. There's a Rorschach quality to rock art that gives a pleasing credibility to even the rank amateur's assertions.

In Wadi Hamra there were acacia trees, a goodly grove of them, our first trees since leaving the oasis. Wadi Hamra was the largest of three north-trending valleys that Almasy said were the location of Zerzura. There were three valleys in the ancient *Book of Treasures* description and here they were. If, as we must assume from all the discarded stone tools and all the rock art, this place was once much wetter than today, then these wadis, with their rare vegetation, must have been the most hospitable place around. There may well have been permanent supplies of water trapped on the surface from rainfall. Even on our trip it had rained three times so far. One night it fell so hard I had to put up the flysheet to stop getting soaked in the cotton tent. I even wore my Newfoundland fisherman's raincoat, which had seemed an absurdity to carry back in Cairo but it had proved its worth against both wind and rain. For the world's most profoundly arid place the Gilf was surprisingly moist – at times. Only hours after the rain, however, all traces of damp had gone. If you pissed in the sand the damp mark would be gone by daybreak. The air just sucked the water right out of the ground.

Had these dry valleys been Zerzura? The question was similar to those periodic assertions that the pyramids had once been a giant heat pump or the Atlas Mountains were once Atlantis or Noah's Ark was now a barn roof in Anatolia. What use were they, these tantalizing, unprovable bits of myth? That they refused to go away meant something. There was something in them, if not the truth. They had a good alluring shape, something for everyone. A hard part of modern life is finding good alibis, good reasons for doing things. Those old myths work just fine. They have the purity and clarity of visions, and they work like visions, guiding lights for despairing souls, or lost souls at least. I already knew that the real lost oasis was the desert itself, that the towns and cities with water where man lived were, by the strange inversions of our time, the place from which we now needed to flee. The nourishment we needed was no longer in those places, it was out here in the vast emptiness. It was the very absence of water that made the desert an oasis, an oasis of light and contemplative beauty that replenished our inner reserves. I thought of my life in England and the escape to Egypt, how I had replaced suburban fear and boredom with chaotic hyper-urban Cairo and yet still felt homeless. Out here I had found what I had been looking for, a place I could rely on, return to again and again, as if I was throwing a leather bucket into a desert well and bringing up life-giving water endlessly. I could come here and somehow see everything in its right place, know instantly, without having to convince myself with words, that I already had everything I needed, re-establish that elusive balance between inner ease and the outside world.

We burnt wood from the acacia trees, fallen ones; it didn't seem too much of a desecration, though I was aware of the habitat-destruction arguments. I sat at night on the rugs staring into the wind-bucketed flames. Old Mohamed always knelt rather than sat, his sandals left at the edge of the rug.

Eight

THE GREAT SAND SEA ADVENTURE

The pretence of 'just looking' at stone tools, showing them around for academic interest and then over-obviously discarding them so that future generations could enjoy them, had long gone. Now all of us walked with bulging, lumpy pockets and clinking rucksacks. Not that we weren't still surreptitious, but I noticed teams had developed. Husbands and wives scoured together and stood in the brilliant noonday sun examining their finds, backs turned to wherever the rest of the group might be. Three maiden ladies from Verona, one a former top mountaineer in the 1950s, the first Italian woman to scale Mount Kenya, formed their own clique of treasure hunters. The ex-climber, Lorrenza, was a sturdy soul; one night when it rained she slept out in just her sleeping bag. She was seventy-two with a replaced hip but she was always towards the front of the walkers in the morning. (That was always the best time for me, not just for the chance of finding things but also because I could get quite clear of everyone, fantasize I was alone in the desert.)

The Great Sand Sea is north of the Gilf plateau and stretches almost to the Mediterranean. It is almost certainly the remnant beach of the retreating Tethys Sea, which had once flooded the desert three hundred kilometres inland. Possibly sand in great quantities had once filled the Quattara depression, then blown south to form the five-hundred-kilometre dunes that ribbed the Great Sand Sea. It's one of the world's biggest sand seas, stretching eight hundred kilometres by five hundred, the huge dunes lying in long parallel lines, with hard-sand-dune corridors in between.

Silica glass, which I was now looking for, supposedly lay in two or three corridors over a stretch of about twenty kilometres around the point 25N 27E. Had Harding Newman and the other Zerzura Club men really cleaned up every piece they could find? With the early-morning sun behind me I set off from camp and almost at once I saw the light reflecting off the pebble-strewn sand, just as light catches broken glass on a lawn in the morning. My first piece was small, but obviously worked, chipped to make the end of an arrowhead or knife blade. I was surprised how clear and see-through it was. Silica glass, or tektite, is also found in Moldavia and Saudi Arabia, but glass from these places is always impregnated with pieces of the surrounding rock. Great Sand Sea glass, however, is always pure. I soon found a big lump, rough on one side but wind-smoothed on the other. It was so clear it could have been used as a small, albeit rather thick, window.

No one knows how it was formed. The current theory relies on an asteroid exploding just above the earth and fusing the sand into glass. If you compare silica glass to trinitite, the glass-like substance left after a nuclear bomb has exploded, you can see how much hotter the asteroid must have been. Trinitite looks more akin to fulgarite, the hollow crystalline sticks caused by a lightning strike. You often see these knobbly grey tubes poking out of dunes. They are only halfway to glass, glassy rather than transparent. Silica glass really is just like glass. A few specimens only are marred by intrusive tiny tiny pebbles.

The best thing I found was a complete glass knife blade, its edge hardly worn by coruscating sand. I wrapped it in tissue, ready to be laid out and gloated over in my tent that night. All of us who found glass lumps too large to hide about our persons were persuaded by the colonel to bury them at a location he marked with the GPS. He already had a few good pieces stashed there. If all the glass in that corridor should be taken he still had something to show future expeditions. I didn't mind complying with his request. Already I was getting choosy. Only the best pieces from now on, quality not quantity or mere size. Only archaeologists or commercial gem hunters want to strip a place bare irrespective of quality. Ghali spoke of a German archaeological dig that had removed every last stone tool from a *playa*, a dried-up lakesite, that had once been layered deep with artefacts. 'And where are those stones now?' he asked. 'Berlin.'

Despite the respectability of archaeology and the highly reasonable justification for scraping a place clean, the result was just as bad as, actually worse than, casual theft by tourists. Archaeology is a classic example of a delinquent activity that is supported and revered by most unthinking people. I am far more inclined to support honest grave robbers, who leave anything that isn't made of gold. In Egypt, at least, they are lazy and incompetent, not systematic and dedicated. In the desert I always found myself siding with the nomads and the grave robbers.

The colonel was more complicated. When I first asked him about the Bedouin he replied, 'I hate Bedouins.' I suppose that was hardly surprising in a man who'd spent eighteen years trying to catch them sneaking across the Libyan border loaded with TV sets and hashish. Which they didn't smoke, said the colonel: 'They prefer to drink whisky or *arak*.' This was possibly worse than smoking dope, from a town-Arab perspective. My father-in-law had once recommended I smoke grass to improve the quality of my writing: 'All artists do it,' he said airily. I can't imagine many ex-army doctors in the UK saying something similar. But if he hated the Bedu as a concept, Ghali also greatly admired certain Bedouin men he had known. He showed me the way a Bedouin guide points the way, with the merest movement of his hand, two fingers together and extended, not speaking for hours, the colonel said. He admired them for their constant activity and strength, how they would go out into the desert alone with just a herd of camels for three months at a time. 'These boys,' he said indicating fat Adil but also aged Mohamed unloading bags from the top of the car, 'they are from the valley. If they lose the way they will die.'

The colonel was proud of being Egyptian, intensely proud. 'This is my country and you can't tell me what to do here,' he'd told Bellini during a contretemps over the cave. Yet he also was proud of having gone to a French school, of dealing all the time with foreigners, of having vehicles equipped with the best European gear including Darr sandplates like the ones I'd bought so expensively from Shaheer and still not used. He didn't like it when I said good-night to him in Arabic; he preferred French or Italian. He loved the desert as a place of emptiness. I could tell he really loved it for the inspirational reasons all mystics espouse, and yet he made a living from bombing around it with noisy trucks and rich pensioners. If he was Brando-as-Kurtz then I was doomed to be groupie Dennis Hopper, ready with my hero worship and extravagant explanations.

Then the pick-up broke down.

It started small, as I imagine all great catastrophes do. 'That iceberg? More like an ice cube. That noise? Mere scratch in the paintwork.' The *Titanic* went down with a whimper, not a bang, and we would too. I could see that as it unfurled in front of me: an accident is a sequence of small unlucky things that keep adding to each other until some kind of critical mass of disaster is reached and it's every man, woman and Italian OAP for himself.

Ibrahim was complaining of a noise in the rear wheel of the pick-up. They took the wheel off and we stood around looking interested in the drum brake and exposed axle. The colonel himself lay down in the sand for a better look. But with the wheel back on the sound just got worse. It was like broken glass in a liquidizer, intensified by being the only noise in the utterly silent desert. It was a sound that even a non-mechanic would recognize as a very bad sound indeed.

After making twenty metres, Ibrahim jumped from the cab with a look of resigned adamance about him. Go another kilometre, he said, and the *roman-belli* would seize for good. *Roman-belli* was wheel-bearing, I knew that much. The pick-up, the trusty 40 Series pick-up, thirty years old but meticulously maintained, piled high with our water and comfy mattresses and the long table, was now just another piece of junk. In an instant worth nothing. There was a brief moment, before thinking of how stuffed we were, when I felt real exhilaration at seeing the desert take over. It was like burning money on an icecap to stay warm: all the values, all the symbols of modern life were obliterated in a moment. A car breaks down on the highway and it's still a car. Our world maintains, in the face of almost everything, the false value of *things*. Objects. Material. We rarely glimpse, and only know as an intellectual possibility that a man is all that survives a shipwreck, a man only needs enough land to dig a hole six foot by three to lie down in. We know this, but the world keeps us from seeing it. But, out in the desert, when the highly complex, revered and expensive machine breaks down you see it's just a piece of junk. Needless to say, the *roman-belli* was the one spare part we didn't carry.

My mind began to race away. The remaining vehicles would now be overloaded. We would be rushing to reach Siwa Oasis rather than driving slowly. Another accident would follow. I thought of a canoeist I knew who had survived a mass capsize on a lake when six others died. Only one boat capsized at first, but in a rush to rescue those in the water every other boat was upset and my friend had been the only exceptional swimmer, though all could swim.

This is how it starts, I thought. And further back, near the beginning, when the pick-up had that puncture and keeled over, maybe that was what strained the bearing in the first place. One accident leading to another. Marino was agitated and off on one side with the colonel, offering his view, his solution. I was intensely interested to see how the colonel, this leader of men, would deal with it. For a start he told Marino in clear and obvious terms to stop worrying and leave everything to him. He started the drivers on unloading the pick-up. Then he summoned the group and broke the good news. 'Everything we need to get to Siwa, even the mattresses, we can load on the other vehicles. This pick-up we will hide here in the desert. Everyone will stay in a hotel at the oasis and I will return and repair the truck. You will have one day in Siwa instead of an afternoon. There are many wonderful things to see.'

That we did not doubt. In fact, I wasn't alone in thinking a night in a hotel would make a nice change from washing my smelly feet in dry sand. There was no sense of emergency. He retained a baffled amusement. 'This is the first vehicle I've had to leave in the desert in twenty years,' he said.

The pick-up was screeched into a depression between two dunes. Would it be stolen by thieving, smuggling nomads or Libyans out looking for hawks? Hamid, the laconic head driver, said, 'If they find it they'll just strip it. They'll take all the best bits and leave it like a camel's bones.'

The colonel knew a faster route through the sand sea, marked out ten years earlier when he worked for a petroleum exploration company. He had set a series of sticks every kilometre or so at the high points of whaleback dunes and along the base of dune corridors. These sticks, about an inch in diameter and about four foot high, would be our rapid escape route. The only problem was spotting them. In a left-hand-drive car I was his right-hand man. Owing to my partial success with the computer, I now had a permanent billet up front with the colonel, with nominal jurisdiction over the tape box.

With the true instincts of the sycophant I tried to select music that would suit the mood of the car, which meant the mood of the colonel. I made a few gigantic blunders based on my own intractable tastes. The overt melodrama of Enrico Moriconi's collected soundtracks of spaghetti westerns just didn't sit right. Neither did the sexy yearning of 'Upside Down' by Diana Ross. I learnt my lesson and if in doubt settled for the middle of the range, even the outright flaccid. Buddha Bar and Café del Mar (the colonel was nothing if not eclectic), Enigma and even the Eagles all made excellent soundtracks to dune-driving at high speed.

But music was now an unimportant side responsibility. I donned my prescription dark glasses, tasked with scanning the horizon for the sticks, or *balises* as the colonel called them. My eyesight isn't great at the best of times and driving at 60kmh through almost featureless sand strained my abilities to the limit. The trick was not to stare but to keep scanning, looking out of the corner of the eye and most of all checking out the places where a *balise* might be likely: high points of long low dunes, straight sections rather than those blocked by sand or the odd rock; always trying to get a bit of horizon between me and what I was looking at, to get at least a little contrast or a sight of something sticking up. After I'd spotted one or two I began to trust my judgement. It didn't do to wait too long for a positive ID: then the colonel would see it too and my role was diminished. He had to concentrate on the nearest bit of sand, making sure we didn't drive over the top of a dune. As soon as I got the slightest idea that I'd seen a *balise* I'd point it out, learnt to cut out the slower mental function of being sure. As soon as I saw I pointed without even thinking about it.

It was in the dunes that I had to concede the colonel really was a master of his art. Even twenty years earlier what we were doing would have been considered a highly risky endeavour with the odds favouring a crash or a succession of deep boggings-down in soft sand. At noon the sun flattens the dunescape so that sudden drops are hidden from view. If the horizon melded into the background as you approached you were safe. This meant there was a gentle slope ahead not a sharp drop off. As soon as the horizon stayed sharp as you moved towards it you had to be careful. A few times the colonel pulled up short and veered away from sudden drops that would have launched us off a hundred-foot-high cliff of sand. 'Have you ever driven off one of those?' I asked. 'Once,' he replied. 'It's part of the job.' Driving becomes like flying into a beige cloud and it's easy to be mesmerized. Even when walking I'd stepped hard off a hidden dip and jarred myself. I'd read of camels taking a tumble while walking at midday. Driving fast raised this particular problem to a new level of potential disaster. But hour after hour the colonel kept it up. It was something like night flying without instruments, and though I was temperamentally opposed to man-and-machine-bonding-as-one experiences, I had to admire the skill. Bagnold had written eloquently of how admirably the motor car is suited to desert travel. His view was that the desert was too dull at walking speed and only revealed its true grandeur when whipping along at high speed. My desert walking experience told me that wasn't true; Bagnold was just a speed freak.

This was a different kind of exploration from that of all previous eras. We covered huge distances; we could do in a day what a camel would take ten days to traverse. It was as much a denial of the desert as an exploration and it called into question just how 'explored' a place is that has effectively been flown over, criss-crossed, but not continuously experienced at a level of normal human interaction – looking, pausing, turning a rock over with one's foot. I thought about the enforced idleness occasioned by the failure of the wheel bearing. Instead of sitting in a moving car I had followed a line of lizard tracks, seeing the outline of the lizard's body where it had rested the night and then the clearer tracks where it set off that morning.

The next day I'd lost my intuitive skill at spotting *balises* and Massimo proved much better. We pulled up just outside Siwa, with its huge saltwater lakes, having powered through four hundred kilometres of sand in a day and a half.

*

There were lots of interesting touristy sites in Siwa, but I managed to see none of them. Like a true world traveller I spent the entire day sitting at Abdu's restaurant watching the world go by, drinking Turkish coffee and writing in my notebook. Our hotel was a clean, government-run joint with showers and TVs, which I watched at night guzzling from my bottle of Old Horse. I invited several of the Italians to join me in my drinking but no one was really interested in getting loaded in front of a satellite-TV movie. Laudable, no doubt, but I had long ago fallen into the trap of regarding any oasis as a place of over-indulgence before a return to the rigours of secret tippling in a draughty dome tent.

In the restaurant, which was open on two sides, affording a great view of all the donkey-cart taxis, tourists, white-clad Siwans and grubby gelabiya-wearing Bedouins, I found it an easy place to talk to strangers. Siwa had a slow, relaxing feel despite the bustle. The boy I hired a bike from (50p a day) trusted me and asked for no money up front. Three elderly men came into the restaurant and sat with Abdu at the back and sang a cheerful rhythmic song, one beating a chair seat as expertly as a drum. When he finished the drummer had a slightly sheepish look on his face which vouched for the impromptu authenticity of the performance, as if to say, 'That's just what we do here in Siwa.'

Ghali had warned me about the notorious gay gardens of Siwa and I wanted to know more. In the past the boys and young men of Siwa were sent out to guard the palm gardens and a homosexual culture involving gay marriage had flourished. The guidebooks assured me it was all over but a local schoolmaster, a large American woman who regularly visited to buy traditional jewellery, and an outrageous German queen called Klaus all assured me it had simply gone underground. Klaus had a thick mane of dyed blond hair and rode around town in flares with a yellow neckerchief knotted at his throat on a bicycle with a shopping basket containing his leather satchel. He was about fifty and had been visiting Siwa for fifteen years. Ruefully he explained that a gay Dutch visitor had put Siwa on the internet as a gay destination and since then you had to be a bit careful – 'But if you want anything just ask the donkey boys,' he counselled. Then he was off on his bike to visit an old boyfriend, a married Siwan shopkeeper whose most recent lover had been an Australian bartender from Port Fairy. 'And I promise you that is no joke!' said Klaus as he haggled over the 20p bill for a Turkish coffee.

At 8.30 a.m. precisely the colonel roared into the hotel compound with the pick-up repaired and everything in order. In a moment of reflection as we boarded the vehicles he said, 'There are only two things you need in this business – a good crew and money to throw at a problem. This hotel has cost me a lot, but they're happy, aren't they?' He was right. From a show-stopping disaster he'd conjured an extra day of rest and relaxation.

We got stuck a lot on the way back to Bahariya. Being the front car we had to find the route, and that often left us bogged down. At first I was so pleased to be well and truly up to the axles in soft sand. For me it was the quintessence of desert driving, the thing I knew for sure would happen, the one thing I'd seen on television, read about and, with my extremely expensive Darr sandplates, fantasized about. The car is winging along over sand that looks just the same as it always has and then the engine note rises and the speed slows. Sometimes, not always, there's a *whompf* sound as the tyre suddenly swims into really soft sand. Usually there is a battle between the driver and the sand. Gears are descended, the car slows; the important thing is to keep moving without spinning the wheels. Every time you are reduced to wheel-spinning you add time to your recovery. Ghali would vary his method of fighting to stay moving. First gears, then a quick slam into four-wheel drive, then an attempt at reverse, but when the game was up he'd stop abruptly, give the gear lever an angry swipe with his palm and climb out into the heat and light.

The colonel had a way of flopping resignedly on to his

knees next to the bogged tyre and then carefully scooping out a channel for the sandplate with his cupped hand. I was so darn excited to be actually stuck I was scooping like a madman, but he took his time. He made a neat trench leading away from the bottom of the tyre. This was not that easy to do, not so that it looked as regular and army-neat as the colonel's. All his scooped channels had the same look, the best way to deal with being bogged again and again.

What appealed to me was the problem solving aspect of a recovery. The key is always to stop before you get too dug in. If you don't, it becomes more difficult but more interesting, especially if the sand is softer on one side than the other, causing a nasty lean. There are several pieces of gear to help when the car is well bogged, a hi-lift jack or even a canvas bag which can be inflated from the exhaust to lift the car with pneumatic ease. But the colonel preferred digging and pushing. You get up a little speed going along the sandplate and with everyone pushing you can usually power your way to the harder sand, which you've already stamped on to make sure it's OK. Ramadan was always the most assiduous pusher, always last to stop, a key role since there is often quite a stretch of soft sand to cover before you're safe again.

We were now making our way past the uninhabited oases that stretch from Siwa to Bahariya, skirting the northern part of the Great Sand Sea. With all the bogging and digging and pushing I was gulping water down. Three litres a day seemed only just enough, despite the winter cool of the evening. At midday it was sunny but hardly scorching, yet still I needed that water. I saw that with camels you could regulate your exertion much better, just keep ticking along, never getting into a sweat. With walking, too, as long as you had no rucksack, it was possible to lope along using minimum effort. It was easy to see that being repeatedly bogged in high summer without water would be the quickest way to die in the desert.

I made it a rule not to drink more than my allotted three litres, but on a few occasions I was so hyper-alert to dehydration that it felt more dangerous than it really was. The slightest symptom of fatigue and light-headedness I put down to a life-threatening lack of liquid. Better safe than sorry. I took to redressing the balance at dinner-time, drinking more than the allowed three tin cups of tea. It was dark, who would notice? Water turns an honest man into a crook so easily. You think, I might die, I need this water and no one is going to stop me.

The uninhabited oases were still uninhabited, except near Areg, where there was a mill-pounding stone for a new asphalt road from Bahariya to Siwa. The present road, which we adroitly criss-crossed on our journey home, was a sad and chewed up piece of disintegrating tarmac smothered in many places with deep sand. It was easier not to drive on it. The uninhabited oases were on either side of the old road in rocky depressions of their own. There were trees and mosquitoes; in fact, with the flat lakes of water and tall palms, they looked the most like an 'oasis' of anywhere I went in Egypt.

The view from the road past the oases was tedious, but only a hundred metres from it we drove through sunlit canyons where castle-like rocks glowed yellow in the afternoon sun. There had been a wild donkey living at Areg, said the colonel, but we didn't see him.

It was at Areg that we had our first human desert encounter: three men from the stone mill saw our vehicles as we parked to take photographs of the dramatic cliff and acacia-lined valley. They set off towards us across the flat plain. It was a hot day and their shimmering image joined together, as if they were a single creature. For forty minutes they trudged slowly towards us as the Italians clicked and fussed over their motor-drive cameras. We were probably the first distraction from the tedium of pounding rock for days, perhaps even weeks. When they were almost within hailing distance, having walked at least four kilometres in the burning heat, their pace noticeably quickened in eager anticipation of human contact. It was at that moment, without any undue anxiety, that the colonel ordered us all back into the cars. Then we drove off. The men stared after us for a longish while, as if expecting us to stop. Then, as the brutal reality of our departure sank in, they turned and started the long trudge back the way they had come.

Nine

OZMAN, OZMAN

Back at home there were several new disasters to contend with. Magoob had helped a neighbour to dump old tiles and bits of concrete on the roof and had fallen foul of my mother-in-law in the process. Mohamed had tried to fix a fuse in my brother-in-law's BMW and caused a small but highly destructive fire. And there had been a murder. Next door.

Hanya, the small wizened man who lived in the electricity box at the bottom of the building, had a son of about twenty-five or so who was a little simple, with a clumsy desire to help and be rewarded for helping. His name was Ibrahim and he had been arrested for the murder of our next-door neighbour. Hanya had gone to the police station to plead for his son's release. He was a small, poor, powerless man and after listening to his plea the officer in charge had him kicked out.

Mohamed the driver had all the details. The man next door was known to be a drinker. He lived on the ground floor of a two-storey villa surrounded by a sturdy fence. A friend had arrived and told Ibrahim, who was cleaning our car at the time, that he was worried about the man. The gate was locked but the man persuaded Ibrahim to climb over and knock at the front door. There was no reply. Then the man persuaded the eager Ibrahim to climb in through an open ground-floor window. He found the owner of the flat in a pool of blood in the bathroom. Shouting at the top of his voice, Ibrahim climbed back out of the window, whereupon the 'friend' roared away in his car. The police arrived quickly and just as quickly arrested Ibrahim for murder and attempted robbery.

One look at Ibrahim and you knew he was incapable of murder, or even planning a burglary. Even if he did do it, which I very much doubted, he would not receive a fair trial if he spent more than a few hours in police custody. I knew from my playboy/judge brother-in-law that the favourite method of solving a crime was to beat a confession out of the most obvious suspect. In one of my favourite columns in the *Egyptian Gazette*, called 'Red Handed', when a true crime is related and the 'perpetrator' caught and often hanged or sentenced to thirty years' hard labour, there is an ominous repetition of the construction 'After questioning by the police he soon confessed.' Magoob had once been picked up as a suspect in a robbery and had been beaten so badly he was now deaf in one ear. And Ibrahim was exactly the kind of simple lad who would confess to a crime he didn't commit just to make the nasty policemen go away.

And even if he did do it, he still had a right to a fair hearing, though I still couldn't believe he did do it. Either way he should be released from police custody as soon as possible. I felt a sense of feudal obligation: it seemed right that as Hanya subsisted on our meagre hand-outs and lived in our electricity box his son was also entitled to our protection. My wife was impressed by how seriously I was taking it. She suggested we couldn't necessarily believe Mohamed the driver's version as he was a notorious embellisher, having suddenly admitted he too was once arrested by the secret police of Mubarak himself and held blindfold at an undisclosed location for several days. This motiveless kidnapping was transparent self-aggrandizement in the face of the greater drama of Ibrahim's real arrest and Magoob's real experience of being tortured. The further complications of the victim being a drinker and possibly an Israeli spy were now added to the story by Mohamed the driver, with relish I might add.

I asked Samia to find a lawyer. There were two candidates. The first was the husband of a friend who had been imprisoned as a leftist agitator during one of Sadat's crackdowns in the 1970s. He was an egomaniac and a philanderer and he had a heart condition, but he was always game for any fight with the authorities. He was terminally angry at the Egyptian system, despite having made a good living for years from running NGOs funded from abroad to counter the inequities of the Middle East. If things improved his funds dried up.

Then there was the tried and tested family lawyer, who had, over a period of thirty years pursued a case worthy of Jarndyce & Jarndyce. My mother-in-law had bought an apartment in a new block on the road to the airport in 1974. The owner was a crook who sold the apartment twice and the second buyers moved in immediately. And refused to leave. Through thick and thin, appeals, counter-appeals, fresh trials and new evidence, the family lawyer pursued the crooked owner of the building. Finally, last year, he had paid up the current value of the flat – about a hundred times its cost so many years earlier. This victory made the family lawyer appear the winner's choice; on the other hand, he was hardly a man of rapid action. And this case needed action. There was nothing I could do, however, until various facts had been ascertained and the availability of a suitable lawyer confirmed.

The day before, when we arrived jubilant out of the desert, Ozman of the Desert Exploration Group, the bald man in the cap and home-knitted scarf who could get me anything, agreed to pick me up at the hotel in Cairo where the Italians would spend the night. Dusty and euphoric and full of plans to get moving, I thought, Why not employ Mr Fixit right away?

The hotel was next to the pyramids, a new Hilton with a golf course attached. It had all the atmosphere of a conference centre and I was keen to leave. I needed more maps than the

116

one borrowed from Richard Head. This seemed a good task to test Ozman's unlimited fixing ability. In the way of such things I had already told Marino, the Italian tour leader, that I could get him maps too. And he had told his girlfriend, who wanted to come along for the ride.

We stood waiting for Ozman to rescue us at the shuttle-bus stop out front. An endless supply of grey-haired men in foreign-correspondent jackets arrived at regular intervals and fussed over golf bags hung with airline tags. Playing golf in Egypt when you could go to the Gilf. Hah! We snorted.

Ozman had mentioned his car in lavish but imprecise terms during the drink-fuelled first meeting of the exploration group. Since he ran a company called Ozman Safari I assumed it was some kind of 4x4. It was with a certain degree of surprise therefore when an enormous low-slung two-door 1978 Buick of that indeterminate colour somewhere between rust and dirty purple puttered to a halt in front of us. A door as big as a wing swung open to reveal a freshly shaven and perfumed Ozman in a smart navy-blue blazer, grinning, his white shirt unbuttoned to reveal chest hair. Marino's girlfriend giggled as she and Marino climbed in the back. Then a policeman in charge of hotel security arrived and started to give Ozman a hard time for taking clients of the hotel away for business without paying a cut to the policeman. Ozman Safari, explained Ozman, no longer grinning, took a principled stand on bribery. He refused to pay the policeman, who uttered dark threats as we rolled away in the spongily suspended car with its great thick doors and electric windows that had to be helped upwards by manually smearing your hand on the glass and pushing to accompany the pathetic whine of the motor, the sound of a thing both endangered and fully aware of the brevity of life.

But instead of becoming merrier as we escaped the policeman, Ozman kept muttering, 'He make trouble for me, he make big trouble.' It seemed that the policeman could impound Ozman's safari licence, whatever that was. I thought

I could bluster him out of this worried state of mind but I couldn't. Fifty metres from the hotel we dropped Marino and his girlfriend, to Ozman's obvious relief. I had met Ozman's reaction before. There is a kind of Egyptian who detests having to bribe the police, yet lives in fear of the repercussions of refusing to pay. I was not impressed. I wanted a man who could fix anything and Ozman had failed at the first hurdle. He hadn't even suggested *I* pay the bribe, but I wondered if that was because he didn't want to accustom the policeman to such gifts. I told Marino we'd get his maps for him and, though surprised by the fifty-metre excursion into Cairo only to have to walk back to the hotel empty-handed, he readily accepted the situation.

It already felt a little as if it was my first day being employed in some way *by* Ozman, but I banished that thought. I was the boss, I was paying, I was giving the orders. But still there were niggling doubts.

With Marino gone Ozman cheered up and drove me home. We agreed a daily wage and Ozman explained several common Arabic phrases. He also claimed to be able to find me a good flat in Maadi and a perfect car too. The car loomed larger in his mind than anything else. In an attempt to convince people I was serious about the desert and could obviously afford a £10,000 car I put it about that I was looking for such a vehicle. I am, I told myself; and if exactly the right car comes along then I'll find some way of buying it. I didn't think there would be much chance of that happening. I both did and didn't want to find a car, though for reasons that still remain obscure I was nothing except enthusiastic about cars. It was like talking about sport in an American bar. In my precarious isolation the car nonsense was a kind of bonding.

Ozman added enthusiasm, bulk and lustre to the car-buying project. He had once worked for General Motors as head of their service department. It was just as he was telling me this that the Buick started to make an odd clicking noise. Ozman was dismissive: 'I know exactly what that noise is.' He didn't elaborate. We returned to the interesting subject of getting a dream desert car for me. Ozman slapped his forehead and said, 'I have the best car for you. Let's go and see it now! Right now!' He fired up a Boston extra-heavy-tar cigarette and handed me one poking out of the pack. Despite a resolution made in the desert the day before to give up smoking, I took one.

'Not a bad old car, this,' I said, slapping the immense heavy door with manually aided electric window right down. 'It's a great car!' exclaimed Ozman. 'I love American car. It's a man's car and not expensive to fix.'

En route to the Map Office we stopped to look at a Jeep owned by a man Ozman knew who was famous in Cairo for off-road driving. The Jeep was heavily modified, with yellow springs and gas shocks in place of the usual leaf suspension. 'It's perfect for you,' said Ozman, then, revealing I felt his true feelings, 'If you drive that car through Maadi everyone will know it. That's a famous car. Parking that car will be a great thing.'

'But I told you I want a Land Cruiser, or maybe a Nissan Patrol, not a Jeep.'

Ozman looked a little sulky and then brightened: 'Do you want to hear the engine?'

'No. Let's get to the Map Office.'

On the way Ozman told me his brother had a chalet in Ain Sukhna, the nearest Red Sea resort to Cairo, and he would be willing to sell for very little. I told him I'd have to ask my wife, which was a stupid thing to say since I knew we were never going to buy a chalet on the Red Sea. But Ozman's combination of enthusiasm and a sort of fragility did that to you. I even allowed myself the thought of arriving at the school and scattering the snotty Petroleum Wives in my snorty off-road monster.

The Map Office in Giza, where Richard Head had managed, with company stationery, to get every map he needed despite there being a law against selling maps to foreigners, sounded like an easy place to negotiate. But from the beginning things

119

got complicated, in a way that they always do in Egypt, complication on top of complication until by some Alexandrine sundering the whole knot is severed and then almost straight away the complications start building again. That's why it's hard even to meet people in Egypt without several phone calls and messages – the situation must be at least a little saturated with complication for it to seem real. If you make a straightforward suggestion to meet it will be viewed as imaginary, unless lashed to both of you with a string of complications. Some Egyptians go right out and start complicating things from the word go; others make a pretence at simplicity whilst complicating things behind the scenes. Even Egyptians who profess to hate complications seem unable to keep things simple.

The first complication at the Map Office was that we needed to pay a character with a huge bunch of keys in one hand so that we could park in the vicinity. Muhammad was a self-elected parking attendant, making a good living from fitting forty cars into the space for twenty by revolving them around constantly to let people out and in. That's why you had to give him your keys. I thought he must make a good living. He was certainly aspirational: on his wrist was a fake Rolex submariner; not a bad copy, I'd got one myself a month earlier in Khan al Khalili Bazaar. After a quick, intense discussion Ozman said that Muhammad could get us our maps for a mere E£10 surcharge per map. I didn't like the look of Muhammad so I said no. Ozman found us a way into the Map Office and we started our own attempt to get maps.

At first I connived in Ozman's absurd pretence that I was an Egyptian. But when the clerk in charge of handing out chits for the right place to go and get your maps asked Ozman who the maps were for he pointed to me. Finding myself addressed in fluent and irascible Arabic my cover was immediately blown. Mistake no. 1, and a black mark against Ozman – he just didn't have the flair needed to be really dodgy. Then mistake no. 2: instead of laughing about the pale attempt at fraudulence, making it seem silly and incon-sequential, Ozman and I went into petitioner mode, even proffering a letter from the British Ambassador that I had taken to carrying around like a talisman. All this seriousness made the man nervous and we were dispatched immediately to a higher boss on a different level. We never saw that boss. Instead, at the entrance to the boss's office, a kind of plain-clothes policeman in a leather jacket took a photocopy of my passport and the letter from the Ambassador that merely wished me well on my enterprise of finding a lost oasis and then returned them all to me after a lengthy wait in a corridor adorned only with a flattering portrait of the country's president.

'We're getting nowhere here, Ozman,' I said.

'They don't like the maps you are ordering. They are too near the border.'

'But they're British maps. They're on the net. It's absurd.' (I didn't add that though identical in information content, the downloadable version was badly scanned into mis-matching A4 segments.) Ozman agreed it was absurd, but then added, 'It is our national security.'

It was time for phase two. Back in the street we sat majes-tically in the massive Buick, drinking tea brought to us by a poor man in a turban. Muhammad arrived and listened gravely to our complaints. He then took our list of maps and was gone about an hour. He returned with the bad news. 'They know this list now. "Uwainat", that is a bad map. Very bad.'

There was a possibility of going to the boss of the clerk and paying him a hefty bribe – E£60 per map, making each one £10 sterling each. This boss was below the big boss, who would never need to know. 'OK, let's do it,' I said. 'Then you must come tomorrow because this boss is not here right now,' said Muhammad. 'I thought the thing about bribery was that it speeded things up.'

Ozman agreed it was shocking to have to wait your turn to pay a bribe. We drove home and looked at a Nissan Patrol

121

owned by a former army general known to Ozman. (I recalled my father-in-law saying that there are more generals in Egypt than soldiers.) I had seen this car quite a few times while walking around the neighbourhood and I had taken quite a fancy to it. Despite its being twenty years old with 377,000 kilometres on the clock and shot rear shocks, the general wanted £9,000 sterling for it. I allowed Ozman to arrange a test drive the next day, kidding myself with such thoughts as, If it's really good I'll get a loan. Before we parted Ozman said that he had paid E£50 on fuel driving me around in his thirsty Buick. I didn't mind the surcharge. I almost liked the fact that I was being obviously overcharged. In a twisted one-upmanship scenario it meant I was superior to Ozman, who had to make up stories just to get a few extra quid.

Back home there was no sign of Ibrahim, though there were new developments from Magoob. The neighbour had been depressed and had called all his old friends, though the police had still not found the particular 'friend' that asked Ibrahim to climb in through the window. Magoob also said that the man was covered in blood because he had cut his wrists in the bath. And apparently there were whisky bottles all over the house. This all sounded promising, but I was still worried about Ibrahim. My wife had spoken to the egocentric lawyer with a heart problem and he had agreed to come and get Ibrahim out of the police station the next day.

I told my wife all about the day spent trying to get the maps and she said, 'Why not just send Mohamed the driver?' It transpired that Mohamed the driver was familiar with the Map Office since in his previous job as a driver/enforcer for a much-disliked building contractor he had often been there to fetch plans and large-scale maps. There was something too simple about this solution. Was I starting to become Egyptian in my need for complications?

The next day, going out of the building with my two children on the way to school, I walked right into Ibrahim, who looked a little stunned and sleep-deprived but otherwise fine.

He explained that the police had found that the man had killed himself. They had found the whisky bottles and the knife he used under his body in the bath, and this proved Ibrahim had not done it. But strangely, knowing the corrupt incompetence of the Cairene police, I immediately began to fantasize that Ibrahim had in fact really done it. Perhaps he really was a murderer. At least he hadn't been tortured and at least we no longer had to deal with the philandering lawyer.

All I had to do was get my maps from the Map Office. We were ushered into the underboss's office, an open-plan affair with drafting tables and a green metal desk bare except for an ashtray full of butts and a flower made from satiny material. He nodded through Ozman and Muhammad's explanation of what we needed. This man, smoothly and in front of all his employees, said that he could get us all the maps we needed for E£100 a map, plus a further E£100 as a facilitation fee. We agreed.

But, back in the car park, Muhammad inflamed Ozman and me with a righteous diatribe against the need to bribe people to do their job. He announced he would get me all the maps I needed and would only charge E£40 per map. It sounded heroic but misguided. Muhammad tapped the side of his nose and explained that if he went in last thing the clerk would be gone and the replacement clerk was his friend, etc., etc. We agreed to come back the next day.

There was ample time left to go looking at cars I had no intention of buying. I test-drove the Nissan. In a move that could not have been better calculated to arouse distrust, the general explained airily that any noise we might hear as we drove would be due to a big sack of loose washers he had dumped in the back of the car, presumably for the exact purpose of masking any noises we might hear. I drove aimlessly around knowing that, despite the loose washers covering up no doubt truly terrible noises, this was a good car with accurate, tight steering and a slick, wobble-free gearbox. For a few minutes I kidded myself I would buy it, but there was something in me, maybe an upbringing where my father always bought cars from dealers, usually brand-new, and where my only privately bought car had died within a week of purchase and been left for dead on the hard shoulder of the M40, that stopped me from even attempting the probably impossible task of getting a loan. I was feeling vulnerable. I wanted security. I didn't know whom to trust. I wanted to trust Ozman but I just didn't and that was that.

We were greeted in the car park the next day by Muhammad. He didn't have the maps, but if we came back that afternoon he would definitely have them. 'Will he?' I asked Ozman. 'Oh yes,' said Ozman, who increasingly sided with Muhammad in these map discussions. We went over to look at a short wheel base 40 Series Land Cruiser owned by a Dutchman leaving the country. This was my lead, via Shaheer, and I was interested to see how Ozman belittled the admittedly old but still tough car. I realized that he was mainly interested in the commission he would get if it was he who introduced me to a sale.

We went back that afternoon to check on the maps. Muhammad said he had them, though I didn't believe him. We waited about an hour and he returned with some, but only three. We had ordered seven. Muhammad explained that the extreme suspicion raised by a foreigner trying to buy maps for the entire Libyan and Sudanese borders of Egypt had made it difficult, even with people who were his friends. We could get two more tomorrow, two more the next day, then another two and finally one. He smiled as if he had finally really cracked it.

'Tell him,' I ordered Ozman, 'that we take forty-five minutes to get here, then we wait an hour and then we drive back another forty-five minutes. Add in time for drinking tea and talking and that's half a day – and he thinks we're going to do this every day for a week just to get some maps?'

They both looked at me as if to say, 'What's the problem?' And there wasn't. From their point of view everything had reached a perfect pitch of complicatedness with the added bonus of looking soluble: a double win!

'Forget it,' I told Muhammad, 'it's not worth the effort.'

And indeed it wasn't. The next day Mohamed the driver went and got the remainder of the maps without any trouble at all.

Now we had terminated the endless employment possibilities provided by map acquisition, there was precious little for Ozman to do. Not that it seemed like that at the time. When you have employees you start automatically thinking of things they can do. You feel you owe it to them to keep them busy. I'd noticed that Ozman's dress code was slipping. Gone were the smart shirts and jackets; some days he didn't even shave. I took to pointing out potential cars as we drove around aimlessly filling our days. We visited Michael Wafiq, who knew Ozman (everyone knew Ozman) and then employed him, and me as I was with him, on a fruitless mission to get some papers out of an army department in Abassiya. We spent days failing to get me an Egyptian driving licence (in the end I got an international licence from the UK). We actually succeeded in joining a holiday-resort scheme my wife heard about, which meant a reduction in hotel prices, but resorts and hotels were just another distraction. Then we looked over a 75 Series troop carrier which Ozman showed me had suffered roof and body damage – you could tell from the welds on the windscreen pillars and the fact that the back doors were misaligned. I'm learning stuff, I said to myself, even if I am engaged in a silly pretence about actually purchasing a vehicle. It's reconnaissance, time spent on which is seldom wasted. Which was true – but there was money too. Ozman plus car cost just a little too much to be a disregardable expense. And I suspected the Buick needed repair work very soon. The strange clicking sound had grown daily to a thundering racket somewhere under the purple-carpeted transmission channel. 'I know exactly what it is,' said Ozman. 'The fuel pump. It need only six hundred pound to repair.'

The imminent demise of the Buick focused my mind on some kind of endgame strategy. I forced myself to be brutally realistic. Ozman had to serve me, not the other way round. I got him up to my 'office' to look at the trolley again. 'How do you feel about pulling that thing?'

Ozman looked panic-struck. 'On my own?'

'No, with me helping,' I said. 'All we need is a rope.'

'This will be a very hard work,' he said, offering me another full-strength Boston. The smoking! Ozman had got me back on the fags again.

Even though I could torment him from time to time with threats to test the trolley at some unspecified time and place in the desert, we both knew he'd expire before we'd tugged the thing five hundred metres. Probably I'd expire too, what with all the Bostons I was smoking and no exercise. No exercise! I'd sworn after my desert trip I'd keep up the walking each day by going to Wadi Digla, the nearest piece of desert to southern Cairo, a place Richard had told me about: he went mountain-biking there most Friday mornings. But despite Wadi Digla being a huge valley that had once been the primary prehistoric trade route from this part of the Nile to the Red Sea, and despite my children's school being built right next to it, I failed to locate the actual desert part of it. For several days I scampered about a dried-up riverbed that looked far too small to be such a vast wadi. Once I was chased by three stray dogs which backed off only when I threw rocks at them. Mohamed the driver, who remained parked as I fruitlessly explored the riverbed, expressed concern that I might be attacked by Bedouins as I wandered about. Somehow my failure even to find something as simple as the nearest bit of desert to Cairo underlined the way my enterprise in search of a lost oasis had gone way off course. And Ozman didn't help.

Fatally, I had begun to feel sorry for him. He had been born into a middle-class family with membership of the Gezira Club and now he had fallen on hard times. His wife worked for a company and I suspected it was her earnings that kept their kids in school and made the payments on their apartment in 6th of October City. Ozman living so far out added to the fuel bill, of course, which I was paying.

Everything was connected. Here was a man, in his late forties, bald, a heavy smoker, relying on a barely solvent writer to give him a career. Daily, I caught glimpses of Ozman's desperation. One night he rang up full of excitement that he had found three Land Cruisers going very cheap in Sharm El Sheikh. 'Buy them and sell two, you'll make a fortune,' he gasped hoarsely down the phone. 'But we must leave tomorrow for Sharm. We can take your mother-in-law's Honda.' Both of us already knew the Buick should never leave the city limits, its very survival bound up with never straying far from home, like a gang member out of its 'hood, the Buick would perish if it ever left a built-up zone, let alone had the temerity to drive through the desert, even on an asphalt road. Hopeless plans, desperate plans. Ozman bombarded me with people he knew selling flats my wife would love to buy, more cars that were in 'perfect condition'. Implosion was near. Ozman was the kind of guy who put all his chips in one basket, banked everything on that basket – and I was that basket.

What I found odd was that Ozman knew so many successful rich people yet he himself seemed only a step away from complete penury. In the West I guessed he would have been ostracized long ago, left behind as his friends stratified into their various economic groups, earning-packs that ran only with each other. Egypt was more benign. He was remembered and looked after – I'm sure Shaheer had put him on to me out of a sense of responsibility for the man. But he was forcing me to live a lie. I wasn't anything like as rich as he assumed. He would have to go.

Once I'd made the decision I felt strangely calm. I ordered Ozman to drive to the Maadi Yacht Club, and was pleased to be able tell him I was a member when he queried my right to go there. As if the club security guard could sniff his desperate situation, Ozman, unlike most other guests I had taken in, was quizzed at the door. But Ozman got the guard smiling and waving him through without my intervention. 'I tell him I know Mr Adeh, the biggest member of this club.' Again the mystery of the connections that had yielded him so little.

We sat down either side of a small table overlooking the grey-green Nile, moving swiftly across to the reedbeds far on the other side. The Nile kingfisher I always looked for hovered near us and plunged from high up. For the first time I saw it catch a small silvery fish and fly off. Ozman just nodded when I pointed this out. Wildlife, as for many Cairenes, held zero interest for him.

'Look, Ozman, we need to make cutbacks.'

'Yes,' he agreed, digging into his *shawarma* sandwich.

'We need to cut costs.'

He looked up and said quickly, 'I know of a Lada Niva you can buy. Only two thousand pounds.'

'Not car costs,' I said.

There was a silence as I watched the painful inward reorganization of his dreams and aspirations take place. His face slumped, but only for a second. He had found something new to hang on to, to grasp at. 'I can search alone,' he said. 'I can go by taxi.'

I remained silent.

'By microbus. Even walking.'

'Look, Ozman,' and the heaviness I felt was like swimming through sludge –

'I know many flats. No middlemen. No *simsars*. No problems.'

'Maybe later,' I lied. 'But right now I can't afford to keep paying you.'

His face slumped again and just as quickly brightened. 'I'll phone everyone I know, then I can call you every day. Every night.'

'Look, Ozman,' I said, 'you're fired.'

I made a determined effort to find Wadi Digla. The day after I fired Ozman I walked along the dry riverbed past great warehouses wreathed in stone dust and emitting the constant hammering of rock being crushed. I found a track to follow and dodged lumbering trucks shifting the stone from quarries up on the hillside. Then I climbed over a wall that was part of an elaborate gatehouse that spanned the widening valley. Down an obscuring slope of boulders I took in the view. A great wide canyon expanded into the distance. I had found my own private desert at last.

Ten

MY OWN PRIVATE DESERT

It wasn't really my own but it felt that way. I rarely saw people, and those I did see stuck near to the entrance, walking their dogs or on one occasion riding a mountain bike. It may have been the time I went – from 8.30 till 10 or 11 in the morning – but almost always I was alone. Mohamed would drive me to the gate (there was an extremely bumpy road, which meant I didn't need to walk from the school any more) and then he'd park, open the boot and hand me my water bottle and my trainers. I'd change, take a swig of water and set out to explore.

It was a canyon of great promise. The cliffs were three hundred or more feet high and rose in a concave curve to an abrupt crumbly steepness at the top. They looked impossible to climb. I was cowed by the canyon's vastness, content at first to leap from boulder to boulder along its rocky bottom. There were plants, but no trees, gravel slides, rounded hillocks of shale and side wadis winding into rocky clefts in the canyon walls. The air was brilliantly clear. Bright blue sky in front and, when I turned to look back, the city squatting under a foggy haze. You could actually see the start of the smog, worryingly near the place where my kids' school was, but as I walked up the canyon I turned my back on it.

In the ultra-clear air of the desert you can see as far as you want to. Small details are visible far away. A falcon floating in the distance above the canyon top was like an inkstroke, a precise piece of calligraphy.

There were two ruined blockhouses in the wadi, remnants of its time as a military training area. These became my landmarks. I would reach them quickly and then decide where to explore. On the ground I found fossils but no stone tools. I followed a path up a rocky defile and rediscovered the pleasure of hauling myself up short boulder-faces. Each sub-wadi was a series of steps that water had once poured down. They looked unclimbable but up close there was almost always a way. Under the cliffs were animal tracks and burrows but for days I saw no animals, only birds, including the black and white wheatear, the *zerzur*, after which Zerzura had been named. At the top of the side wadi I was on the plain, flat and gravelly. In the far distance were new tower blocks being built. Ahead it was clear to the horizon and behind, in the hollow of the Nile valley, lay Cairo under its pall of greyness.

I had been keen on rock-climbing when I was younger, but it had been years since I had done any. I was surprised to find I'd become trepidatious about heights, nervous about scrambling up shale cliffs. Slowly I regained the old skills needed, not pausing too long on a hand- or foothold, not thinking too much, just moving upwards. Instead of seeing unclimbable vertiginous cliffs I began to see routes, ways up and out of the canyon. I deliberately sighted up a possible route and found my way quite easily to the very top edge. The drop made me keep clear of the edge, gave my knees a slight wobble. Looking across the canyon, which was maybe a half-kilometre wide, the plains on the other side stretched away to hills marked only by a distant radio tower. Coming down the same way I saw my first desert fox, not a big-eared fennec, but a red fox. I sat still and watched it as it watched me. The time spent watching in the cool clear high-up air was like an inner breath to some neglected part of me, which neutralized the heavy sense of self, made me transparent again.

As my confidence grew I went further afield. Around one

great bend in the wadi was a solitary tree. It was an acacia, with a few sprouting leaves and a green, scarred trunk. The sole tree, it took on an iconic significance, like the famous tree of Ténéré, a landmark for hundreds of years in northern Niger. Even here, so close to the madness of Cairo, the way the desert pared everything down to its minimum was apparent. The tree in its lonely splendour ceased to be a piece of scrub, instead became something wonderful, a focus point for wonder without distraction.

The desert makes us see things newly. Just as fasting makes you see the wonder of simple food and clean water, the desert brings home the magnificence of things, their essence, which is occluded by the information overload of ordinary living in ordinary places. Shamans in their madness talk about the way all living things communicate. I'd even read about a potential use for junk DNA, that part of the gene code that scientists can't fathom a use for, which was as a kind of energy transmitter connecting all life on the planet. Nutty stuff from a scientific point of view, but perfect sense when you see THE TREE, or THE FOX, or THE LIZARD running away on its long thin legs and pad-like toes.

One day I came down, full and satisfied by the immensity of the place, and heard thunder in the distance. Or was it some kind of machinery? A kind of rattling with a distant echo way over on the right outside the canyon. Then the first bullet whistled overhead, quickly followed by the second. Shit! I was under fire. Those old dented bullets with rusty metal jackets I'd found weren't a remnant of the '67 war – they were still using this place as a firing range. More bullets zinged overhead and I went into a stupid crouching run. I knew from all my reading that the bullet that hits you makes no noise, but such knowledge is only partially reassuring. If only I made it to the entrance gate I'd be OK. I dodged through boulders to get as close as I could to the wadi cliffs. Any bullets flying overhead would surely miss me there – unless they were firing in a high arc and these were projectiles raining down at the end of their trajectory. People were regularly maimed by bullets falling from the sky at Afghan weddings. Only in Egypt, I fumed, would a protected area (Wadi Digla was one of the few successful conservation areas near Cairo) actually be the backend of a firing range. I crouched and ran and after a while the dream-like quality of the zinging bullets made the prospect of being hit implausible. I had to keep reminding myself what they really were.

When I made it to the car I pointed out the crackling of the distant range to Mohamed. He smiled broadly: 'Maybe two kilometres away.' Not far enough, not nearly far enough. Though it probably did help to keep my private desert deserted.

On another occasion I was picking my way down past some fox burrows when I saw a metal object that looked like part of an engine exhaust. I picked it up and saw that it was cylindrical with metal flaps that folded out like ... little wings, and then I saw the end had a dull dented head. Oh-oh, I was holding an unexploded rocket grenade. My first instinct was to fling it as far away as possible but this I quickly cancelled by laying it as softly as I could in the sand. Then I walked rapidly away. Once I was a suitable distance and a number of boulders away I thought, What if some kid picks it up? But there's no way I'm going near it again. I told Mohamed and he folded his hands back at the wrists, miming a handless man. While he guffawed I realized I probably should have marked the spot where it was, but though I often looked for the bomb I never saw it again.

I took my kids to Wadi Digla, but owing to a conversation with Uncle Mahmoud they were convinced the place was full of snakes. 'It's winter,' I said. 'The snakes are all hibernating.'

'Where?' asked my six-year-old son.

'Under the ground,' I improvised.

'In that hole?' he asked.

'No.'

'Where then?'

'Maybe under a rock.' For the rest of the walk they skirted every pebble with absurd precaution.

I never saw a snake in Wadi Digla, summer or winter, though wadis are much more likely habitats than the open dunes. Snakes the world over prefer the night to the day; in the winter the desert at night is too cold for them to move, and daytime dune temperatures in summer would cook any living thing lying on the surface. Sand vipers burrow under the sand and wait for their prey that way, knowledge of which should make you cautious about ploughing down dunes joyously in bare feet, but never does.

I got so adventurous I decided to invent a new sport: wadieering. In wadieering the object was to ascend each wadi as far as you could go. I advertised on a website called Saharasafaris which was a user group of mainly youngish Egyptians who liked diving or going into the desert. I got one reply to the advert but despite making plans with this woman, who was mainly interested in learning how to rock-climb (I sold wadieering as the ideal introduction to the more taxing demands of real climbing, without the need for a rope and other pieces of specialist kit), we never managed to kick off this new world-changing sport. It was doomed to remain a sport with one practitioner, highly localized, like Eton fives or that game they play in Afghanistan with a dead goat. Every time I did what I would do in England – try to start a group of like-minded souls – I met with conspicuous failure. Perhaps the desert wasn't as popular as I thought it ought to be.

I had met the founder of Sahara Safaris, a studious young guy called Mohamed Mabrouk, who had picked up the hiking habit while a postgraduate in England. He was immensely bright, an expert in computer satellite navigation, and obsessed with exploring the desert. Others nicknamed him 'the Headmaster', but a casual group always needs a leader to do the boring stuff and he suited the role well. Most weekends and every holiday he was off with friends in his battered Jeep Wrangler, the long-wheelbase version only assembled in Egypt and China. He boasted, with evidence, that he had spent more time in the desert than Hassanein Bey, whose two major trips added up to about three hundred nights in the Sahara. This was an equivalence I didn't take seriously. Long trips into deep desert count for more (even though you may do just as much exploring on repeated short trips), perhaps because of their symbolic likeness to a pilgrimage. You can get deeper into the desert and you can go deeper into yourself on a long trip.

The desert wasn't about what was out there. It was all about what was in here. The lack of noise, distraction, things, allowed you entrance to the overlooked part of yourself whose function was simply to observe. The lost oasis was the place where you hit ground zero and started learning what really made you tick. Without knowing how your machine worked everything you did was just so much displacement activity. The desert fathers had it right; they just went a little overboard. Until you find that lost oasis you're just flailing, unable to get a real grip on anything. Once you know, and knowing follows from simply observing without prejudice, what your ego+body+inner desire needs to function, you can set about doing something beyond mere self-maintenance. It's as if you don't know what food really is and how much you need so you spend all your waking hours dreaming of food and pursuing it and suffering indigestion and never doing anything else. That rested simple space inside allows you to observe your real needs. Fasting is a metaphor to help you find this space. So is the desert.

Things I found in Wadi Digla:
  A lump of quartz crystal
  A goat skull
  A fox's jawbone with teeth
  Two caves, one obviously enlarged by human hands
  Fossilized coral
  Fossilized cone-shaped shells
  The rocket-propelled grenade round
  Numerous 7.62mm AK47 shell casings
  Numerous steel-jacketed rounds

Many odd-shaped stones of a pleasing hue
A canister of tear gas (used)
A large paper target with the bull's-eye shot away
Stone-martin nests
A log of petrified wood
A family of foxes.

All the foxes I had seen in Wadi Digla had been very wary. I had never managed to get up close to any of them. I had been going to the wadi for several months before I even saw my first fox, though there were plenty of their trails, so I knew they must be there. Then one day I was exploring a series of sandy overhanging caves at the base of the cliff when I saw two foxes coming towards me. They stopped and went sideways, then on my left a third fox with a silvery tip to its tail appeared and came forward with a determined growling set to the jaw even though it made no sound. The younger foxes saw me and backed off but this one just kept coming, trying to make me back off. Was this a mother with nearly full-grown cubs, or an old fox that had learnt it could scare humans? Not that I was *scared*, but you do think about rabies when an old and grizzled-looking fox is advancing towards you with its yellow fangs revealed. I'd had ludicrous animal face-offs in my time with black swans, elk, small dogs and even a cornered rat (very high-pitched squeal). It shows you how much of a confidence trick is involved in such an encounter. I mean, I was huge compared to that measly little fox, but there I was, almost backing off because I had an excuse to do so. The decision to back off precedes the excuse. You think, I don't like this, and then it comes to you: Ah yes, it might have rabies therefore it is *not* cowardly but rational to run away.

Not that I did run away. This was my desert too. I picked up a rock and we circled each other, neither giving ground, our pride intact. But after that I ceased to think all animals would necessarily run. I'd seen jackals outside Siwa. Ghali called them wolves, which is what the Bedouin call them, but they were too small and were almost certainly jackals. Real wolves have not been recorded in Egypt for over a century. Ghali put the decline in wildlife down to the Bedouin getting 4x4s. 'Now they can hunt every gazelle in their area by just running it down in a car.' At Areg Oasis he said you could once look down from the cliff-edge and see the gazelle scattering in front of you. Now there are perhaps one or two, and we saw none. Leopards, too, had not been uncommon up until the 1980s. These too had suffered from being shot, skinned and stuffed for the Cairo bazaars, avaricious for such trophies.

There was also the occasional human encounter. Once I came down the side of the canyon on the other side of the big curve and saw a whole tented encampment, including camels, around the tree. They were filming an episode for a historical drama and the wadi was now part of the Sudan.

Not often, but sometimes, I met white women with dogs who said hello in English; also, once, a school party of Egyptian kids with an American teacher and two soldiers who looked lost but also said hello.

If I saw anyone I took to keeping my distance, just like Ghali in the desert. It is a place of outcasts who go there to be alone. If someone wants to talk to you they will make a sign, welcome you over.

The desert encourages this desire to be left alone, a desire supported by the smuggling, gun-running and police nosiness that goes on there. When I was with Ghali I tried to get a picture from him of just where the police and army patrolled, in case I needed to avoid them in future. The nearer you got to the coast and the borders the more likely you'd meet a patrol. Old tracks, well worn routes – these were the places that were frequented. Keep away from tracks and checkpoints and you'd probably be able to travel the desert without seeing a soul.

I went to Wadi Digla three times a week. I enjoyed the routine with the shoes and the water bottle, which, when I returned tired and thirsty, Mohamed would hand to me to glug from like a marathon runner at the finish.

In winter there was a grey dust over everything in Wadi Digla, over the plants as well as the discarded plastic bags and pieces of broken-up concrete. But as spring approached it began to change. The weather grew hotter, the sun bright enough to burn by ten in the morning. The desert began to come alive. The plants, all grey and listless, became green, some with tiny yellow flowers. New shoots broke through the hard ground. There were more birds and lizards; you could feel the burgeoning vitality of the place. I had always assumed, because of the heat, that the summer in the desert was the dead time, but it wasn't. In the Gilf, the big rains, according to Tubu tradition, came in the summer, not the winter. Nowadays, no people went there at that time. It was deemed too hot. I imagined everything blooming in that empty place with no one to see it.

One night my son wanted to appease me because of some annoyance he had caused. 'Show me your desert things,' he said. 'Show me your crystals and stones.' However tired and grumpy I might be, he knew how to revive me. I unwrapped my treasure from its newspaper roll. The chipped flint axes, the silica-glass arrowheads, the granite pestle, the ancient pottery shards I'd found in the Gilf, numerous fossils, petrified wood, the jawbone of a gazelle, date kernels so desiccated they were hard as stone, and a flake of obsidian, minutely worked ten thousand years ago into a blade that perfectly fitted my hand.

Eleven

THE RUSSIAN WELL

I was getting to know more about the colonel. He liked to have people around whom he got along with, who thought the world of him and didn't challenge him. That was my role and that of another freebie taker, Paula from Vicenza, who brought software, roofracks, electronics and other gear hard to find in Egypt in return for free trips into the desert. Paula had been on eight different expeditions with the colonel and yet she had none of the pomposity that might accompany someone with so much desert time under their belt. 'I just like coming out here with these people,' was how she put it.

Her desert stripes were on view in subtle ways – she wore leather-sided aviators like the colonel and was the only person allowed to lift that natty front passenger seat. I was hoping I would receive special instruction in operating the seat now that I was in the in-group, rather in the way kung-fu masters pass down secret moves to favoured pupils, but alas I made no further progress than being entrusted with lowering the seat after everyone was back in the vehicle.

This trip was less serious than the last. Shorter, too: only two weeks and with less time away from water. I had written something for a newspaper and the colonel said he always had room for journalists. Now I felt I knew something about the desert I made a plan. This time my aim would be finding stuff. It had become an obsession.

I had formulated several rules for beachcombing in the desert.

1) You're always looking, everywhere, even during a coffee break on the highway. Eyes down, looking for anything.
2) When someone else finds something the natural reaction is to give that area a miss, on the vague statistical grounds that it has already yielded its gold. Actually what people do is go to the same rough area but studiously avoid the exact place the find was made. *Do not do this*. Some of my best finds came from exactly the same spot as someone else's good find but they were so excited with what they had they didn't keep on looking.
3) Don't assume interesting piles of rocks will yield things. Sometimes it's just as good to aim for pure, empty sand. I've found a perfect Acheulean axehead sitting on a dune as if dropped by someone a few hours previously.
4) Near the asphalt is as good a place as any. My most intricately worked Neolithic flint knife was four metres from the well travelled tarmac road in the White Desert, itself the most populous piece of the Sahara in Egypt.
5) Lower places tend to be better than higher places.
6) Places that resemble dried-up lakes are often good.
7) But most of all keep looking so that when you are looking somewhere good you're neither hopeful nor pessimistic. The best stuff is always found by the least desperate.

That said, I was a little bit keen to find a shark's tooth. There is something primordial and yet familiar about the shark. Owning a shark's tooth conveys some element of being a successful hunter or warrior, even if the thing is fossilized. Shark's teeth, too, had a special significance for me after a telling experience I had at a publisher's party I once attended at the London Aquarium. The notion of an aquarium was good, but the reality was disappointing. Aquariums are too dark and too low with too many rooms for a party. You can't see who is famous and who isn't and even if someone tells you a famous person has arrived you can't find them because there are so many rooms. At this party I had a miserable time because I was driving and not drinking and trying to interest (in a novel I had written) one of the famous (in publishing terms) people whom I couldn't find though everyone told me they had just finished having a lovely chat with them next to the giant carp/octopus/catfish.

Towards the end of this non-party I observed the novelist Ali Smith surrounded by people, with a man in a wetsuit handing her something. I pushed through the crowd to find out what was going on. Earlier I had seen two divers in wetsuits inside one huge tank, swimming about feeding the fish, but I scarcely paid them any attention since my own fishing mission required all my attention. Ali Smith opened her hand to reveal a shark's tooth. I can barely recall what it looked like owing to the crush and the poor lighting but it was big and white and sharp-looking. She told me that she had seen a tooth at the bottom of the big tank when the divers were in there and she had asked them to recover the tooth for her. I would have been as happy as she was with such a prize. The place was full of people but she was the only who spotted the tooth, as well as the method for retrieving it. There were lots of other writers at that party, including some who were very well known, but none of them got the shark's tooth, they were all too busy posturing and positioning themselves.

The symbolic nature of the shark's tooth was further underlined when, after finally finding the publisher and making my miserable pitch, I was pointedly avoided by two very well known writers, both of whom I had brazenly asked to puff one of my books in order to promote its sales. Writers are shy folk generally, and aim to please, so instead of saying, 'Fuck off, your book stinks,' these two demonstrated the same eagerness to escape my company that a wounded flying fish shows in the presence of a sharp-toothed dolphin, its main predator.

But all these famous and not-so-famous writers missed the

real prize, which, in a poetic sense, was of greater significance than even the Booker prize, for which Ali Smith has been shortlisted several times and indeed was 'up for' that year. I sensed that the shark's tooth constituted part of the real texture of things, was a real coordinate, unlike the false nonsense of flattering dealmakers and puffing books you couldn't be bothered to even read. In Aboriginal folklore, and also the mystical traditions of many cultures, a man may be given a stone to carry somewhere and deliver to someone. Or he may find a stone that is connected to someone and by moving that stone he affects their fate. I liked this version of the world. That there were objects, some valuable, some nondescript, that connected to the other half of reality, the invisible world of our dreams, ideas and aspirations. The visible world was no more real than this invisible world, and, in fact, much of the visible world, despite being visible, 'didn't count', was inert in some way because it didn't connect through the fabric of space-time to the inner world of human beings. But these 'power objects' did. The shark's tooth at the aquarium was such a power object. I wouldn't at all be surprised if Ali Smith, almost incidentally, goes on to become the most revered novelist of the twenty-first century. The shark's tooth, as well as its mystical quality, had value as a symbol of her willingness to live the life of a writer 100 per cent, even when she was engaged in something basically antithetical to good writing, i.e. is sucking up to publishers looking for the next big thing. I instantly knew from the shark's-tooth incident that I was living the wrong sort of life. I had become a writer to get freedom to live the right kind of life for me. The right kind of life, which would be reflected in the books I wrote, was one where I grasped the full potential of any situation, including any shark's teeth going.

Now I was in the desert again, in the right place, and I knew it. I was making the most of the present. I didn't want to be anywhere else. On this trip we drove down through the Great Sand Sea following for a while a series of oildrums left on crags and dunes by Russian prospectors in the 1960s. The drums had been placed very carefully. They had been placed to break the horizon with their unmistakable outline against the light. As you drove past one you just had to scan the horizon for the next. Even a drum three kilometres away was visible if placed in this way.

The drums led to a surprise 'for the ladies', the colonel said. After two days following them through dunes with no vegetation at all, just white sand everywhere, we came around a slight hill to see, in the middle of nowhere, an oasis. It was the classic image I had of an oasis. Sand everywhere and then a circle of palm trees and acacias and a stone trough full of water. De Lancey Forth and Wingate had postulated that Zerzura must exist somewhere in the Great Sand Sea. It looked as though we had found it.

'This is Bir Russie,' said Ghali, 'the Russian Well. They drilled for oil and they found water instead.' A bent pipe poked out of the ground and artesian water under pressure gushed out in a thick, profligate spray. The trees had not been planted: they just grew up as soon as the water started its non-stop flow. The treat for the ladies that Ghali promised was that they could wash their hair in as much water as they wished.

I wandered past the concrete floors, all that was left of the Russian drilling camp, and down a hill of shale-laden sand to something white in the distance. It was the skeletons of two dead camels. Where the bones poked through the sand they were bleached white. Where sand covered the carcass it still had a leathery brown furry covering, the flesh mummified in the dry sand.

That night we camped in a wide depression in the desert with *yardangs*, wind-eroded shale protrusions. Their shape perfectly resembles the body and neck of the Sphinx. Perhaps that enigmatic statue is a relic of an older culture that came out of the desert. In this radical version of history, the Sphinx and the Great Pyramid have nothing to do with Cheops and date from a far older period about seven to ten thousand years ago. This is borne out by the weathering on the Sphinx's body, obviously caused by rain, which hasn't fallen in sufficient quantities to do this for seven thousand years. The so-called earlier pyramids of Sakkara and Darfur are in fact later, incompetent copies of the earlier, perfect Great Pyramid at Giza.

Crazy theories for crazy minds intent on finding treasure. In the campsite depression I found several large circular fossilized anemones. They were beautiful, like fragile ornamented biscuits, and soon my pockets were full. I knew I was in tip-top beachcombing mode. I was utterly sure of finding something valuable yet I didn't care – a state of mind that is hard to will: you can only increase your chances of being in it by spending all your time hunting. I walked across a stretch of pebbly sand and instinctively bent down, picked up and recognized all at once a perfect shark's tooth. It was the rarer kind – white, not black – and neither its tip nor the fossilized gum was broken. News of my discovery excited the Italians and they all began searching. I showed the tooth to everyone, just like Ali Smith did, each time cradling it back in my trouser pocket. I showed Ibrahim, who was the cook as well as a driver. He grinned and said, 'You are lucky man.'

Twelve

WHO OWNS YOU

I came back from my trip with a new plan that involved the colonel. I would try to gather like-minded people from Britain who wanted to search for rock art, and the colonel would make a profit. I went up to Alexandria to see his expedition garage and to talk business. It seemed to me that finding a new cave would be just the sort of thing a book about the desert required. That is, if I didn't find a lost oasis first.

This was exactly the kind of thinking that assailed Almasy. In letters he is always banking on finding Zerzura or, later, the lost army of Cambyses (a Persian army that supposedly perished in the Great Sand Sea marching on Siwa). He wants to find these things because he's convinced that he will then be of sufficient reputation to be appointed director of King Farouk's Cairo Desert Institute. He hungers after the respectability of this role but also the opportunities it will bring him for spending unlimited time in the desert. You see this hunger, or greed, feeding itself. You find yourself searching for more and more ways of being able to spend more time in the desert. But these ways often bring you away from the desert, from what attracts you to it in the first place. I was about to discover that with my attempt to enter the semi-commercial expedition market.

While I had been away in the desert my 'office' had not been empty. A friend of the family, Dr Naguib, had been in hiding there, escaping the long arm of the law owing to a bank loan he had failed to repay. In Egypt you can still get a custodial sentence for such civil crimes as defaulting on debt and flaunting building regulations. One member of the family spent two years on the run – in her own house, never answering the door and always leaving after the all-clear had been given by the *bawab*. This was for building an illegal fourth floor on a three-storey villa.

My office was perfect for Dr Naguib, who always dressed impeccably in three-piece Italian suits, fluorescent silk ties and highly polished Clarks shoes. For some reason Clarks shoes signal high status in Egypt. The office was a good bolt-hole because it could not be connected to Dr Naguib in any way. It seemed strange that a mere two weeks was enough, but he said once the police couldn't find him at home they would give up. Dr Naguib liked his creature comforts and left the fridge well stocked with cans of Birel, chocolate bars, halva and other delicacies, and on my desk a vaporizer of cologne labelled 'Victoria's Fruity'. Despite being a qualified surgeon of urology and owning two clinics in Upper Egypt he did no work apart from a little dabbling on the stock market (unsuccessful, if the bank loan was anything to go by).

Uncle Mahmoud and Aunt Zaza had returned in a hurry from their usual three months in Alexandria after the balcony in the flat next to them fell off in the night and crashed first into the lower balcony and then the street. This was more than worrying – the building had been erected by my mother-in-law during her property developer phase and there was a chance that a) all the balconies would fall off and b) the owners would sue her, the builder and freehold owner of the block, for gross negligence.

The balcony disaster had a positive effect in human terms. Aunt Zaza had fallen out with her sister, my mother-in-law, over some trivial matter involving a mutual friend. Their estrangement was making everyone in the family uncomfortable, but both were stubborn in refusing to speak to the other. When the balcony crashed down they started talking without hesitation, as if they had been waiting for something like this, of sufficient moment to overwhelm their petty differences. Disaster free economies could be losing out in the potential they have for building human relations.

The semi-commercial expedition ground to a slow halt. Though I garnered a few keen souls I did not garner enough. It also became increasingly obvious that it would require lots of work doing things I hate doing (phoning, checking, posting, booking flights and hotels). And I wouldn't make any money from it unless I organized several such trips – but to popular places in Egypt I didn't want to go to myself.

I kept having to remind myself that the real experience of the desert was very simple; it was getting out into the desert that seemed to complicate things. You needed cars, fuel, camels, jerry cans and fodder and, above all, other people. You couldn't go alone and yet it was to be alone that you went there. I needed to strip back my endeavours to the basics. I reassembled the trolley and pictured myself towing it. I was in pretty poor physical condition owing to sitting down and being driven everywhere. I decided to improve my strength by joining a gym. A real gym. I had long ago given up on the genial OAPs in the moribund weights hut at the Maadi Club. I wanted somewhere where youth and vitality provided a spur to pushing myself that little bit harder.

There were several gyms favoured by ex-pats but they were all expensive, full of women in leotards running on treadmills while listening to self-improvement audiobooks on earphones, and instructors who gave personal training advice at UK prices. Through a younger cousin of Samia's, I found exactly the place I wanted: a hard-core body-building gym in the poorer part of town run by a genial giant called Captain Mustapha. The captain's head was the same width as his trunk-like neck, he was six foot six and his shorts were like a

147

pair of Bermudan-rigged sailing boats each racing around its own Eddystone Lighthouse. Each leg was chest diameter in dimensions, each arm leg-like in its massiveness. There were no running machines with natty computers to tell you you were about to have a heart attack, no bicycles, no prissy weights machines with five-kilogram increments, no step-aerobics steps, no Nordic ski machine or rowing machine, and nothing at all that smacked of bending or stretching. The only aerobic option was skipping; there was a little dungeon-like corner where Captain Mustapha forced fatties to skip for hours on end. Otherwise you just had the bench, free weights and a few hulking old machines, well oiled, with ten- and twenty-kilo minimum weight increments.

The captain pushed me hard. For a £5-a-month subscription I got one-on-one tuition every time I went. For the first time, after years of mucking about in gyms, I discovered the right way to lift the bench-press bar, to do wrist curls and even to skip. And I liked the fact that there were no women. It gave a wholehearted seriousness to the business of pumping iron, a seriousness always deflated by the sight of super-fit house-wives running a treadmill half-marathon before breakfast.

My wife had intensified her search for an apartment. We needed our own place and in Cairo we could just about afford it. In England, our £50,000 (a generous gift from downsizing parents) would have bought one-third of the former public lavatory in Oxford that had been granted planning permission to become a one-bedroom flat. In Cairo that money would get you a four- or five-bedroom apartment in the area where we wanted to live. Whilst it is true that only a raving optimist would imagine that buying a house in Egypt was as simple as in Britain, there were some aspects to buying that were simpler. For example, Egyptians never bother with a survey. Instead you trust the fact that others are already living in the same building. Mortgages had only been available for the last three years and were still a novelty. And in Egypt you don't exchange contracts, with all that nonsense about gazumping;

you exchange cash, physically like in the drug-buying sequence in *Scarface*. There then follows a rush to change all the keys.

The real difference however was in how you found a house. There were some ads for houses in magazines, but they were paid for by expensive developers and all aimed at foreign companies. There were estate agents – but they catered for the very rich and, again, for foreign companies. The advertising of houses for sale was a novel innovation, and advertising always brought out the latent greed of Egyptians. Instead of the humble 'or nearest offer' you got 'highest price only'.

The Egyptian way of buying a flat is to walk around an area you like and ask to see the local *simsar*, the middleman. *Simsars* take a cut, which is why Ozman had promised he would keep one out of any future deal. The *simsar* has no office; people simply know where to find him. He takes you to properties for sale. Every *bawab* knows who the *simsar* of their street is, and asking the *bawab* of a building you like will get you to the *simsar*.

I did not hanker so much after home ownership as a rent- and mortgage-free existence. Rent had always struck me as immoral, in some way only Marxists, anarchists and Irish travellers have come close to defining. Mortgages I'd always been wary of. I'd never had a job with any mortgage-attracting qualities. Though I had fantasized about buying a house during periods of very low mortgage rates, I had lacked follow-through. I knew from one building society interview, which in many ways resembled a job interview (the kind of job interview that brought out a desire to tell whopping lies), that mortgage companies thought they were doing you a *favour*. They acted as if they owned you, or would shortly, once they had generously stumped up the thousands you needed. Instead of holding my wrists up to be ritually hand-cuffed by a smirking mortgage adviser I had long dreamed of walking into a house-purchase deal and simply slapping down a plastic bag full of money. Now we had the money, all we needed was to find the right place.

Many were incomplete, nestling at the top of shell-like buildings without windowpanes or even doors, with piles of sand in the corners of what the *simsar* tried to make you imagine would be your living room complete with wide-screen telly. Penthouse flats came with the promise that the roof was ours too, to be made into a garden if we could stand staring twelve storeys down as we watered our begonias.

Everywhere we looked at was deeply flawed. Perhaps we were trying to get too much bang for our bucks. I was determined to get a place with plenty of space and high ceilings. Though modern buildings in Cairo follow the global penny-pinching trend towards troglodytic crampedness, older buildings can have superbly high ceilings. When we found one that had views – admittedly on one side they were of a vacant lot used as a car park and on the other of tower blocks of a Stalinist simplicity – we decided to buy. As I walked around the neighbourhood I couldn't keep from thinking that despite the dust-laden avenue of trees in our road the area bore a striking resemblance to West Beirut before they rebuilt it. Garbage-filled lots and half-finished blocks filled every vista, run-down shanty shops stood across the road from a new McDonald's and a KFC. I was not a fan of fast food, but I grasped at straws. McDonald's make good landmarks for visitors, I extemporized lamely. At the end of our street I found a Mobil gas station that also sold a big selection of Havana cigars. I bought some cigarettes and thought how convenient to have such a fine range of cigars within a few hundred metres of my front door – it was a pity I was just about to give up smoking. Right up until that moment I was still in two minds about the place. Resigned to buying but hardly happy about it.

I then experienced a revelation or, more accurately, a shift in the way I looked at the world. And being truer, it was better than what I had coerced myself to believe before.

Coming across the roundabout, holding up the traffic but moving fast, were two men in gelabiyas and turbans with a great flock of goats, some raggedy-looking sheep and four untethered donkeys. Unlike most donkeys these looked healthy and strong. There must have been forty goats and sheep running across that roundabout, skittering on the concrete pavement, bunched up in groups against honking taxis and trucks. That's when I decided we had bought in exactly the right spot. We could eat a Big Mac while watching the goats and goatherds go by. Cairo wasn't traditional, rural and quaint. Neither was it modern, convenient and reliable. It was both. I felt then that the desperate shoehorning of Cairo into a more traditional picture than it really was had been the cause of self-inflicted misery. It was no good trying to squint with half an eye closed down Talaat Haab Street and imagine Groppi's café in its heyday in the 1930s, or sit in Fishawi's in the bazaar and ignore the man selling wraparound shades, or take tea at Mena House while imagining you were in the Stranglers' video for 'Golden Brown', ignoring the smog and the tour guides with mobile phones.

Cairo was bigger than all this, encompassed all this, and it was OK to live in a place that looked like a slum just as long as there were goats, Mercs, Big Macs and shoeshine boys, ATMs and a woman roasting corn in a hubcap, an English bookshop and an open-air mosque, a *bawab* with five kids in the basement and an ADSL connection, a knife sharpener with his grindstone over his shoulder, Radioshack, Kall Kwik and a family on a donkey cart loaded with *birseem* fodder.

Opposite the goat crossing where I formulated this new world-view was a restaurant cast exactly in the shape of a ship. Unfinished but already in use, there were remnants of desert sand (New Maadi, where we live, used to be *all* desert until recently) piled up in the car park. It was like one of those photos of the former Aral Sea where you see a ship high and dry on a dune. The name of the restaurant: Titanic, of course. I resolved to eat there as soon as possible. A real ship of the desert in modern Cairo.

In the troubling days before I accepted that Cairo had actually changed since Bagnold and Almasy lived there, I took to

151

having the odd nostalgic beer in the Windsor Hotel's lounge bar, a place virtually the same (if you squinted and ignored the TV set and the photo of Michael Palin, who stayed there) as the officers' club it had been during the war. The Windsor stands next to the old site of Shepherd's Hotel, burnt down in 1952 as a gesture of contempt towards the soon-to-be-departing British. I talked with the owner of the Windsor, Mr Doss, a gentle, middle-aged Copt, who mourned the great days of the recent past when Cairo's downtown streets were as smart and beautiful as anywhere in the world. The Windsor was a monument to that vanished past. 'You know,' he said, 'once every hotel had Greek and Italian waiters, and even the pharmacies had English assistants.' Though the Windsor sometimes smelt of petrol its charms were undeniable. It had that dark, contemplative, leather-and-wood silence you expect from a good bar. It was spacious with a high ceiling. The lift was see-through metal scrollwork with a rattly door that expanded and clicked shut, the handle rubbed through to a pure brass shine. Downstairs the telephone system was all jack-plugs and a wood-faced socket board with a bakelite cone to talk into.

It was during my Windsor phase that I met Holland's leading desert explorer, Arita Baaijens. Legendary in Egypt and Europe but sadly little known in the English-speaking world, Arita is a successor to such extraordinary desert cameleers as Wilfred Thesiger, Theodore Monod and Michael Asher – all of whom she has met. If this sounds like the introduction to a laudatory article, it's because my first meeting with Arita was intended for just such an article. But, like many obviously great stories, the piece never got published.

I was meeting Arita at the self-imposed end of her eighteen-year desert-exploring career. She must have been about fifty but she looked younger. She had light blue eyes, full of fun, used to looking a long way into the distance. She radiated the cheerful, buoyant energy of a dancer, and I was only half surprised when she told me that in her twenties, before she got into the desert, she had trained in her spare time as a dance teacher – the tango of course.

After one visit to Egypt the desert enmeshed her in its attractions. She gave up her job as a research ecologist to become a full-time traveller.

She wore a red leather motorcycle jacket and I thought of George in the Famous Five who dressed as a boy and was better at boy's stuff than the boys. She carried a gun when travelling in the wilder parts of the Sudan. Another time we were in a bar with a pool table and she announced, 'I'll beat you easily' – kind of matter-of-fact and triumphal at the same time. I believed her (besides I'm crap at pool). She liked to win. Her journeys had been made alone, with just three or four camels, through country I had driven in my cosseted convoy of 4x4s. As I said, the pics were great. Very wind-blown and wild-looking, sun-browned in loose clothing; small campfires with a sharp-beaked, blackened coffee pot; she looked happy.

Now Arita wanted a new challenge and had settled on the shaman-rich expanses of Siberia. Shamanism can get to the best of us, but I didn't say this. I had even read and perused with initial interest the books of Philippe Morel, a British based teacher of shamanism. Morel offered courses in shamanism as well as weekend seminars in Fairey Magick (his spelling). What little I knew about shamanism included the sure knowledge that it couldn't be bought and sold with a slot-machine mentality. You couldn't self-select to be a shaman. Also I was dubious about Fairey Magick: even for an open-minded pro-shaman kind of person Fairey Magick sounded very silly, the kind of thing that gave shamanism a bad name.

Arita was too well travelled and perceptive to be taken in. She wanted the real thing. She was still searching and that was a very attractive characteristic. Searchers are people who haven't given up. And this world is littered with people who have given up. And people who are too afraid even to try.

I was, however, a little sad that Arita was turning her back on the desert as I had nurtured a slight hope of making a trip with her.

Within a few minutes she had outlined her own desert apprenticeship under (literally under) Carlo Bergmann, who exchanged desert knowledge for sex out in the high dunes. 'You see,' said Arita, 'I really wanted to learn and he was the only person who could teach me. It was kind of a trade at first but then I grew to love him.'

In the staid surroundings of the Windsor bar (dark wood chairs, yellowed prints of old Cairo, an elderly man drinking anise) I was somewhat stunned by this revelation. But stunned in a good way. This was a side to the desert experience I had not really expected.

It seemed that Bergmann turned Nietzschean once he got out in the dunes. 'I am the King here,' he used to shout. 'I make the rules.' At first Arita had resisted his demands for sex, but when she saw how much she could learn from him, she gave in. But her matter-of-factness doused his burning sexual urgency, which only further maddened him. The way she talked about Bergmann, he sounded like a cross between Fassbinder and Saint Simeon, or maybe Thesiger and Morrissey – definitely an intriguing figure, an outsider's outsider.

Not surprisingly Arita's first book, which revealed the whole sex-in-the-desert apprenticeship, was a bestseller. She had then gone on to travel in the Sudan and to live for a year in Farafra Oasis, which she loved despite its isolation.

Arita had been deserted in the desert by her camels and then painstakingly found them over a period of twenty-four hours. If she hadn't she would have died. She had had many encounters with armed and possibly dangerous nomads in northern Sudan. Almost as an aside she said to me, 'I don't care if I die tomorrow. I learnt that in the desert.' She had really been out there and *done* the desert, the desert whose surface I had barely scratched.

I expected I would be envious, but I wasn't. Partly that was because Arita was such a positive, encouraging person who did not belittle others. But it was also because of the nature of the desert. It would have been nice to have made the trips when she did – pre-GPS – so there were no cars and no car tracks to spoil it. But the desert wasn't like a jungle that was being logged. The desert would always be there. I took it as a good sign that it was big enough for the both of us, so to speak, that it offered the possibility of a multitude of different experiences. The car tracks were nasty but the wind blew some of them away and there were always places where cars couldn't go. There was no oil south of Bahariya Oasis, so the one product that could attract the despoilers wasn't there. The desert protected itself; that was the beauty of it, that was its secret.

And here I landed on a metaphor I was unwilling to let go of. The desert resisted ownership. No one wanted to own it, because there was nothing of 'value' to own, and even those who did (governments) quickly lost interest and ignored it. That refusal to be owned, that slipperiness in the face of acquisition, made the place an example to everyone.

Thirteen

THE CURSE OF ZERZURA

In Egypt, I was surrounded by people fearful of curses. Every house has an evil-eye decoration or a hand of Fatima hanging over the front door. And everyone knows of the curse of the pharaohs, exemplified by the untimely death of Lord Carnarvon, the financier of the Tutankhamun excavation. Three months after they found the mummy, he lopped the top off a mosquito bite while shaving and developed a fatal fever. In England his beloved one-legged fox terrier keeled over and died at the exact same moment. Other deaths followed. By 1929, twenty-two people connected directly with the disinterment of King Tut had died prematurely.

Of course it's nonsense. But then you start thinking – especially as you are ducking down into KV62 (King Tut's tomb) – What if it isn't?

I noticed that all the Zerzura hunters, apart from Bagnold, tended to die young, sometimes from illnesses contracted while searching for Zerzura. Bagnold believed that Zerzura would never be found, that it was a necessary chimera. Those who didn't switch their attention away from Zerzura tended to succumb to the curse. The death toll was eerie. Robert East Clayton died from a rare form of polio aged thirty-two, though Almasy reports it was 'from a disease contracted from an insect bite in Egypt'. Dorothy East Clayton, his wife, died a year later mysteriously jumping from a taxiing plane she could have halted by simply switching the engine off. Dorothy East

Clayton was the real-life model for the character played by Kristin Scott Thomas in *The English Patient*. Almasy, the real English Patient, only survived into his fifties, dying of liver problems exacerbated by years in a Soviet prisoner-of-war camp. Shortly after Dorothy East Clayton's death both Harding King and De Lancey Forth died from diseases contracted in the desert. Then there was Squadron Leader Penderel, Douglas Newbold, Hassanein Bey, Prince Kamal al-Din (suddenly, while on holiday in Toulouse), and General Orde Wingate in a strange plane crash in World War II. Zerzura, it seemed, was an unhealthy obsession.

I half-heartedly sought to protect myself from any curse that might accrue to Zerzura hunting by telling myself, I'm not really searching, but it sounded strangely unconvincing, a bit like Lord Carnarvon peeking through his fingers at King Tut's coffin and saying, 'I'm not really looking at this.'

I was once cursed, by a west African juju man in Paris, on a big-skyed April day near the Pompidou Centre. I was sitting in a plastic-cane chair next to a tiny steel table in an open-air café, with a Malaysian friend, Charon. From a distance, through the hundreds of similar tables and chairs and people, the juju man bore a resemblance to one of those poor sods at TGI Friday's decked out in badges and 'fun' ephemera. As he got closer, weaving aggressively through the tables, I saw that, despite my averted eyes, he was clearly aiming for me. When I looked up he was there, chanting in Creole. Senegalese Creole, we agreed later, inferred from the Senegalese national football team badge on his beret. He had a haughty face and a wide scabby nose, and his eyes were hidden by too-small Ray-Ban-type sunglasses. Around his neck were juju strings of plastic beads and even a rubber Dracula on a piece of elastic. Either mad or dangerous. He shook a gourd rattle and a grubby tambourine in a semblance of entertainment. Then he thrust the tambourine under my face for alms. My friend Charon, in a gesture both resigned but somehow still dignified, slid five francs out of his jeans back pocket. I refused, with a curt shake of my head. That's when the cursing started. A rising wail interspersed with vituperation which drew bored looks from other cool-seeming tourists, inwardly desperate that the juju man should not visit them next. The performance went on and on, with hand signals and head-shakes as the bad spirits were multiply invoked. We sat without moving, as if this sort of thing usually happened in Paris. Then it ended, with some drama, when the juju man threw brown *stuff* (later conclusively identified as Samson rolling tobacco) in my direction. He raised his Ray-Bans for a final look at me with his dull, bloodshot eyes, bad eyes. A gangster cliché announcing, 'I know your face,' but still disturbing. Then he stuck his tongue out, a great grey long tongue, and was gone. This tongue business should have been funny but it wasn't. Neither childish nor suggestive, it was plain disturbing. It reminded me of the vengeful Mayan deity Chacmool.

'I think you've been cursed,' said Charon, when the juju man was out of earshot. We laughed it off. Sort of.

I've only gone into this in detail because being cursed is *not pleasant*. Despite knowing it's all cobblers you are left with a nagging question, What if it is true after all? After quantum physics, iPods, Richard Dawkins and home shopping channels? What if, despite all the assurances of the modern world, cursing really works? When you've been cursed, especially in public, that nagging suspicion doesn't go away quickly.

On and off the curse of Zerzura played on my mind. Quite a lot of the time it wasn't on my mind because my mind was being dragged elsewhere. Mostly into the all-encroaching details of buying an apartment in Cairo.

In Britain all the negotiating is about price, the strangely reluctant-to-bargain Brit going into haggle overdrive, spurred on by greedy estate agents. In Egypt agreeing the price is the least of your worries. Price is almost secondary to the physical reality of getting the money. Price can also be undermined by taking things, or leaving them behind in the house. In Britain we expect to find a kitchen, heating system and bath. In Egypt, you have to make sure that they're leaving the doors and windows. Everything is negotiable. Then someone can agree to your price but then announce they want to pay in two instalments, or six. The fat woman selling our apartment knew all about instalments as a stalling device. Money up front, cash not cheque, that was what got attention – until then the price was mere idea.

I rammed all the money we had into my laptop case. Five hundred thousand Egyptian pounds fitted easily. I had taken it out of the bank the day before and had been nervous of being the victim of a sudden heist, though this feeling quickly faded. It's amazing how blasé you can get about a ton of money after only a few hours.

Next day I went with my mother-in-law and Samia to an open-air coffee shop to finalize the apartment deal. Mohamed, in his preferred role as bodyguard, sat in the car, parked right in front of the café with the door half open, obstructing all passers-by. The fat, gasping, grasping old woman who was selling the apartment made demands until the very last. She wanted the fixed mirrors, the taps, the air conditioners. She wanted the briefcase to take the money away in. She'd seen the movies. But that was my laptop case and I had grown rather attached to it. It was strange to get niggly after, or rather, moments before, handing over £50,000, but that's the way it was.

The woman broke the impasse by sending her driver off to get her own bag. He returned with several black bin liners. I picked up with some haste, in order not to attract attention, each paper-sealed wodge of a hundred Egyptian pound-notes, and passed it somewhat reluctantly over. The fat lady examined each seal for flaws and then dropped them without ceremony into the bin liner. Male coffee-shop regulars ignored us and read papers or puffed away on their water-pipes. For added security the bin liner was placed in a second black sack.

Samia quickly put up a mirror in the corridor outside the apartment, in the shape of an evil eye. A day later, without explanation, she also hung a rather natty modern version of a hand of Fatima. Mohamed the driver also changed the locks on the apartment – though theft was the least of our worries: the fat woman had left nothing. All the air conditioners had been ripped out, leaving holes the size of TV sets in the walls. Even the doorknobs were gone. The woman had also left us several unpaid bills and was in dispute with another flat owner over the use of the lift. For a while we were denied use of the lift which was controlled by a special key only certain favoured members of the building had access to. Then a neighbour who disliked the man who controlled the lift slipped us her key to copy. As an even more Egyptian twist, when we got a man in to varnish the floors he showed me how to use the lift without needing a key. One person stands outside and pushes the SUMMON LIFT button in synchrony with the person inside the lift, who pushes the button of the floor the lift is at. Then, in a moment requiring timing and some panache, the inside person very quickly pushes the destination floor button. The lift then works despite any disabling security-key system. The whole lift saga seemed to contain within it a microcosm of Egyptian life: power struggles, deceit, creative ways around seemingly insoluble problems. It was like the jams on Road 9, when cars parked on either side would make it impossible for two-way traffic to proceed. Sometimes the traffic backed up behind two cars that could not pass each other. In the West such situations are always made worse by there being at least one driver unable or unwilling to drive extremely close to other drivers. We demand our personal space. In Egypt the first skill all drivers possess is the ability to squeak by with a centimetre to spare. And because of this, despite all the foolishness and selfish thrusting of drivers in vehicles of all kinds, these jams, which would be terminal, utterly insoluble in Europe, melt away almost magically. In Egypt, in the most hopeless situations, there always seems to be a way.

The flat became the focus of new disasters, almost daily. Mohamed found the new address of the woman who had sold us the place (which she had kept secret from us). He wangled it from the *simsar*, who felt he'd been cheated by the woman. Magoob, dressed in his only suit, went round to her house and impersonated a plain-clothes policeman demanding the money for the unpaid bills. The woman told him to come back later when she had got the money; of course she never again answered the door. Several sets of contractors fleeced us efficiently and left the flat in varying states of redecoration. Eventually I settled on a policy of only employing anyone who was both recommended by someone I knew personally (no friends of friends, please) and whose work I had personally seen completed. Unlike in Japan, there is little sense of responsibility attached to making intro-ductions. And if there is any ongoing business relationship between a recommender and a recommendee then a kickback is usually involved. I kept remembering Ghali's words: all you need is a good crew and money to throw at the problem.

It took many months before we were able to move in. As the date approached I noticed we had one more lucky charm outside our front door: a small square frame containing a picture of an eye inside a triangle with five blobs hanging down. I recognized immediately its combined power – evil eye in magic pyramid with hand of Fatima thrown in for good measure, an excellent anti-curse symbol. I did find it surprising that Samia put this stuff up and never mentioned it. She was a Western-educated, secular-inclined woman who had lived and worked in the US and England for over ten years. 'How could you condone this tawdry local super-stition?' I mock-berated her.

She shrugged: 'They say it works even if you don't believe in it.'

Fourteen

HARD AND KEEN ON THE TRAIL OF ZERZURA

In the early twentieth century Zerzura was not the only lost oasis in the desert west of the Nile. There were two others, known as Arkenu and Ouenat. These were found in 1923 by Hassanein Bey, an Egyptian explorer educated at Balliol, a champion fencer and an adviser to royalty. Two out of three wasn't bad; it looked very likely that Zerzura would be found.

But Zerzura was never quite like the other lost oases. For a start there were so many of them. The fifteenth-century *Kitab al Kanuz* or *Book of Treasures* listed two sites, as did the early-nineteenth-century Egyptologist Sir John Gardner Wilkinson. Both were either near, or connected to, Dakhla Oasis. *Murray's Guide to Egypt* in 1896 gave four possible locations: some days south of Dakhla Oasis; five days west of Farafra Oasis, 'a foul and gloomy place'; three days west of Dakhla; two or three days west of Selima Oasis.

W. J. Harding King, who spent three seasons in Dakhla Oasis just before World War I, devoted much time to sifting out fact from fiction in the quest for Zerzura. Harding King, whose name the people of Dakhla could only pronounce 'Hard and Keen', wrote the funniest book on the subject, *Mysteries of the Libyan Desert*. He was a lively eccentric who wore Canadian snowshoes, 'with which I have found it perfectly easy to cross even the softest sand'. Much of his time he spent wandering around Dakhla, being led astray by various Bedouin guides. He was a great recorder of 'native information'. One place he never visited but heard about was called 'the stone temple', which was supposedly eighteen hours by camel from Gedida village in the Dakhla Oasis depression. It caught my imagination but I was not the first to consider looking for it. In fact, only a year or two ago, the stone temple had been found by the ubiquitous and energetic Carlo Bergmann. *Dr* Carlo Bergmann.

Arita told me he always liked to be called 'doctor'. He was a doctor of marketing, though, not archaeology. He came to Egypt in the early 1980s to further his studies at the American University in Cairo and fell in love with the desert. He left his wife and child to live as simply as he could, spending each winter in Dakhla Oasis and the summers in Germany. On his website he announced his discovery of 'Wilkinson's second Zerzura', which he had found after following a map engraved on the wall of Harding King's 'stone temple'.

The stone temple turned out to be a rocky hill two days by camel from Dakhla, with engravings that combined early hieroglyphics, mentions of the Pharaoh Cheops, and a network of lines identified by Bergmann, using his intimate knowledge of the area, as a neolithic map. The map, which with his talent for hyperbole he called 'the oldest one in the world', led Bergmann to ten 'wells' or rain oases. The wells were close together in an area where clay was interbedded with sandstone so that when it rained the water collected long enough to be useful for irrigation. This, he claimed, was Zerzura.

He also found several hills with giant amphorae hidden among the rocks. These he called 'water mountains'. They were located along an ancient desert trail with evidence of donkeys, not camels. This put it firmly in early dynastic times, before camels arrived in Egypt. The giant vases were water dumps for a route that led towards the Gilf Kebir.

But at the bottom of his website it read: 'Due to treachery and intrigue this manuscript [Bergmann's unpublished

180-page treatise, referred to on his site] got into the hands of a faction of the German archaeological community in Egypt which, for no obvious reasons, strictly opposes the field-work of the author (beginning the moment when he discovered the spectacular site southwest of Dakhla oasis.)'

I felt for poor old Carlo. *Dr* Carlo. He had devoted years to trudging around on camels and had, according to Arita, an amazing ability to find old routes and archaeological sites. No doubt, in seeking some recognition, he had tipped off his fellow countrymen and they had ripped him off. Archaeologists and settlers cause all the problems.

Despite his complaining, Bergmann has recently been credited (*New Scientist*, 13 Jan 2007) with reversing our ideas about where ancient Egyptian culture came from. His donkey trails (which could have brought the silica glass to Tutankhamun), 'water mountains' and early hieroglyphic inscriptions are sufficient evidence to support the idea that the pharaohs came out of the desert, and not from the east. This confirmed my instinct that sphinxes and pyramids were inspired by the desert. I was also pleased that there was still room in this world for such talented amateurs as Carlo Bergmann.

Judging by the words and pictures on his website, it looked as if Carlo Bergmann had pretty much sewn up the whole hunt for Zerzura. Or had he? The more I pondered his findings, studied the old maps, read between the lines of Harding King's inconclusive desert excursions, the more I realized that Dakhla Oasis was surrounded by intriguing, unexplored desert. Explorers in the past, including Bergmann, had stuck to the edges of the main piste heading towards the Gilf. But that was only scratching the surface. There had to be much more down there. I would have to visit.

Unlike in Libya and Algeria, Egyptian nomads were clustered around the coasts and the oases. The caravan routes going west had not been used for a hundred years. The Bedouins who lived in Dakhla Oasis never travelled west. This added up to a huge ignorance about what lay in the surrounding desert. The Tebu, who had once travelled as far as Dakhla, had long ago retreated to Libya and Chad.

They were the real masters of this super-arid desert: Almasy and Hassanein Bey had both obtained new information from Tebu tribesmen. But the Tebu were long gone. Bagnold had been wrong to call this desert 'dead', but it was unpeopled.

Now I had decided on Dakhla as my jumping-off point, I needed to get back there. By car or camel? Bergmann preferred camels but I was not convinced I could handle camels on my own. Arita's stories were full of hair-raising escapades with camels stuck in quicksand (*sabkha*, waterlogged salty sand) or camels running off having chewed through their rope hobbles. I had little experience of big animals and even feeding horses a lump of sugar as a child had never appealed.

When Arita met the great desert explorer Theodore Monod he was a hundred years old and still working on new problems of the Sahara. He had travelled with Colonel Ghali and Samir Lama to the Gilf when he was in his nineties, but it is for a series of very long camel journeys in the unknown parts of Mali and Mauritania in the late 1930s that Monod is most famous. Yet when Arita tried to enlist him as a fellow mourner for the lost days of the camel's supremacy he answered, 'But cars are so much better! You can get a ton of rock samples into a car.' Characteristically, when I asked Wilfred Thesiger, the last of the great British camel explorers, what he thought of the Frenchman, he replied, 'Never heard of him.'

So, despite the many excellent reasons for preferring camels to cars, I completed my move into middle-class normality by finally buying a vehicle. I did a total reversal and decided on an Egyptian-assembled Jeep Wrangler, on the conformist grounds that there were lots of them around and I knew several people who owned them. They were short enough to park and beefy enough to make desert trips. The desire to explore in a noisy, polluting car was ameliorated by the realization that the main function of the car was to get you to the place where you could start exploring on foot. An ordinary reliable car could get you to any of the oases; from there it was just a matter of walking. All along it had been that simple. And the money? Just as it always had in the past, as soon as I made a committed decision the money appeared. The bank offered me a new way of restructuring (and increasing) a loan that suddenly made the overpriced junkheaps in Egypt a viable option.

But a strange thing happened when I ran my ads for a Wrangler on the Saharasafaris website. Even though people had earlier ignored my tentative appeals for a second-hand Toyota, I was now emailed by several people all concerned that I was making a big mistake by buying an Egyptian Jeep. Unreliable, they all said: what you need is a Toyota Land Cruiser, old but not too old, short-wheelbase for the city but with toughened suspension for the desert. And by some strange process I still can't exactly figure, I ended up buying exactly the car I needed from Mido, a young engineer who also loved the desert and had taken said car to the Gilf Kebir and back. With its four-hundred-litre fuel tank – four hundred litres! – I was sold before I saw it, which was at twelve mid-night, hardly an optimal time to be buying a car.

Needless to say there were several very good reasons why I ended up scratching the chassis for signs of rust using street lighting and an electric torch rather than normal daylight. I was leaving for England the next day and I just *knew* this car was it.

I had been expertly sold, I have to say. I found no rust on the chassis but as a word of advice to future midnight car shoppers I can say that although chassis rust shows up in the dark, rust on the body doesn't. On the positive side of night car-buying, unrusty cracks show up better as the bare metal strongly reflects street lighting. I found several such cracks in the roof, a sure sign of roofrack overloading. Cabin interiors look a lot better in the dark than in the unforgiving light of day. But I had no choice and, as I knew from my assiduous reading of Chris Scott, as long as the chassis was fine I could replace or repair everything else. I scratched for rust and hit bare metal; I decided to buy.

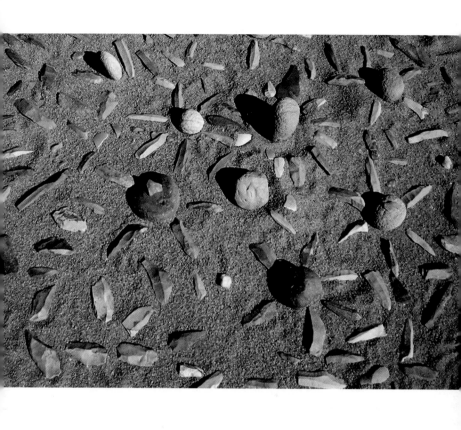

In preparation for driving this massive 4x4, quite the biggest car I had ever driven, I acclimatized myself to the Egyptian roads in the family Honda. Some foreigners are so unnerved by the sensation of being driven in Egypt that they never drive themselves. Obviously I couldn't allow that to happen. One of the more unsettling things was that there were few accurate road signs, even in Arabic. Also, in our neighbourhood the roads looked very similar. Plus, and this was very Egyptian, despite being labelled as if following a grid system the roads did no such thing, leading one astray as easily as the false lights set by wreckers to lure ships on to the rocks.

The first time I drove in Egypt I steeled myself, as if expecting a fight. This was not helped by a last-minute request from my mother-in-law to buy a Christmas tree 'while I was out'. Good grief – this was my first time ever venturing forth alone into the wild west of the Egyptian road system and I was being asked to bring home something I'd never seen nor even heard of before in Egypt, namely a Christmas tree. I knew that if I searched too assiduously for the Christmas tree I would get lost and probably have to spend Christmas alone in a neighbourhood of tower blocks with no glass in the windows and feral dogs browsing rubbish piles as high as telegraph poles (and there are several such neighbourhoods quite near Maadi). On the other hand I realized that the Christmas tree would be very welcome to my kids, who were, if truth be told, a little homesick for the crass commercialization of Christmastide they had grown to know and love. There was no such crass commercialism in Egypt because there was no Christmas, except the muted Coptic Christmas twelve days late on 6 January or thereabouts. So, torn between getting lost for ever, crashing and getting involved in an argument that would be resolvable only with the iron bars I had seen drawn by even quite civilized-looking drivers, and finding a Christmas tree to please my nippers, I set out.

I made a big deal of making sure my seat belt was properly on. I looked down at my *A–Z* of Cairo, which is always regarded with wonder and admiration or puzzlement by Egyptians, as if such a document could only be designed to defraud them in some way. Mido remarked, when he saw my *A–Z*, 'Is that *really* any good?' Only in Egypt could an *A–Z* be instantly expected to be an A–K or even an A–B, i.e. a real let-down. Actually this *A–Z*, which was available in all good bookshops, was excellent. Aided by my mother-in-law's directions and the *A–Z* I identified Road 150, the supposed site of the Christmas-tree seller, which lay only a short distance from Road 100, where I now was. Braced for violence, I pulled away and barged into the main stream of traffic at the end of the road. People let me get ahead, as if sensing my aggression and nervousness. I duelled with a battered Fiat and he relinquished the lead instantly, far faster than a pig-headed English driver would. I relaxed a fraction and swam in the stream of traffic. I even allowed myself to think there was something almost gentle about the way Egyptians drive. Then someone swooped up from behind, real close. That was bad. Then it happened on the left-hand side, almost but not quite clipping the wing mirror. Many taxis in Cairo have an extra big mirror fitted on to the reversing mirror in the windscreen, and now I knew why: wide-angle vision was needed to see all the cars zooming up from behind. I leant forward, a gap between my sweating back and the back of the seat. I felt some strange new organ of perception growing, prodded into existence by the extreme evolutionary pressure I now felt myself under. All-round vision, like that of an owl or an octopus, was what I needed, and miraculously it started to develop. Twitchy as a bird expecting a cat to leap on the bird table, I piloted my way to the Christmas-tree seller.

I had been dreading parking but fortunately there were several gaps about twice as long as the Honda, which nevertheless felt like a very tight squeeze. The Christmas-tree man had a roadside arboretum. I knew he would have no Christmas trees but he inventively suggested a Cyprus fir in a big pot. At least it was the right colour. I drove home with the boot open and the fir poking out, truly relaxed, at least, about that minor infringement of the law.

Apart from the nasty zooming-up-from-the-rear it was OK. People were pushy but not hostile. Make a mistake and you might get hooted or even berated, but you wouldn't encounter the sheer venom you can witness on British or European roads. The horn was used to warn others, let others know you were there, as an exclamation even, but never as a punishment. Being hooted was no cause for shame, unlike in Britain, where a loud parp signals the triumphant discovery of yet another driving incompetent. The horn blowers in England see themselves as self-appointed driving instructors. No such role exists in Egypt, since road regulations bear the same relationship to driving as a recipe does to a four-year-old's mud pies. In Egypt it's accepted that the normal way to drive is to use every method to get ahead. The reason kerbs are so ridiculously high is that without them Egyptians would drive on the pavement. Red lights are merely decorative, unless there is a policeman there too. Reversing on motorways is OK as long as you go slowly.

The big Toyota was even easier to drive than the Honda. Other people were evidently scared of its bulk, noisy engine and solid steel bumpers which extended several inches all around the front. In the first week a saloon car cut round me and impaled itself on these bumpers, tin-opening a wound in its soft metal skin. Very few cars are insured in Egypt; some consider it un-Islamic. The injured saloon car didn't even stop, the driver just slowed, looked at the damage, shrugged and roared away.

Quite quickly, almost overnight, I became obsessed with my car. At the expense of almost everything else I spent hours combing the internet for user groups to join. I visited many different garages to get all the different oils changed: there was oil to change in the gearbox, the transfer case and both diffs, not to mention the steering that needed regular greasing. After the trepidation caused by driving wore off, I began to notice the mechanical defects of the car. But these I ignored:

the loose steering, the coughing and hiccuping the engine made when cold, the rock-hard suspension that needed a thousand kilos of payload to react normally to a bump or hidden sleeping policeman. With no load the car leapt into the air at the slightest excuse, the merest wrinkle in the road's surface.

I got used to driving by day, but night driving was another matter. However careful I was there were always nasty surprises in the form of suicidal pedestrians, cyclists or trucks thundering towards me on the wrong side of the road with no lights on, not helped by me having no lights either. Mysteriously all my lights, bar the full beam, had blown almost as soon as I took delivery. Since most of the police cars in Cairo also drive around without lights this was never a legal problem, even if it further reduced my safety.

I've owned cars before, three to be precise, but this was the first car I really loved. I loved the big fuel tank and the jerry cans and the grab-bar on the dashboard; I loved the claw towhook, the extra-strong suspension and special shock absorbers. Just looking at it parked made me smile secretly to myself. Even if I was just driving to the shops the car seemed to vouchsafe my serious intentions to get out into the desert.

I emailed Arita Baaijens and joyfully told her about my new desert-ready machine. Straight back she wrote: 'You've managed what I never have – buying a car has always seemed such a grown up thing to do.'

From the 'woman of the dunes', being 'grown-up' was about the worst possible insult.

In *The Book of Treasures* it is written:

'Account of a city and the road that leads to it, which lies east of Qa'ala es suri where you will find palms and vines and flowing wells. Follow the valley until you meet another valley to the west between two hills. In it you will find a road. Follow it. It will lead you to Zerzura. You will find its gate closed. It is a white city like a dove. By the gate you will find a bird sculptured from stone. Stretch up your hand to its beak and take from it a key. Open the gate with it and enter the city. You will find much wealth and the king and the queen sleeping the sleep of enchantment. Do not go near them. Take the treasure and that is all.'

Something that few of the Zerzura hunters consider when poring over this information is the old and well attested practice of treasure hunters never leaving a desert village in the direction they really intend to take, so as to maintain secrecy about their destination. If the lost oasis was full of treasure why tell anyone where it is? It would seem, therefore, that any public mention of Zerzura is unlikely to be accurate. Casual enquiries would also guarantee obfuscation, unless arrived at in the way Harding King used to extract information from his native guides, slyly and obliquely and without hurrying the man with the knowledge.

Harding King actually did discover another stone temple, which, confusingly, is not the place now referred to as Harding King's Stone Temple, which he never saw. The temple he did see was found using a treasure-hunting book owned by his Bedouin guide Quaytin. He revises his dismissive opinion of such books, but he also adds that people have been hiding treasure from tyrants for so many years that almost any building may contain lost loot.

That *The Book of Treasures* worked as a guide was probably coincidental. Ancient texts might be repositories of genuine information about buried treasure, but more likely they worked as metaphorical texts, rather in the way alchemy was used by mystics as a metaphor for the transmutation of the soul and other practices that could be viewed as heretical in a climate of religious oppression. It seemed far more likely to me that *The Book of Treasures* contained information that needed to be recorded and saved for future generations. What better way than to employ greed? Tell someone there is buried treasure hidden in his garden and he's unlikely to forget it. In one Arab tale this is precisely the method used by a man who had three lazy sons he wanted to help. He tells them about the treasure in the fields and after he dies they dig and dig but find nothing. Having dug the fields they decide to plant corn. It grows and they harvest it, as they plan to dig the field up again to find the treasure the next year. But no luck again, so they make use of the unintended effect of their labour and this time plant more corn than before, the result of even more energetic digging for treasure. After a while they become rich farmers, but only in old age do they realize that the real treasure was all along their effort and energy and all that that brought them, and not some rusty box full of stones and shiny metal.

Fifteen

THE SWEDISH DIRT
BIKERS' COLLECTIVE

But still I shied away from just walking out into that desert.
I had a vehicle. Finally. It was desert-ready. It had been to the
Gilf. If I wanted I could strap in the four-hundred-litre tank
and blast off there this very afternoon. But strangely, I felt
no closer to my goal. Something I'd learnt about goals before
was coming back to me.

When you think you need something to get you to your
goal you probably don't. The key is in the word 'think'. When
you have a properly defined goal you know what you have
to do and you do it. In the general management accounting
sense of the term, searching for a lost oasis is not a properly
defined goal. My search was both inner and outer, which is
fatal for anyone with a tendency to prevaricate or, my spe-
ciality, to move sideways until I end up doing the opposite
of what I intended in the first place.

I took the vehicle, which made all the right noises, up Wadi
Digla. I burnt up a few joggers and cyclists. I was with my
daughter, who loved it apart from the bumps. 'Let's call this
car Mr Bumpy's car,' she suggested. The thing about the desert
is that you can't get away from the bumps. They're everywhere. The human form is naturally designed to make
light of bumps; we have the best suspension system going.
But cars are crap at bumps. Even the biggest, fattest-tyred,

monster-Chevy-engined supercharged monster hates bumps. Car freaks, and a part of me was a kind of unformed childlike car freak, a sort of throwback to when I was twelve and loved *Autocar* and knew the 0–60 figures for the Morgan Plus 8 and the Jaguar XJ12 5.3, that part of me did battle at the wheel with this grown-up part of me that kept thinking, These bumps are fucking horrendous. Car freaks get round the bump problem by preferring to fly over them, turning the driving experience into something like snowboarding or BMXing. Rallying is the natural home of the car freak who accepts bumps without question. The thing is, bumps that look like nothing when you're walking can pitch you forward and bounce you up so hard your teeth get chipped. And slopes that are nothing to a walker assume all the terror of a first ascent of an overhanging pitch on the Eiger. The challenge is not to go where no man has gone; the challenge is to go where no car has gone. It would be even more of a challenge driving a double-decker bus over such terrain, so the challenge is limited. It's a very precise sort of challenge. But it's also about speed, doing it fast for the buzz. And for the buzz there is little to compare to the dirt bike.

Richard Head had a dirt bike and he was always taunting me with offers to have a go. I always said no because as a seventeen-year-old I had spent some time riding dirt bikes owned by friends who were more cautious than I. Two crashes, including a near-death experience with a Mercedes on a country lane that sent me flying into a barbed-wire fence like Steve McQueen in *The Great Escape*, had left me with a healthy aversion to furthering my dirt-biking career. I wasn't after danger. I was averse to breaking my collarbone, which seemed a pretty common dirt-biking injury. I was actually glad I felt no need to prove myself aged forty in the arena of dirt-biking. I told Richard, 'If I have to ride a bike to get somewhere I can't get to I will. But otherwise count me out.' I had once met a former special-forces soldier who told me all about the horrors of low-level parachuting at night. He'd done it but it had left him with a passionate hatred of sport parachuting and sport parachutists. I was relieved: I no longer had to feel like a weed for disliking thrill sports. Though I hadn't the credibility of having been in special forces I decided to follow one of Uncle Mahmoud's maxims on the subject – ordinary folk learn from experience, whereas wise men learn from the experience of others. Dirt-biking was out.

But I still wasn't getting any closer to the desert. My excursion with my daughter ten kilometres up Wadi Digla had brought home something I had only been vaguely aware of: you can't go alone. What if the car gets stuck? What if it breaks down? Suddenly in this independent quest you are dependent on this machine, which is complicated and heavy and hates bumps. It wasn't like climbing, which you can practise alone on boulders or trees; with desert driving you need company. So when Richard told me he was going off with the Swedish dirt bikers' collective to the nearest big dunes to Cairo I said yes, I wanted to come too. He said that the collective were into off-road driving as well as biking so there would be something for everyone.

The rendezvous was at 8.30 a.m. in a shady street in Maadi outside Tron's villa. Tron was Norwegian, and one of the leading members of the collective, which, though dominated by expatriate Swedes, accepted all who loved using machines in the desert. Tron greeted Richard and me as he sipped from his Thermos coffee cup. It was a little awkward as he was on crutches with one of those contraptions that look like a hockey mask on his foot, confirming the common fate of dirt bikers. Tron was short with a bullet head and a crew cut, tanned, wiry and small. He wasn't soft and tubby like the other members of the collective, but then they weren't on crutches. He dismissed all enquiries about his injury and when Richard asked if he was driving he said, 'Of course' with the dismissive air of a Viking captain questioned about his ability to hold the tiller when he had a mere splinter in his hand. There were bikes on trailers and 4x4s and men drinking coffee with their wives sitting in the cars ready to go.

I met Nick, who was towing a quad. He was cheerful, thin

175

and wiry and English. He said he'd never towed a trailer before. 'It's the bumps you want to watch out for,' I said, sporting my only piece of experience as soon as possible. Some of the group hadn't yet arrived. Tron was looking at his watch. 'I've been waiting forty minutes for these clowns to show up. I think we should go. They're Germans,' he added, and I got the distinct impression that the further south the collective members hailed from the less acceptable they were. Peter, a Swede, shook my hand amiably. 'Nice car,' he said, clocking the off-road status of my ride at fifty metres. It certainly looked the business, even if I wasn't.

We set off, convoy-style, and sped through Cairo as if we were on a mission. I brought up the rear. 'Why aren't we at the front, Daddy?' asked my son. 'Do they know more about the desert than you do?' It had taken me years to discover that my father wasn't the absolute best at everything in the world but my son already had inklings, aged six. 'I know more about the desert from books then they do,' I told him, to maintain a small shred of daddish dignity.

We arrived at the second rendezvous – the last petrol station before the desert. Tron wasn't happy that they had sold out of 90-octane fuel and only had 92 or 85. He spoke in English to the gas-pump attendant as if it was the attendant's first language and the lack of the right fuel was a fuck-up rather than a normal part of Egyptian culture. Tron, I could tell, couldn't be arsed with going native.

The Germans arrived on their dirt bikes and with several more vehicles, including a brand-new 78 Series Land Cruiser. Its owner was tall and bearded and wore glasses. With that car, I thought, he must be seriously into the desert. But he told me, 'I just make the short trips. When I hear about these thousand-kilometre drives I say not for me. I always take my family so it is not possible.'

We followed Tron at high speed along the desert road to Bahariya. He drove fast and I had to floor it to keep up. After sixty kilometres we turned off into the desert. You could see the white line of the dunes in the distance, showing up like snow against the gravel-strewn yellow-brown of the flat desert that was all around us. Richard split off to one side and drove in parallel, flying along, but I felt obscure need to follow Tron's tracks; that way I got some warning about the bumps ahead. In fact, there were hardly any. The gravel gave way to easy hard flat sand and soon we were at the dunes.

There then followed a long indeterminate period where a tent was set up in the considerable breeze and bikes were unloaded and tinkered with. Engines puttered and roared all around. The kids ran up and down the dunes in bare feet. I was torn between childcare duties and wanting to do something.

Richard's wife Jo lay on the sand sunbathing. 'There's always a lot of waiting around with this sort of thing,' she said drily.

Slowly the bikers came into their own. They puttered around in increasingly large circles, then, at a moment known only to them, it seemed, they roared off into the distance. I wasn't really sure what to do. 'OK, kids, let's go and get stuck.' My son and Richard's sat in the front and my daughter sat behind as we drove off from the base area.

I went precisely eight metres. I knew all the theory: don't rev too high, stop as soon as you get stuck, try to reverse out. I forgot it all. Hitting the gas, both in front and reverse gears I quickly succeeded in digging myself in up to the axles. 'How did you do that?' asked Richard's son admiringly. Instead of replying, 'Sheer incompetence,' I laughingly jumped out and said, 'I told you we were going to get stuck. Now the fun part starts!'

And in fact the kids did enjoy burrowing away at the sand under the car, and I might have got away with it but, at a moment known only to the collective, they all arrived back after their first spin coated with sand just in time to view my ignominious bogging. Partially remembering what I had learnt with Ghali, I laid out my sandplates in front of the car. At this point Richard detached himself from the silent mockery of the bikers and kindly suggested it might be easier to place the plates at the back, since in front was limitless soft sand whereas behind was hard gravel. That suggestion saved me from an afternoon of misery under the cool scrutiny of Scandinavians sipping beer in special thermal sock things.

I got clear and roared away along the foot of the dunes. It was just as I remembered with Ghali, how you can't see what's ahead, how the horizon kind of melds with the sand in front of you, how it's like flying in a sand cloud – except I was doing it myself and the experience was not entirely pleasant.

Back at base after half an hour of tentative mucking about, we had lunch. The kids had already stuffed themselves with crisps and biscuits and were playing in the sand. Richard had told me to be 'self-sufficient in food and drink' and, perhaps interpreting this too literally, I crouched in the back of the wagon like a refugee munching on his last hidden crust. Richard arrived back from another spin, his dust-caked face already sunburnt. I noticed he had a beer and was glad he didn't offer me one. I was already thinking about going home and the last thing I wanted to do was drink-driving over bumps.

The bikers sat on each other's bikes, drank beer, smoked and revved engines. Tron took the quad out for a spin and when he got off he was laughing and wincing with pain. 'My God that hurt,' he chuckled, straightening his bad leg as his crutches sank into the sand.

By the same mysteriously-arrived-at common consent it became apparent it was going-home time. One biker, a big tubby Canadian, had hardly ridden his bike at all, as far as I could see, but that wasn't the point. The actual riding was secondary to just gathering and chewing the fat and being out in the desert. The whole escapade seemed like a vastly complicated and expensive way to drink a few beers with your pals. The bikes and the cars were focal points for chat. The riding was a nice quick thrill. The whole thing felt manly and 'out there'. It was one more way Western man has come up with to square the fact that he spends most of his life in an office with the need to feel tough and capable.

Richard, with the barest of explanations, took off for what I assumed to be the road. But instead of heading back the way we came, or even taking a dirt track that followed a longer but similar route, he headed north, out into the wastes. Fast.

Many cars had been the same way, but that was little consolation. He was burning into the distance visible only as a puff of beige dust. I was stupidly in 'Lo' four-wheel drive and by the time I had changed up he was even further ahead.* I gunned my faithful motor and quickly realized I was doing 60kmh in second gear. But the cab was so noisy I hadn't noticed that the engine was screaming. I was also still in four-wheel drive, and began to be assailed by ungrounded fears of 'wind up'. This is when you drive in four-wheel drive too long on a surface that is insufficiently loose and the transmission explodes. On most modern 4x4s there is an extra differential to cope with this, but mine was the basic model (simpler, stronger – remember?) and you only engaged four-wheel drive when you really had to. Was this now? I didn't know. And just as I was fretting (of course unnecessarily) I hit the mother of all bumps.

It was a double bump, like those ones that BMXers launch off and land on. It loomed far too instantly. I hit the brakes and probably the clutch too, which is definitely the wrong thing to do as you actually sense the loss of control as a speeding up. The front end flew off the top of the bump and smacked into the crest of the second bump with a horrendous, bone-jarring smash. 'Are you OK?' I screamed to the kids, whom, although they were strapped in, I had visions of being hit by the jerry can of fuel, or their seats actually ripping free. The car was still going forward. The crest of the second bump had disintegrated in a cloud of sand as the front end ploughed through it. Amazingly the wheels were still turning. I was so intent I didn't dare take my eyes off the few metres in front of us. The kids remained silent. 'Are you OK?' I shouted again.

---

* Off-road cars have a second gearbox with two settings, 'Hi' and 'Lo'. This acts like the second chainwheel on a ten-speed bike, multiplying five gears into ten. But in my car you need to be going slowly to change from 'Lo' to 'Hi' and also from four-wheel to two-wheel drive.

'Yeah, yeah,' drawled my son from the back. My daughter up front, whom I had caught from the side of my eye being catapulted out until the seat belt restrained her, managed a wan smile. 'Mr Bumpy,' she said.

I slowed down and took stock. I began to recognize bump-type situations. Even Richard Head's dust cloud was no longer visible. Bumps appear when you cross other tracks, where the sand looks overchurned and when you go up hillocks you can't see over. I was learning fast, the kind of learning situation that gives you a splitting headache.

And where the hell were we? We could be heading deep into the desert for all I knew. Our only survival rations were four litres of water and a few chicken-nugget sandwiches the kids had rejected earlier. I pressed the milometer. If the shit hit the fan at least I'd know how far I was from ... the bump. I slowly built up the speed and saw Richard again in the far distance.

Driving madly, taking stock. You arsehole. Out with your kids without even a jack and foot pump for the tyres. Richard had all the rescue gear and I had none. Never again. The kilometres sped by. The dust cloud was still in view. Then my son piped up, 'Dad, can we stop? I want to do a wee-wee.'

'No.' Brutal. Thoughts of pissing in empty beer cans while driving to a party as a student, throwing them out of the window. But the ride was so bumpy you'd have a hard job aiming at a waterhole, let alone the narrow orifice of an Evian bottle, which was all there was in the back. 'We can't stop!' I yelled. Why the hell were we going so fast? Richard liked to say calmly, 'Speed is your friend in the sand.' Speed is not my friend, I thought, speed is my worst fucking nightmare. It was like a grotesque off-road version of holidays with my parents when we'd be lost in the pouring rain in French cities where the whole town centre was cobbled and my dad would be going frantic trying to find his way to the N13.

Finally, out on the far distant right I saw an oil refinery or some other massive industrial plant which I remembered seeing from the road. We were getting close. If we broke down here we could walk to the oil plant.

And then, almost without warning, after jinking a bit through soft piles of sand and being pleased I did it with a semblance of *élan* rather than getting stuck, we were back on the road.

And when we saw Cairo, its fume-laden, crowded, overbuilt, hideously ugly beauty struck me so forcibly I shouted to the kids, 'I'm a city man. I love the city. The city is my place.'

I flashed Richard to let him know I was stopping and my son scampered out of the back to take a leak. I sauntered up to their sleek air-conditioned Prado. The electric window crawled down. I felt like Ben Gunn seeing his first sailors for years. Richard and Jo both had their shades on. The interior of their car was air-conditioned, upholstered, carpeted and unruffled. 'Nice drive,' I said in a high-pitched whisper.

'Yeah, I picked up that track on the GPS and saw we were converging on the road.'

My capacity for small-talk was exhausted.

'You enjoy yourself?' asked Richard, smiling.

I nodded dumbly. Never again.

Sixteen

DUNE RAIDER

The car sat in front of the building. My longest journey was to the new Carrefour hypermarket and back. At least there was plenty of room for the groceries. Then the phone rang. It was Mido, the Mido who had sold me the car. Mido was a busy young man. He had a family business to help run; he raced in the Pharaohs Rally; he knew everyone. Though he was only thirty or so he'd been desert driving for ten years. Now Mido wanted me to go on a trip with him. Deep desert.

Hossam, a friend of Mido, and Mido's girlfriend Salma were in on the trip. Hossam in my car, Salma with Mido in his huge 80 Series, much modified, a real dune raider.

Owing to my competent chat Mido assumed I was at least semi-experienced in the world of off-road driving. He didn't know my sole experience was driving like a terrified madman after Richard's dust trail. And that piece of desert was nothing, *nothing*, compared to what else was out there.

Mido had a plan and I was flattered to be involved. He wanted to visit the Djara Caves, but by a new and difficult route. The caves were discovered by the German explorer Gerhard Rohlfs in 1874. They were vaguely marked on the map but since the entrance was no bigger than a double door hidden in a shallow depression they were lost again until Carlo Bergmann and Arita Baaijens refound them in 1989.

I was tasked with buying all the food and supplies. This was fun and I bought way too much. We left at dawn and drove out towards Wadi Rayan over easy sand, four full jerry cans roped down securely in the back.

Then we hit the first soft sand. I got stuck and over-revved trying to escape. Basic error. The others looked a little concerned: this was the easy part. Then we pulled up at the top of a sixty-foot dune. My first slipface, the steepest side of a dune where the sand is loose all the way to the bottom. Slipfaces, depending on moisture levels, are never more than thirty-five degrees, but to me, from the top, it looked almost vertical. Mido cruised down it easily. I knew the theory. But I also knew that one wobble and you can roll.

In at the deep end. Hossam, a genial guy in his mid-forties, an engineer by profession, a man entirely at home with broken machinery, had quietly departed my cab as I pondered the slipface. He and Salma sensibly slid down to the bottom on their backsides and waited. At the last minute Mido, realizing the true extent of my incompetence, climbed up the dune and jumped in my cab. There are some situations you only face because of peer pressure. On my own I'd have been back at the asphalt and heading home. I once read in an account of courage during WWI that soldiers are more fearful of looking cowardly in front of their mates than of the actual danger ahead. This was my battlefield then, if you can excuse the exaggeration, and of course I did know the theory. Engage the lowest gear, 4x4 'Lo' first, and crawl towards the edge. Make sure you are lined up absolutely straight and then over you go.

The sensation was extraordinary. The car simply slid. It skated sedately on a cushion of collapsing sand. The engine did not protest. We never gained speed. By lucky coincidence cars slide down dunes at a perfectly controllable slow speed. It's not like sledging as you go very slowly; maybe it could be compared to riding a big heavy sledge through very deep soft snow. The bottom of the car sits on the sand and the wheels pointing straight ahead give it directional stability.

And though the bottom looks so steeply angled that you are sure the front end will simply dig in and you'll pitch over, it doesn't happen. The car simply rolls off the slope, ready for more.

I'd been in a car with Colonel Ghali when he'd made a similar manoeuvre and it had seemed harder. But it was only hard when you thought of all the things that could go wrong. With adequate care it was easy. I was going to crack this thing.

The rest of the day was all along bumpy terrain, nothing difficult, and with a heavy load of fuel and water in the back the bumps were easily ironed out.

We camped at an old well right by the side of Abu Moharik, at six hundred kilometres the world's longest sand dune. Mido's plan was to drive several hundred kilometres along the dune until we were opposite the cave and then just hop over its six- or seven-kilometre width. No one had done this before.

After only twenty kilometres following the dunes we could see the other side and it looked close. We were also lagging behind Mido's optimistic schedule. Hossam suggested we cross now while we had time. If we stuck to the original plan we'd be crossing late in the afternoon, perhaps even at night. Madness, especially with me along. The plan was changed. We went for the crossing: maybe seven lines of dunes separated by sand corridors about three or four hundred metres wide, sometimes more, sometimes less.

I started to get stuck at regular intervals and in places difficult to escape. Mido got stuck only twice – and one of these was trying to help me get free. Time was disappearing.

The secret of crossing dune barriers was worked out by Bagnold seventy years ago. On the principle of a rollercoaster you use the momentum gained screaming down one dune to reach the top of the next. Slipfaces are avoided except in descent. You drive back and forth up and down corridors looking for the least steep slope to climb. The worst place to find yourself in is a boxed dune corridor with soft sand in the bottom. As soon as you descend you have to get out. If you get stuck at the bottom there is no way to build up enough speed to get up any of the four slopes that seal the corridor off.

It was the last ridge of dunes and we were boxed in. The flat desert was all too visible in front of us, diminished further by the harsh bright light of early afternoon. Mido made it down and screamed up the slope ahead. I followed and made it almost to the top, the engine making a noise of harsh mechanical protest. No good. I had to reverse at high speed, across the soft stuff at the bottom and back up the slope I'd just come down. Another attempt. Then another. I dropped my tyre pressure until the tyres bellied right out. We laid sandplates up the slope so that I could get more grip. Still I kept conking out just clear of the top, the engine groaning and dying within a few metres of the crest.

There was nowhere to turn and though I reversed a long way back, there was no way I could reverse all the way to the top of the slope behind. If I didn't make it soon I'd be stuck. My failed attempts were leaving deep ruts up the dune. I chose a new path, a little steeper but with more of a run-up possible. This time I didn't waste time changing into third, I just screamed the engine all the way in second. And made it. Then I got stuck at the top – but it didn't matter, because I was off the slope. We had crossed the dune barrier.

It was about then that the car started to go wrong. It became a real haul to change gear. Hossam said it was the master clutch cylinder. We bumped the fifty kilometres to the cave in third without changing gear. He also added, by way of conversation, that it sounded as if my exhaust had a leak in it. I threw in the fact that my lights only worked on full beam. 'Oh, that's easy to fix,' he said. I liked Hossam. He had no fear of cars or engines. His own car had been to the Gilf (with mine when it was owned by Mido) and had drunk a litre of water a day through its leaky radiator. 'The thing about these cars,' said Hossam, patting the whining, vibrating carcass we were encased in, 'is that they always get you home.'

Despite talking in detail about his cars, Bagnold restrained himself from waxing too long or too lyrical. He surmised, correctly I think, that most people do not read books about exotic places only to take an intimate tour of the inside of a bonnet. Cars aren't good literary companions like donkeys or camels. They have personality, but it doesn't translate well on to the page. They answer back only when upset. When they miraculously get better we impute it to luck or a mechanic's skill. We want to ascribe intention to a car, but it sounds fantastical to do so. For example, I was suspecting that Mido's car, now mine, had been driven like a demon. Now that I was treating it so considerately it didn't, she didn't, like it. Like a naughty dog used to discipline but now off the lead, she was playing up. She wanted correction. That's what I suspected, but it could just as well be imaginary. Cars cleave to us in this strange intimate way which can't be communicated except through passionate talk about cylinders and horse-power. When people go further and name their cars and talk to them it's silly. You can't kill a car so it can't be alive. It just seems so.

At the caves we descended to look around. They were huge, church-big with stalactites drooping down into the sand. The cave had been dry for thousands of years. There was a visitor book which announced the caves' rediscovery by Bergmann. (Later Arita told me she had been with him at that moment. They had celebrated their discovery by making love in the cave.) Mido told me Rohlf's original log had been taken back to Germany and the tin box he left had been nicked sometime in the mid-1990s. Hossam pointed out the scorpion tracks which look like wavering mountain-bike-tyre tracks. Despite this evidence Mido and Salma said they would sleep in the cave. Mido said, 'In twenty years I never once heard of anyone being bitten by a scorpion or a snake in the desert at night.'

Hossam and I weren't so brave. Both of us crouched in our frail nylon domes, glad of the groundsheet and the tightly zipped doors.

Next day we descended another cave through a hole in the ground the size of a manhole cover. The cave was like a huge dry bottle. We made a rope ladder to get in and out but it was a rough battle to get past the overhanging shoulder of the 'bottle' and into the neck. 'Do you think there are any more caves?' I asked Hossam.

'Look around,' he said. 'These caves are on an old camel track. That's how they were discovered. But off to the side there could be many more. Notice how the ground sounds hollow when you walk on it.'

This short conversation stuck in my mind, and after we got back (driving on full beam along the desert road to Cairo; I don't think I've ever been flashed so aggressively and so often by so many trucks before) I got in touch with a TV company in the UK who were interested in shooting a screen test about hunting for new and unnamed geographical features. The plan was to use my car and another, possibly Hossam's, to go searching for a new cave. But as the plan progressed my car sat outside, watched over by Magoob, cleaned by Hanya, a pool of something black and wet spreading out in front of it. Mohamed the driver pointed it out most mornings as I left with him in the Honda. I dithered over a repair manual, in between improving my Arabic with a wide selection of Toyota mechanics in Cairo. My dream car. Get you anywhere. A real desert car. A real lemon. Yet I couldn't quite force myself to believe this. That I spent an absurd amount of money on something destined to be useless. Even worse than useless: requiring constant money and never getting properly fixed. Mohamed had ceased to be gleeful when a new problem arose. In his own clumsy way he felt for me, for my humiliation, and he wanted to help. But even he, an incurable optimist, knew that this thing, this lump of metal manufactured far away in Japan, might be beyond him, beyond any of us, far and away beyond the bodgemanship of even top Egyptian mechanics.

After the lights and the clutch and the exhaust had been fixed, the steering lock jammed and the ignition refused to work. A brutal mechanic who had been recommended with the caveat 'but he's a little rough at the edges' used a ball

187

pein hammer to smash away at the ignition-key barrel. Amazingly, the thing was only partially destroyed. When he finally left off smashing at the dashboard I discovered as I was about to drive off that he had taken the steering-wheel nut with him. The ignition-key barrel, not surprisingly, was the rarest made since 1948. With no spare available, the car had to be started using a complicated double action involving a key and a screwdriver. It would have been easy to steal – except the gearbox was now playing up, and, depending on the day, you could only get into fifth, which required starting up in Lo 4x4 drive and then adroitly flipping to Hi, preferably on a soft surface otherwise the car protested horribly. Then there was the bendix, a wheel I'd never seen that engaged the starter motor – except it usually didn't. Then the cause of the black oily patch – the power steering was leaking.

Therein lay the clue. The steering had always been wobbly. Many Egyptians have told me this is normal on Toyotas as people don't grease the top steering bearing. No problem, they say, *mafish mushkellar*. But what happens is that, over time, all these loose bits start to wear out the non-loose bits, and so the car spirals into a state of constant disrepair.

I want to believe the guy I bought it from. I want to believe that as long as you have a chassis you can rebuild the thing. But then there's the small problem of spare parts. For my model they are strangely unavailable. I have to face it: I bought a lemon, despite all the warnings. I can feel myself getting a little hysterical here. Of course it can be fixed.

Oh, and I have a suspicion the clutch is on the way out. Again.

The trouble is I was weaned on modern cars that never go wrong. Change the oil and go. With this car I've bought into history. But still I love it. Still I believe that at some point in the future I can get it into perfect condition. If only I can find that Mecca of spare parts in Port Said everyone talks of but never visits. I cling to that last possibility.

Maybe it was my driving. Maybe I treated it too well. Maybe it thought it deserved a holiday. There I was, giving it a personality when all it was was a heap of nuts and bolts and hot metal.

The conversation about looking for a lost cave grew into a reality just as the car began to look less and less suitable as a desert conveyance. By happy coincidence the film people liked the sound of the trolley better. They said it would look more exploratory. I explained it would also allow for better and closer on-the-ground exploration. Everyone was happy as they arrived in Cairo to make a short film about looking for a new cave.

I now genuinely believed what I had told the film people: cars have severe limitations for desert exploration. They go along too fast so you miss lots of things. When they stop you are so shaken up and so intent on checking under the bonnet for the cause of all the new strange noises that you pay little attention to where you are. I always wondered why the people who travelled with Bagnold always made so much of sunset and sunrise in the desert, and now I knew: it's the only time on a car trip when you really notice the desert. The rest of the time you're caught up in that state of mind that characterizes searching for a parking space in Sainsbury's on a Saturday morning. Cars get you into the desert, but then they get between you and the desert. I didn't want that.

But if it had to be walking then I needed a suitable companion. My friend Steve volunteered. He had been on a previous expedition when we crossed western Canada in a birch-bark canoe. In an accident on the river the top of his thumb had been cut off. He had never complained even when the pain must have been terrible. Steve had been in the US Navy and still kept fit. He knew about towing from pulling our canoe through rough waters in Canada. He was the perfect man for the job.

Steve and I would head west into the desert with just the trolley and try to find Zerzura. Suddenly it was all beautifully clear and simple. We didn't need several cars and lots of complicated kit. We didn't even need camels. Just us and the desert and the faithful trolley, which was going a little rusty, having lain outside on my mother-in-law's balcony for a year.

Steve arrived and we set off with my two kids to the dunes where the dirt-bike collective had taken me. I had learnt something since that last desperate foray. It seemed almost tame driving the five or so kilometres from the road, the bumps negligible and easy to spot.

It took a while to assemble the trolley. The bearings seemed stiff and the nuts rusted to the bolts. When we were finished it was midday and burning hot. The kids sat on the trolley and Steve and I tried pulling them up a dune. It was killing work, almost impossible. Steve was bright red from pushing at the back and I could only haul the thing a few inches at a time.

We let the tyres down and this time I was at the back, turning them as if they were wheelchair wheels. We made it up the dune, but it was still hard work.

'How much do your kids weigh?' asked Steve.

'Not as much as a hundred litres of water,' I replied.

I was sure the trolley would work, even though it looked quite hopeless. On the flat, hard, gravelly sand it was perfect. 'We've just got to steer clear of the dunes,' said Steve, ever optimistic. I thought about the dune barrier that Harding King mentioned surrounding Dakhla on the west. We'd find a way.

My son ran around the dunes in bare feet and then came running back. He'd found a scorpion on a discarded egg box, and we went to look. It was a small one, but it had its tail up ready to sting. I recalled something Hossam had said: 'If you get stung by a scorpion early evening is worst because it's been sleeping all day and hasn't stung anything.' We backed off but my son chased the scorpion down the dune bombarding it with handfuls of sand.

The arrival of the film crew delayed things awhile, but they were keen to search for a new cave with the trolley as long as we had cars as back-up. We drove direct to the caves along the bumpy track, this time in Hossam's car and another driven by a guide called Mahmoud. He was taciturn but cheerful and an excellent driver. Despite being in heavy old 60 Series Toyotas we hardly got stuck at all.

The film crew had certain shots in mind and these did not feature Steve. I had to pull the loaded trolley up dunes with Hossam pushing from the back against the boxes of water and provisions. I found that if I paid out the tow-rope to its full extent and then hauled the thing up hand over hand it worked reasonably well, if terribly slowly.

We camped again at Rohlf's cave. Around ten at night there was a noise in the distance. Then we saw lights. A hundred and eighty kilometres off road from the nearest oasis and we had company. The car wove through the small hillocks around the cave, almost driving right into it. It was a 55 Series Toyota, maybe forty years old, the model renowned for being the ugliest Land Cruiser ever built. Mahmoud greeted the driver, a thin-faced, ebullient man called Sobhi. He had with him a single tourist and a boy to do the cooking. They made camp around a hillock from us, a place which Steve, the film crew and I had earlier used as a convenient toilet.

The crew were tired and so was Hossam, but I was curious. Steve, Mahmoud and I paid a visit to Sobhi's campfire. The tourist was an elderly Italian called Giorgio who gave Steve and me a beer. That he had trusted Sobhi to drive through the desert alone and at night seemed extraordinary. 'I trust him very much,' said Giorgio, pouring himself a beaker of Chianti. Sobhi had intense piercing eyes that he fixed on you as he rattled off his tourist shtick. When he learnt that I lived in Cairo he changed tack and showed me a photo of his 60 Series Toyota which had been stolen at the pyramids two months earlier. 'It is gone, Sobhi,' said Giorgio, 'it is cut up and sold into a thousand pieces.' Sobhi ignored this and declared that I must search for it for him in Maadi. I said I'd look out for it. Then he grilled me about what I did. I have rarely experienced such a probing inquisition before. Thin and wiry and ageless, though at least forty-five I guessed, Sobhi looked pure Bedouin without a trace of the soft features of most Nile Egyptians. He announced we should visit the cave, even though it was about eleven at night.

He set about trying to fix a propane-gas lamp by firelight borrowing Giorgio's glasses so that he could see better. He seemed to encapsulate in a pure form the intensity required to survive in the desert, where either strength or guile were all that would keep you alive. He had no interest in us as anything other than 'meat', tourist fodder or people who could recommend him to other tourists. After unblocking the pipe with a needle he sealed the join with a tight wind of thread. Though he was obviously a master at bodging things the lamp still didn't work as intended. Flaming and belching black smoke, it was carried down into the cave, where it cast mysterious flickering shadows. 'They're mad aren't they?' said Steve. 'I wouldn't be surprised if that lamp explodes, the amount of smoke it's making.' While the amiable Giorgio schoolmastered Steve and me around the rock formations, Sobhi, Mahmoud and the boy did their level best to smash one of the larger stalactites off using a heavy spade. It was a flat, spear-shaped stalactite and it boomed like a bell every time they hit it, filling the cave with echoes.

The next morning we met Giorgio as we were leaving. He looked kinder and younger in the dawn light. 'Are you sure you're safe in just one vehicle?' I said.

'I trust that man Sobhi with my life,' he said. 'In all our trips he never let me down.'

Hossam told me later that Sobhi would have left word in Bahariya when he was likely to return. If he was two days late they'd send out a search party. 'And he would burn a tyre – you can see the smoke for thirty kilometres.' I looked at Sobhi on the roof of his vehicle tying things down with quick movements. I knew whatever happened to Giorgio he would always survive.

*

And, though the film crew didn't require us to find a new cave (just looking was enough for their short film), we did. Driving at speed past some rocky outcrops the director noticed an odd shadow. We climbed up the short hillside and found a wide, low cave. On the ground, in front of a lower tunnel that none of us wanted to crawl down, were the lower leg and hoof of a gazelle. Around the base of the hill I found a flint-knapping station with hundreds of broken and discarded palaeolithic stone tools. Just when I'd been spouting on about the impossibility of finding things in a car, we had done precisely that.

We stopped in Bahariya Oasis on the way back. By the kind of coincidence that I was beginning to expect in the oases, Richard Head was there. He had just finished a ten-day bike safari to the Gilf with renowned Italian motorcyclist Franco Pico. Richard roared up to the outdoor seating at Bayoumi's wearing his sand-caked leathers. It was his big trip of the year, he admitted ruefully: he'd now used up all his holidays. He dug in pockets and showed us some of the flint implements he had found.

We sat there drinking beer and talking freely about making desert trips, knowing that the 'real' world was looming back in Cairo, waiting to swallow us both up in a myriad of details one sensed were unimportant and yet couldn't get free from. Richard had a wife and two children and a full-time job. He needed the job to keep his family in the style he thought appropriate. I was no different. I had more freedom to bunk off but I was caught in the same trap, and it did seem like a trap, spending most of one's time doing things one didn't want to do in places one didn't want to be.

Was it simple discontentedness? Many Egyptians would have thought us mad to be complaining about doing such relatively high-income work. But one look at Richard's beaming face, the sunburnt chops and the bubbling enthusiasm, explained everything. Hossam had told me earlier: 'The desert recharges my soul.' Then he added, 'When I come back I find that people and things that used to irritate me no longer do. I can live better after I come back from the desert.'

Back in Cairo, I needed a map of the Dakhla area. I decided to try using Muhammad, the car-park man outside the Map Office. Months had passed and softened the memory of how he bilked Ozman and me. This time we only needed one map, but it still involved a protracted wait and multiple 'gifts'. In the end I paid £10 for a map that should have been £4. After a heated row over money with Muhammad, he suddenly embraced me, which surprised Steve. But seven months on I was used to the strange way an Egyptian can simultaneously like you, want to be your friend and want to rip you for every penny they can get. We drank tea from grubby cups as we waited. 'That was good tea,' said Steve, 'but I hope the last bastard who drank from it didn't have TB.'

We bought supplies and gas canisters for the stove but the car only started after an annoying bout of pressing the clutch and advancing the rotor arm before pressing the ignition. Watching this routine, Mohamed the driver went and found a slight, well-mannered young man who fiddled under the steering column with a bent screwdriver and fixed it perfectly, it seemed. Mohamed told me to pay him E£10, less than £1 sterling. It was the night before we were due to leave, about 10 p.m., and I couldn't imagine such a thing happening in England. 'But then your car would probably be working if this was England,' said Steve.

Seventeen

JOURNEY TO DAKHLA

We set off at dawn the next day, the best time to be heading for the desert. Steve was excited: he'd never been to Egypt before. But we'd been so busy the only sight he got of the pyramids was as we screamed past to hit the desert road at six in the morning. They looked like rough stone hills poking through the mist. 'Well, at least I can say I saw them,' said the uncomplaining Steve.

We took the turn-off for the Bahariya road and there was hardly any other traffic. Our plan was to drive down to Dakhla, make a reconnaissance, possibly try to meet up with Carlo Bergmann if he was there, leave the car and set off with the trolley into the desert. My only worry, or rather my main worry, was the checkpoints we would have to go through. I knew that as you got closer to Dakhla the checkpoints became more numerous and more interested in where you were going. If there was a security alert foreigners were forbidden from driving the road without a police or army escort. And whatever the state of alert, no one was allowed into the desert west of Dakhla without military permission and, if foreign, an accompanying soldier. Steve looked nervous when I mentioned that our whole plan involved travelling in forbidden territory. 'It's just cars they want to stop,' I said, recalling what Arita Baaijens had said about checkpoints: just keep your distance and even if they see you they'll look the other way. I hoped this would be true.

The first checkpoint was at the top of the Bahariya depression. The policeman took the licence-plate number and our names and passport numbers. The last time I had been through they had simply written down the car's number and waved me through. Perhaps since the recent bombings in Jordan they were on a higher state of alert.

In Bahariya we had the regulation beer at Bayoumi's restaurant. He now recognized me by sight, though I noticed he still charged me the tourist rate for drinks. A young guide called Mohamed brought us tea and told us he made more money taking backpackers into the desert and guiding tourists around the Cairo sights than he ever could as a lawyer, which is what his brother did. 'Some kids pay me, like four hundred Egyptian pounds a day just to drive like crazy through the Cairo traffic. Without seat belts.'

Mohamed had identified a neglected niche. For every ten tourists scared of the Middle East, who came to lurk in the Mena House Oberoi and play golf at Katemaya Heights, there were one or two who came for the perceived danger and craziness. 'My Japanese tourists are best. They love the pick-up. We just crank up the Madonna and head for the horizon while they smoke all the *bango* (grass) they want.'

'You guys, I can tell,' said Mohamed, 'are my kind of guys.'

But if Mohamed was making so much money, why was his car a piece of shit? wondered Steve after he left. 'Maybe he's just starting out,' I said, and then added with feeling, 'Besides, cars are fucking expensive out here.'

Another young guide sidled up to us as we walked about town and spoke of his experiences of taking predatory foreign women on desert trips. 'They come for the desert fucking!' he told us. One Japanese girl had given him £1,000 sterling after such a trip, as a present, he said. I had similar stories from other guides and whenever I saw a lone woman, Western or Eastern, sitting proudly in the front seat of a desert-bound Land Cruiser, Bedouin tent and firewood strapped to the roofrack, I couldn't help thinking of what she had planned.

The guides themselves were in their early twenties and rather innocent, they didn't mind being paid for sex, but they were not exactly proud of it. Do women head off to the jungle to have sex with remote tribesmen? Or to South Sea islands? Perhaps. But with nothing like the numbers that still find the desert sheikh fantasy so compelling – even if he's just a kid in a borrowed Land Cruiser driving through the much-visited White Desert.

The White Desert had been the initial focus of my desert enthusiasm but I now spoke of it rather slightingly. It was a strange and beautiful place, replete with land-forms that looked like moulded icing sugar, but it was just too *visited* for my liking. It was the number-one desert tour destination in Egypt and for that reason alone I didn't want to even stop there. We blasted through early the following morning and then hit our first military checkpoint.

Finally, after months of wrangling with various traffic authorities, the car was street-legal, or as legal as I could make it – in Egypt legality is always a matter of degree; there's always some bit of paper you haven't got if people want to be difficult. The soldier was young with a thin, sprouting moustache. Unsmiling though.

'Passport.'

I handed them over from the battered metal glovebox in front of Steve. Steve grinned at the soldier. 'Nice day, mate.'

'Licence.'

I handed over my international driving licence which, owing to being a constant companion in my trouser pocket, looked as if it had been through a complete wash cycle. He waved it away.

'Car licence.'

I proffered the piece of plastic that said that I owned the car, or rather that my wife did.

'*Merati Masri*,' I said helpfully. '*Arabiyat*.' Her car.

'Where go?' he asked.

'Dakhla.'

He pointed to the trolley wheels on the roof with a quizzical look on his face.

'It's for our water,' I said, 'like an ice-cream trolley.'

The soldier looked at me as if I'd just said I was going to urinate on his lunch. He held on to the papers and waved us through. Power games. I rolled forward, parked, walked back as he wrote down our licence number. Then he handed me a blank sheet of paper. 'You sign you have no police escort.'

I wrote: 'We the undersigned wish to strongly advise the authorities of Egypt that we do travel through her unpopulated wastes neither desiring nor transporting a policeman as escort and protection against such villainous attack as might occur.' I underlined 'policeman as escort' in case he thought I was taking the piss. Steve and I signed the paper with great ceremony. The soldier looked at it both upside-down and the right way up, grunted and turned away.

'Friendly bloke,' said Steve. 'Do you think next time we should have music playing? I read once that war correspondents always play popular local music when they go through checkpoints.'

That's why I liked travelling with Steve. Always full of good ideas.

From Bahariya we drove the 180 kilometres to Farafra Oasis. It was all empty desert and we stopped halfway to brew up some tea. I drove about three feet off the road and immediately got stuck. I tried and tried but because the car was on a slope I just kept sliding further down towards the soft sand.

'Shit,' said Steve. 'I hope we're not going to get stuck here for ever.'

'Nah, we've got the sandplates,' I said, though I knew it could be a lengthy process to get clear, especially if you buried the car to its axles. Then I realized I hadn't even locked the front hubs into four-wheel drive. A real beginner's error. With all the wheels connected we soon got clear of the soft sand.

In Farafra we went to the main coffee shop, where men sat drinking tea and holding small evil-looking sickles. 'That bloke's definitely a foreigner,' said Steve, nodding with his chin at a sunburnt man with a bushy moustache. He had the slightly hostile aloofness one learns to recognize in foreigners in Egypt, but he was wearing a grubby grey gelabiya, albeit over jeans and trainers.

'Nah, he's one of those Egyptians with a skin disease that makes their skin pink,' I said. But when I asked him in Arabic the way to Badawi's Hotel he replied rather haughtily, 'You can speak English to me.'

He was Austrian and had just made a ten-day camel trip from Bahariya – a distance we'd made in three hours. He didn't really want to talk to us tourists, as he saw us, but I was persistent. Tomorrow, he admitted, he would fly back, ready for work in Vienna the next day. He was rightly proud of his camel trip – just him and two Bedouin. His Arabic was atrocious but he spoke it with admirable gusto. Having intruded into his Lawrence of Arabia fantasy, we were allowed to play the role of lowly admirers. Steve hated him, but I could see that, like Richard Head, he'd spent his hard-earned holiday doing something uncommon and admirable. Even self-satisfied Austrians are allowed to recharge their souls.

Back on the road, we drove the remote three-hundred-kilometre stretch to Dakhla. We stopped for tea halfway and in half an hour not one truck or car went by. The car was making strange sounds whenever it started: the bendix was skidding and not engaging as it should. By experiment I found starting the car with the clutch in usually solved the problem. I was learning how to bodge, a skill all Egyptians have by necessity. Steve was a little nonplussed by the bendix problem. 'What if we get stuck out here?' he asked.

'We'll just wait,' I said. 'After all, we've got enough water.'

That was certainly true. In Bahariya we'd bought four boxes, each contained twelve bottles of one and a half litres. Using boxes rather than jerries resulted in the horrible waste of plastic bottles, but it was light, clean and safer – it's easy to upset a jerry and find it's leaked away twenty litres without you noticing. The bottle system meant the most you might lose in an accident was a litre and a half.

For food we had sardines, tuna, corned beef, dried soup and twenty-four packets of bread sealed in plastic bags. It was the kind of bread I hoped was steeped deeply in noxious preservatives. To save weight we carried no other carbo-hydrates, so if the bread went off we'd go hungry.

Steve had a small appetite and never complained about eating rubbish food; it was another reason why he made such a good expedition companion.

More checkpoints. We'd developed a cheery attitude by now and mostly the young soldiers in their tight camo shirts and trousers were friendly back to us. Many of them could not read English numerals and asked me to copy down my passport number for them.

Dahkla is a big oasis, filling a depression seventy kilometres across. On the left is a great high scarp and on the right lie the dunes: desert all the way to the Atlantic, four thousand kilometres away. There are many small towns and villages in the oasis but the main one is Mut. We headed there to drink a beer at the Gorgeous restaurant, the place where I had rejoined Colonel Ghali's expedition months, years, it seemed, earlier.

We pulled up alongside the tree-lined hut with its outdoor tables. A young, skinny foreigner came out to greet us. Before he could speak I said, 'You're Paul, the English guy, aren't you? The one helping Yusef?'

He grinned and nodded shyly but when he spoke it was in curious broken English. 'I call Yusef now and he come straight away.' Living in Dakhla for five months, he'd started to go native. Paul was reticent at first but warmed up as Steve chatted to him. Meanwhile I ducked into the restaurant to use the single internet connection. It was slow but

I had no difficulty getting on to Carlo Bergmann's site.

The latest news was disquieting. The Zerzura curse had struck again. Earlier that month Bergmann had been in a very nasty bus crash on the way from Cairo to Dakhla – Upper Egypt buses, the same company I'd used when I took the bus with the hole in its side. He had ridden the day bus, perhaps believing that it was safer than the night service. The driver hit a parked microbus on the roadside at 130kmh and nine people were killed and a further fifteen injured. Bergmann suffered injuries to his eye which, he wrote, required a macular operation. Presumably he was now back in Germany. It was disappointing. Despite his fierce reputation, I had hoped to meet him. Strangely, Carlo Bergmann, who was so secretive about his discoveries, whose website sports not a single accurate map or lat. and long. position, included in his account of the bus disaster the GPS coordinates of the crash site.

I showed Steve the photo on the website of Bergmann's Zerzura – an area of hundreds of closely packed conical hills. There was also another arresting image: two mummified donkeys lying side by side in the sand. I pointed to it and Steve said, 'Hope we don't end up like that.'

There was the sound of a bicycle bell ringing and Yusef arrived, breathlessly happy, it seemed, to see us. I thought he remembered who I was but it became apparent later on that he had confused me with someone else. When he heard I was looking for Carlo Bergmann he told me he now had a small child and had left somewhere on a trip, maybe to Germany. I took all this in as Steve gestured to me with a discreet whirling finger at his temple that all was not right at the Gorgeous restaurant.

Quite slowly, over two beers and a meal of omelette, soup and vegetables, it became apparent that Paul was a little strange. He made several references to his 'problem', which seemed to revolve around a bus he had once owned in Dorset. While living in the bus he had spent four years studying shamanic healing. He asked me with beady intent if I knew Philippe Morel, his teacher. I said yes – well, I'd glanced at some of his books. At this Paul began to shake, just perceptibly at the elbows, the kind of shake you make when you hold yourself so tensely you can't help shaking.

'I study all Philippe Morel courses,' said Paul.

'Even Fairey Magick?' I said. Paul nodded in a matter of fact way, as if studying Fairey Magick was as normal as studying business Spanish or elementary carpentry.

Steve said he felt tired so we paid and left. As we drove back to the hotel he said, with a glance in the mirror, 'I'm not really tired. It's just that guy Paul was giving me the creeps. Did you notice that shake he had?'

'Yes,' I said. 'There's something weird about that guy. The way he talks like a German who doesn't know English too well. Too much time talking to backpackers, I expect.'

I had more pressing matters on my mind, however. From the hotel garden I could see the dunes, as I remembered, but there were also lots of gardens and small fields in between. Towing the trolley over these would be difficult and very conspicuous. We set off in the car to look for a way into the desert from the village of Gedida, which was about twenty kilometres back up the road. This meant going back through the checkpoint and I immediately saw that returning this way with the trolley assembled would excite far too much attention. Gedida itself was also surrounded by fields. No good. We could see the desert, but how to get into it?

Night fell and Steve and I got lost somewhere near Qasr, another village in the oasis. Finally we got back to the checkpoint where the friendly concerned policeman on duty insisted on giving us an escort back to the Mebarez Hotel. At reception we were grilled by a tourist policeman on how long we intended to spend and what we intended to do in Dakhla. 'Oh, just looking around for a few days,' I replied.

Sitting in the warm gloom at Yusef Farid's that evening, Paul told us more about his 'problem'. 'You see, Philippe Morel is inside my head. He tell me to do things I don't want to do.'

'Philippe Morrel very bad man,' interjected the benign, mustachioed Yusef.

'Is he French, this Philippe bloke?' enquired Steve. Everyone ignored him.

'Philippe Morel he tell me to smash up my bus. He tell me to break my CD player. Only here I feel safe.'

Yusef gave a doubtful smile.

'At least here you can do work, learn Arabic,' I said placatingly.

'Oh, I don't speak Arabic,' said Paul.

'And he don't work,' said Yusef. 'Philippe Morel tell him not to work.'

I looked at the skinny form of Paul, unconcernedly suckling on a bottle of beer I had bought for him. He'd been here five months, doing nothing. He'd made one camel trip of ten days but even that had been a wash-out.

'This guy told me we would visit the desert but all we did was wander from village to village seeing his relatives. I got really angry so he gave me half my money back at the end.'

Five months and he hadn't made it into the desert.

'I visited that hot spring two kilometres up the road, too,' he added.

'And he have no money,' said Yusef. 'He tell me his mother will pay when he go but I don't know.'

Paul seemed quite happy for his problems to be discussed freely by all.

Steve said, 'You need help, mate. There are people in England who can help you.'

Paul looked vague and said, 'Philippe Morel wants to kill me but I know he's going to be crucified on 20 July 2007.'

This gave everyone pause for thought.

Steve rubbed his temples and said, 'I'm feeling a bit tired. Got a bit of a headache.'

'That's what he does,' said Paul. 'He gets inside people. He could be in those shadows. He could be behind that beer bottle.'

Yusef took it all in very calmly, I thought, for someone

burdened by a paranoid probable schizophrenic. 'If I don't help him who will?' he said. 'But it cost money. I am not rich man. One fellow, Sheikh Ahmed, he come and touch Paul and he was better. But for full treatment it cost money.'

'How much?'

'One hundred pounds.'

Ten pounds sterling – four beers in an English pub – to cure someone of their madness. But then, wasn't it equally mad to believe chanting bits of religious verse, burying a ring that Paul wore and blowing smoke over him would really cure him?

'There are people that could help you in England,' repeated the ever-reasonable Steve.

'Sheikh Ahmed could help me,' said Paul, but with little conviction.

'If I paid, would you go to him?' I asked.

'Oh, I couldn't take money from you,' said Paul. There was another pause, but a hopeful one rather than a stunned-into-silence one. 'Not unless you were like throwing it away, like it meant nothing to you.'

I whipped out a hundred-pound note and gave it to Yusef. 'Get the cure. It might work. You never know.'

Walking back to the hotel, Steve said, 'They're scamming you. It's a double-act to get money from unsuspecting tourists.'

'If they are it's superb. Except they aren't. You saw the way he started shaking every time he mentioned the dreaded Philippe Morel.'

'Who's going to be crucified.'

'On 20 July 2007. Christ. Do you think we should warn him?'

'That's when I knew he was nuts. He needs all the help he can get.'

'Exactly.'

'But this magic stuff isn't the answer. What if it made him worse?'

I admitted that, bad though Paul was, he could indeed get worse. 'He's so wrapped up in the whole shamanic thing that he really believes in magic. You heard how it made him a little better when that sheikh touched him?'

'He needs drugs,' said Steve, 'powerful drugs.'

'Probably. But he's not going to get them out here.'

'Just tell me we're never going back there,' pleaded Steve. 'I don't think amateur psychiatry is up your street.'

Eighteen

OFF OUR TROLLEY

We spent another day searching for a way through the fields to the yellow dunes beyond. Past the hot spring we drove along a track which ended at an irrigation ditch. Across the way were two big excavated lakes and a collection of huts. Dusty yellow digging and dredging machines lay as if abandoned. A friendly bearded man in a gelabiya came out of the little enclave of the huts and invited us across the drainage ditch for a cup of tea. He had two friends, or fellow workers, a short tubby chap and a tall fellow in a tight blue jacket, who were guarding the equipment. Sometimes the one in the blue jacket, who seemed vaguely in charge, drove the machines. But you could tell this happened very rarely. Most of the time they sat in the shade, drank tea and did nothing.

I explained what we wanted to do. The bearded man pointed up to the dune at the end of the access road to the lakes. 'There is the Sahara,' he said. Steve and I walked up and climbed the dune. There was one salty-looking field beyond, but it looked passable; after that there was desert. We unloaded the trolley and packed the water and all the food and gear on it. I then drove back to the hotel to leave the car. The man on the desk was doubtful about my 'walking tour' around the oasis.

'You take man with you?'

'Not exactly.'

'You go with group?'

'No.'

'You alone?'

'Yes, but we don't have the car and we have sat-phone and we are very, very experienced. We've done the same thing in the Sinai and ... Jordan,' I lied.

The ratty-faced man made a phone call to the tourist police. I gathered the main thing was whether we were taking the car or not.

'You not take car?'

'No.'

He beamed. 'Then you are free to go.'

I parked the car and removed the rotor arm from inside the distributor cap for good measure. We were free to go.

Because I had implied our walking tour was amongst the small hills and rocky desert on the eastern side of the road, I was reluctant to give further information away by taking a taxi back to Steve. It was a five-kilometre walk in no shade at midday and by the time I got there I was hot, tired and already suffering from an incipient blister.

Steve looked a bit desperate when I arrived. 'What's "*meshi*" mean in Arabic? They keep saying it.'

'It means OK.'

'Oh. They wanted to phone. Thought you had run off and left me.'

'Had to calm the fears of the police,' I said.

'They let me smoke their water-pipe,' said Steve, pointing to a *gooza*, a hubble-bubble pipe made from fitting a brass tobacco holder into an old plastic water bottle. 'They're good blokes. Made me another tea. That one, the one smoking, he's a real laugh. I couldn't think of anything to say so I pointed to that dog over there sleeping in the shade and he suddenly jumps up, bends over and says, "You like doggy style, Steve?" We all cracked up.'

The guards waved us off as we trolleyed along the dirt road to the dune. In view of several farmers planting in their field we lumbered the monstrous weight up the ten-metre-high dune.

'First one's always the most difficult,' I said breathlessly.

Down the dune was easy enough but then it was soft sand rising slowly for another two kilometres. I was towing but I had to beg for an increasing number of rests. My heart refused to stop beating extremely fast. I drank three litres of water. I slumped next to the trolley in the pathetic shade it offered.

'Are you all right, Rob?' Steve asked warily.

'No. Do you mind if I push from the back for a bit?'

'Not at all. No problem.'

I could tell from Steve's concerned expression that he thought I was about to collapse and abandon the expedition there and then. I leant my weight on the back of the trolley, which now had a pushing handle contrived from a rucksack frame, and pathetically paddled along as Steve towed manfully at the front.

We made horribly slow progress. If this is what it's going to be like, I thought, we'll be lucky to make three or four kilometres a day. Such thoughts were interspersed with self-chastisement for lack of fitness, walking that five kilometres without drinking, not having decent footwear, etc.

The last inhabitants of Dakhla we saw were two young men on a digger. As we trundled past them across the last dirt track before the desert one of them gestured with his hand: 'What are you doing? Why?'

'*Ana magnoon*,' I shouted over the din of their engine: 'I'm crazy.'

Now we were climbing steadily out of the depression, but up sand that was harder than the soft dunes closer in. The tyres were at very low pressure and now it was getting towards evening it was marvellously cool all of a sudden. I had another go pulling at the front and as long as I moved slowly, with small steps, ignoring the pitiable progress we made, it worked. By nightfall we had our tent pitched and water brewing in a convenient way on top of the trolley, our camp at the top of a huge dune of hard sand that overlooked all of Dakhla Oasis. We had come about four kilometres.

Things always look more rosy when you have sweet tea

inside you. The direction we would take the next morning, now we were clear of Dakhla, looked slightly downhill. Our path through the dunes had been dictated by the easiest route. South-west lay Bergmann's water mountains and rain oases. But if we headed west-south-west we'd be exploring new ground. I was glad to see there were no car or even camel tracks. Steve's splitting headache – he had them almost every day – had abated after dosing with painkillers. I had had time to get used to the difference in heat between scorching midday and chilly night. He hadn't, and this was perhaps the cause of the pain. True to form, he didn't complain.

I felt revived after my near-death experience out in the soft sand. 'Do you think I'm getting too old for this game?' I asked Steve.

'Yes,' he replied, adding several more spoons of sugar to his tea.

'It's not age,' I protested from my prone position next to the trolley wheels, 'it's lack of physical conditioning hastened by having to spend too much time sitting down earning a living.'

'Perhaps you should work standing up,' said Steve, 'like Hemingway.'

'He only stood up because he had piles, which, by the way, is a common ailment of anyone man-hauling a sledge. Ranulph Fiennes suffered terribly from piles.'

Steve was silent for a moment. The night sky, moonless, was spread out in all its brilliance above us. The Milky Way was an opaque cloud of light. Venus was like a tiny keyhole, sole evidence of a brilliantly lit room behind a shut door. 'It's great here, isn't it?' he said.

It was cool in the morning but, despite a dawn start, we were not away until 7.30 a.m. By 8.30 it was getting warm. In the dark early-morning shadows, staring out across the pristine sand, there was a powerful necessity about the place, as if this was all there ever was, or had been. It was hard, even, to imagine anywhere else existed; we were travelling through a perfect image of the infinite.

Steve made two little caps of duct tape to cover the sunburn on his ears. It made him look like some silver-eared alien. I caught a glimpse of myself in the mirror of the sighting compass: my sunburnt nose was like a huge red beacon. An alien and a drunkard wandering through the wasteland.

Though it was November the weather was still hot and both of us were soon sweating. Sand gave way to rocky stretches of shale interspersed with small hills. As we bumped over the rock the trolley flexed admirably, as if picking up each wheel in turn to cross the uneven ground. Its bombproof construction, though murderously heavy, meant we could tackle any terrain without fear of damaging the thing. Then Steve noticed we had.

'We've got a flat, Rob.'

No problem. We had a spare tyre and two spare tubes. For the time being I thought I'd just pump some more air into the tyre, to check if it was a slow puncture or not. I broke out the footpump, bought by Mohamed the driver for E£30 and bearing a sticker saying it was 'made in Bavaria' – my arse, it was a Chinese rip-off copy and already useless. Despite spraying its insides with WD40 (the bodger's best friend, next to his mole grips and duct tape), the thing was pushing out less air than an asthmatic dormouse. Sand was probably the cause, but sand getting in at all was due to the poor quality of the pump.

'If we can't blow up the tyres we're stuffed,' said Steve.

'We can always pack them with the crushed-up remains of the water bottles,' I suggested without conviction.

At the last moment I had thrown into my bag an old bicycle pump, just in case. I retrieved it and screwed in its flexible connector.

'Does it fit?' said Steve.

'No. Bugger.'

Time for some Egyptian-inspired engineering. I took the car valve connector off the broken pump and carved the plastic nozzle so that it would fit into the end of the bike-pump connector. One advantage of non-German engineering:

on the real thing that nozzle would have been brass. I then duct-taped the whole thing together. It worked. The tyre seemed to hold its air so I put off changing the tube until it started deflating more quickly.

We were making slow but steady progress. By lunchtime we had arrived at a strange flat-topped hill. I hoped to find rock engravings in its sandstone cliff but there were none. On top was a pile of large flat stones, an *alem*, an old marker of a caravan trail, though Bedouin still use them to make modern trails. But here it had to be ancient. There were no car tracks to indicate present use. Nowadays most traffic west tended to first take the road south through two checkpoints that required military permission.

Now the weather was sweltering and we both glugged constantly from the same water bottle. We took it in turns to push and pull the trolley. Pushing was far easier. As soon as I got thirsty, maybe every half-hour, I'd start glugging again.

We towed on and on. I found another *alem*, this time only a few metres from the ground. I sighted it up with the one behind us on the hill and then looked in the other direction; sure enough, there was an anomalous bump on a silhouetted hill maybe five kilometres away. Another marker; we had stumbled upon an old trail. Who knew where it might lead?

By mid-afternoon it was Steve's turn to feel bushed. I checked the water with growing concern. We had been drinking from the same bottle, replacing it every so often from the opened box. But when I counted I thought there must be some mistake. We had drunk almost an entire box – eighteen litres – in under twenty-four hours. Just that day we'd drunk about six or seven litres each. I had bargained on less than three per twenty-four-hour period.

Steve's face was bright red and his hair was dripping with sweat. It was clear that whatever we drank we were just sweating right out again. But on this, our first day, I had been determined to find out just how much water we might drink if there was no restriction. I had my answer and I brooded on it. At seven or eight litres per man per day, using the trolley was impossible except for very short trips. We had to find a way of drinking less.

That night we camped at the edge of a new set of dunes. They were marked on the map as being '6–9 metres high', but they were widely spaced so it was easy to find a way through that didn't involve too much hauling. We were learning to be canny, taking a downhill stretch at a run in order to build momentum to scale the next dune. These were all dunes with deep ripples, with the kind of crest you associate with Mr Whippy-type ice-cream. But the sand wasn't soft. In a vehicle it would have rattled us to pieces, but moving slowly on the trolley it was very easy going indeed. Going down dunes we sledged the trolley as if it was a car, skidding it down through the collapsing morass of sand. On one such steep dune we suddenly heard an eerie, deep booming sound.

'Is that an earthquake?' asked Steve.

The booming seemed to come from within the earth. It was quite different from any noise you might associate with moving sand. But I had read enough to know what it was. 'Singing sands,' I told Steve. The sand, over time, becomes so close packed it acts like a solid. Walking sets the interior of the sand mass resonating like the soundbox of a guitar. 'Sometimes you can set it off by just stamping across the tops of dunes.'

Steve had another terrible headache by the evening and after our hearty meal of tuna, soup powder and bread I suffered from a worrying and increasingly painful stomach ache. Stumbling behind a dune I voided everything in an excremental spray. Was it all the water we had been drinking? I didn't know.

That night, despite our ills, we slept without the tent, watching the stars overhead. You always see shooting stars in the desert but then we saw something quite extraordinary: a bright star that shot horizontally across the sky rather than in the usual downward track. It went through an arc of at least sixty degrees, as fast as a rocket, and then disappeared.

'Bloody incredible,' said Steve.

'Just like an alien spaceship.'

In fact it looked so like an alien craft that we then and there solved the whole UFO issue. There are simply rare and bright shooting stars that go horizontally rather than vertically. The supporting evidence is the preponderance of sightings in desert areas, places where the sky is clear enough to see such things. Having solved that pressing problem of the modern age, we fell asleep.

Next morning I knew I shouldn't eat anything. I drank one tea and we set off. We made a decision to turn back when we had consumed half of our water supplies. Steve was still sipping regularly from a water bottle but I didn't drink a thing. I slipped into a lower gear, minimum rather than maximum exertion. As we plodded across the hard sand I shut my body and mind down to just the slight activity of shuffling one foot in front of the other.

Following the ancient stone-marked way I sighted up on a convenient landmark, two conical hills that looked to be about five kilometres away. The map showed a hill at that distance, but it soon became clear that the hills were much further than that. I remembered Ghali saying that one of the hardest things in the desert is judging how far in the distance mountains are. We trudged for three hours and these hills seemed only marginally closer. We stopped for lunch and drank only tea and half a piece of bread. I didn't feel in the slightest bit hungry or thirsty, but I drank a cup of water. Steve was still giving the pulling and pushing everything he had and that made him sweat, and I could see now the sense behind the Bedouin habit of never drinking during the day – you just sweat or piss it right out. If you're so hot that you need to sweat to cool down then you must drink, or suffer heat death. But the secret is *not* to sweat. Do everything slowly if it requires effort. Wear dark glasses to make the land look cooler (bizarre though this sounds, it works – the days when we drank seven or eight litres were ones where I was squinting into the glare); wear a headscarf wrapped loosely, even if it looks ridiculous. No shorts: cover up when it's cold and only remove clothing when you really have to. Eat oranges and drink tea, which stays in the system longer than undiluted water. Take a cup of salty water at night if you sweated in the day.

The ground was now perfectly flat. Hour after hour we made 4kmh, and by day's end we had gone twenty-eight kilometres. I wasn't thirsty and had only consumed about two litres, including tea.

The trolley system worked, but only if you planned it carefully. Travelling in January would give cooler daytime temperatures. You needed to be up and moving before dawn. Plan a trip when there is a good moon to aid moving at night. Take dunes very very slowly and always late in the evening or at first light. Stop for four hours in the middle of the day and do nothing, having first erected a tarpaulin for shade. Following these rules I could see no reason why one couldn't make thirty kilometres a day across reasonable sand while drinking a maximum of three litres a day, with an aim to only drink two.

But learning all this had taken time, and water. It would have been foolhardy to keep going with our diminished reserves. We had to turn back. Steve was both disappointed and relieved. 'I was kind of hoping we'd find that Zerzura place,' he said.

'We already have.'

'I know what you mean: the stars and the emptiness and everything.'

'We could always come back and see where these stone markers lead. Get more supplies in Mut. Drink a beer at Yusef's and come back out again. Now we know how to do it.'

'Not Yusef's, please. Even if that mad bastard Paul has been cured.'

We followed a new trail back, testing the compass and our knowledge of how far we were going each hour. The mirages were extraordinary. As well as the usual endless reflective lake-like strip ahead there were shimmering blocks like castles hovering just before the horizon. As an experiment I took a bearing off one of the mirage castles to see if it stayed in the same position as we approached. It didn't: as we got closer it moved to the side.

In the early evening I tried to navigate by the stars and learnt for the first time that the Great Bear is opposite the W of Cassiopeia and revolves like a clock around the pole star. Whenever I looked up at night I could now guess the time within twenty minutes without looking at my watch.

We had given up using the tent. Now we were immersed in the desert, and I felt I was learning its reality for the first time. Throughout the day, instead of kicking wind-blown branches of dead thorn away, we gathered them and stuck them under a bungee cord on the trolley. At night we always had enough for a small fire, enough heat to make tea and boil our soupy stew. The desert was teaching us to dispense with things, stripping us down to the essentials. We were losing weight and getting fitter, needing less water, breathing in time with the level desert sands.

Steve pointed out what looked like a jet-black rock, sitting on the sand in the distance. He was towing and I walked alongside as we approached. By strange jump-cuts of perception I saw it was much closer and smaller than we imagined. We were upon it far sooner than I expected. The 'rock' was in fact a thick ring of solid iron, perhaps part of a lorry engine, but about the diameter of a side-plate. I guessed it might have been left there since the more intense vehicle activity during World War II.

At one point we came across wheeled tracks no wider than our own. They traversed black gravel, the surface that keeps a track longest. No modern vehicle could ever have made such tracks. 'You know what these are?' I asked Steve.

'A donkey cart?'

'Not this far out. These are Almasy's tracks when he made his sponsored Baby Ford expedition in 1936.'

Our trolley was about the same width as a Baby Ford. There was no other explanation. Even more than the ancient camel tracks we'd seen earlier, those tracks brought home the way the desert distorts time to make the past a part of the present. You sense the clever illusion of time. Its bonds are loosened and the soul spreads out. Words that seem used up in ordinary life acquire their ancient significance, become your own for the first time.

Nineteen

GOATS ON THE ROAD TO ENLIGHTENMENT

Back in Mut, at Yusef's resthouse and internet café, things had taken a dramatic turn. Despite Steve's warning the prospect of a cold beer had grown into an image so enticing we had sidelined the madness of Paul. When we arrived, skinny, sunburnt and thirsty, Yusef and Paul were playing dominoes at one of the front tables. They were pleased to see us and I ordered beer for everyone. But Yusef seemed agitated. He ushered us into the restaurant; towards the back a cloth sagged over a huge depression in the floor. Beside it was a great pile of sandy gravel and broken concrete. Yusef whipped back the cloth to reveal a half-filled hole. It looked as if the water main had burst and been excavated.

'Paul, he have a dream,' babbled Yusef. 'He tell me, "Yusef, there is gold under your restaurant." He tell me that the Queen of England tell him. And the pharaohs.'

Paul looked a bit shame-faced. 'It was a dream I had when I saw that there were tunnels connecting this place to the pyramids.'

Yusef interrupted, 'Last Ramadan, a man come into my restaurant and say there is gold under the floor. This is Islamic man. I never tell Paul. Then *he* say there is also gold here so I think it must be true. I ask Paul where and he point here. We dig and dig. One metre and a half. More! Paul, he works so hard. He is digging and digging. Then we find water. Water comes up through the ground. Then Paul says the gold is somewhere else.'

Yusef took us on a quick tour of the other potential gold sites in the restaurant. Beneath the solitary dusty computer. In the shit-besmirched toilet. Under some sacks of rice in the storeroom. Luckily they had yet to start excavating these new sites. 'What you think?' asked Yusef. He seemed both keen to keep looking and disgusted by Paul's involvement. 'I wouldn't dig up the shitter,' said Steve, 'You never know what you might find.' Yusef nodded at this sage advice and pointed at the disinterested Paul, 'He dig and dig but he refuse to fill the hole in.'

'It just didn't feel right,' said Paul, rubbing at the obvious blisters on his soft hands.

Yusef started moaning. 'And there is no customer for two days. I think if Philippe Morel leave Paul's head he come to me and spoil my business.'

Paul nodded at the dangerous complications of his condition.

'What about the cure?' I asked.

This was a mistake. Yusef thought I was questioning his honesty with regard to the money paid. 'OK, we make cure, but what if Philippe Morel leave Paul and come to *me*?'

'Did you do it?'

'No.' Yusef thought for a moment. 'But today we can go at four o'clock to a man who will beat Paul and make Shaitan leave him.'

Paul looked nonplussed. 'What about Sheikh Ahmed and burying the ring?'

'Yeah, what about Sheik Ahmed?' I asked.

Things had obviously moved beyond the sheikh's competence. Now Paul required more drastic treatment. Beating a man who is possessed by a jinn, or evil spirit, is supposed to only hurt the jinn, not the man. That's the theory.

'Do you want to do it?' I asked.

'Well, I can't say I'm that keen on being beaten about the arse by some bloke with a stick.'

'He must use stick!' cried Yusef.

'But if that's the only way to make Shaitan go then I suppose I have to do it,' Paul continued reasonably.

'Four o'clock, then?' I said.

'We go by bicycle,' said Yusef, and then, to emphasize his own sacrifice, he added, 'I shut restaurant. Say no to customer and go with Paul.'

As we left, with a prearranged excuse to visit some rock paintings on the Kharga road, Steve whispered, 'Whatever happens, we've got to be out of here by four. God knows what those guys are going to do next.'

'But Paul seems to be getting a bit better,' I said lamely. 'He's even helping out a bit, he told me. I mean as well as digging that hole.'

Steve snorted. 'Helping out? He told me he was now bringing the chairs in and rolling up the tablecloths every so often. Not exactly the nine-to-five is it?'

Paul and Yusef seemed bound together in a strange compact of greed and dependence. Yusef had captured Paul and was convinced that somehow he could make money from him. He couldn't let go of this idea. And Paul had become dependent on the restaurant as a 'safe place'. He used the word often: 'I started to feel unsafe down there,' or 'I feel safest right here in the restaurant.' Somehow he had changed the meaning of the word, given it sinister overtones. When Paul said 'safe' it flashed up in my mind as 'unsafe for anyone else'.

We visited the rock carvings. They were near to the road – too near: tourists had defaced them with their own signatures and smiley stick-men. Now I knew why I had been to the Gilf.

Then we had to get fuel, but the petrol station was out of stock and what with finding another garage and having a cup of tea and buying oranges we were driving through Mut at 3.45 p.m.

Across the road, cycling through a herd of goats, was the

determined form of Yusef Farid trailed by the languid Paul, for all the world like a couple of tourists rather than two desperate men on their way to an appointment with Satan.

Yusef saw us immediately and waved madly. He turned and started riding after us.

'Quick!' shouted Steve. But the herd of goats had now re-formed around our front wheels. I slowed to a halt. Yusef and Paul were gaining on us.

Jamming my hand on the horn, I hit the accelerator. Goats scattered and my last sight of Mut was in the mirror. Yusef and Paul astride their bicycles surrounded by milling goats, hands raised as if in uncertain salutation, and sad recognition that they were once again alone in their crazy world.

'Christ,' said Steve, 'that was close. I was sure that if we stopped we'd never get away from those two. Or this place. Ever.'

We drove on and didn't stop until we were a hundred kilometres along the desert road. Flat white horizon all around. I stopped the car and the silence was instant. No wind. Nothing.

'You know what?' said Steve.

'What?'

'I love the desert.'

'Me too. How about a nice cup of tea.'

As the kettle heated up Steve lay in the middle of the road, hoping to tempt some traffic to appear. None did. We drank the tea, and like cyclists in the Tour de France made a leisurely display of urinating in full view of the tarmac. Still no cars appeared. We took as long as we could packing up the tea things. I stood in the road looking both ways, like Wile E. Coyote expecting Road Runner. Nothing. Emptiness. Complete silence. Blacktop, blue sky, white sand. We got back in the car and started driving.

Twenty

THE CONTENTS OF THE CONTAINER

It is exactly a year since my close encounter with the container. I still feel emotionally burnt by the experience. It still feels uncomfortably close, as if I might have to do it again soon, even though I intend never, ever to pack a container without an army of paid help. Of course I was in a pretty bad state when I started those long solo drives out to the airfield, deciding what to keep and what to chuck. I'd been away from my kids for several months and assumed they missed me as much as I missed them. But, it seemed, I suffered more than they did. It was the thought that *they had a right* to be not suffering, even though they weren't, that was making me feel bad. Having to empty a house you've lived in, where your kids were born, full of the accumulated junk of years, and size it down to a metal box 20×8×8 feet – that's hard. What makes it hard though is, or was, all in my head. I beat myself up. The self-pity I felt was like all self-pity – self-generated. The container wasn't the problem, I was. It was as if all the accumulated bad faith of living where I shouldn't be living reached its height during the moving out. As if the cosy, suburban, convenient life was fighting for its existence, desperate to keep me in its thrall. It was like that old life was saying, 'Look, this is a foretaste of a big bad world – it's nasty and cold. Stay home and watch television.' The TV was the first thing I got rid of; I sold it to our next-door neighbour – it was either that or the skip, the other container in my life, the outbox, so to speak. Trash the TV. Pack up your bags. Hit the road. Do that and you can do anything – but don't think it will be easy, 'cause the easy life will keep taunting you from its position of safety.

Today the container arrived. A year later and everything I own is here in Egypt. And the whole saga of its arrival is both a microcosm of Egyptian life and an indication of a change, the biggest kind, with far-reaching consequences, a change of mind, or mindset, invisible on the outside.

Shipping the container from England had felt like a cross between buying a house and taking too much through duty-free. It was full of ifs and maybes and dire warnings about taxes, duties, correct packing and insurance – if we got caught. Lots of phone work to Jackie in the office. Not to mention the impossible-to-ignore memories of anxiety and stress that almost did me in packing the thing.

Meanwhile in Egypt, at four-thirty-two in the morning, I gulped a coffee just after the call to prayer; it was Ramadan and there wouldn't be an opportunity to eat or drink until this thing was over, one way or another. I drank some water but could swallow nothing. Mohamed the driver had agreed at one o'clock the previous night to come early, at 5 a.m., to help us magic the container to our new flat. Finally we had a place to put all that stuff I had stored a year ago. But that was only the beginning of our woes. The problems ahead of us at this point seemed insoluble. The problems behind us, already surmounted since the container had safely landed at the wrong port on another part of the coast, seemed dream-like, already fading.

The problems ahead. The container was chained atop a full-length lorry trailer with a full-size tractor unit pulling it. Even trucks half this size are banned from entering the reasonably upmarket area of Maadi where we lived. Trucks a quarter of this size have to get a permit to enter the town, and all entry points are guarded like Colditz – a machine-gun post, a parked

Toyota pick-up, the death-squad special, and three or four black clad cops with nothing to do except water their vegetable garden. Strangely, and fittingly for a nation of uprooted farmers, every police post has a well-tended vegetable patch next to it.

Needless to say we had no permit, nor would getting a permit have been possible because (a) our truck was too large and (b) we had only heard that this huge truck was coming about five hours earlier and the time-frame for getting permits is measured in days if not weeks.

Problems we had solved, mainly with money:

Getting the container from Port Said to Alexandria on a lorry rather than a ship sailing in a year's time

Paying off customs officials

Paying off dock officials

Paying off policemen

Paying off every other parasite whose sole job is to kidnap people's dearest possessions and ransom them for the highest amount.

As far as Customs was concerned we were very lucky. We'd been scalped but the container had not been detained. Most people who import their stuff to Egypt have it stolen, or left until it rots in the corner of a container park no one will tell them the exact location of, or resort to getting letters from ministers just so that their boxed collection of Popeye videos isn't seized as evidence of a pirate porn ring. You have to pay, pay the right people, and then pay them some more since the very act of payment reveals your crucial weakness, the one you want to keep hidden until the last moment: you have money and you *really* want your stuff.

These problems had been surmounted. The truck was supposed to arrive at eight the previous night. I left a rather interesting discussion of the Cairo Desert Exploration Group, which had suddenly begun to attract new people each week, a welcome contrast to those dark months of three beers, ten fags, a bit of carrot and cucumber and dry-roasted nuts courtesy of Hesham the unctuous welcoming manager, my desert books laid out and ignored on the table. Yes, things were changing. My desert-ready car (finally fixed by a decent mechanic, now much more reliable) was parked outside. I was inside talking to interested people about my walk with Steve into the unknown. I drove to my appointment with the container feeling cheerful and utterly disbelieving that it would arrive. No, that's not quite right. I neither believed nor disbelieved. I just knew that by the time the evening had ended things would have developed beyond anyone's prediction, would have spiralled far into the realms of adventure, involving both fantastic luck and swingeing adversity.

Subsidiary problems: The flat was in a side street. The street was full of parked cars. The lorry would block the street for as long as it took to unload. I envisaged horn-honking like nothing before heard, like a full migratory flock of trumpeter swans heading south for winter.

We had been assured that the driver would have an unloading crew. A complete lie. I was faced with unloading an entire container just as I had packed it, alone.

My wife and I and faithful Mohamed waited for the container for three hours. Mohamed waited downstairs as befitted his situation. He went to buy ant powder for the ants and cockroaches already scenting new occupancy of the apartment. I smoked cigarettes, sitting on the only chair in the entire flat. Samia sat on a paint-spattered stool.

Of course we had been told by our fixer at the docks in Alexandria that the driver had left at 5 p.m. the evening before on a journey of about three hours. At 11 p.m. we spoke to the real driver for the first time (his number withheld for precisely this reason) and found out he hadn't even started. And wouldn't, for the simple reason that he knew his truck was illegal in Maadi.

Now, ratcheting up the complication level to one where everyone began to feel more comfortable, we got the landlord of my old writing apartment, which in another century had also been Dr Naguib's hide-out, to plead, berate or otherwise persuade the lorry driver to set off. The landlord, who had a sideline in importing used Vauxhall spares, had recommended the shipping company as one with a problem-free track record. Later I came to nurture dark thoughts about the landlord and the shipping agent splitting the exorbitant fees between them. All transactions in Egypt can be clouded by such thoughts, even the most mundane, like the time I was persuaded by a roadside honey seller that the honey he had indoors was much better than the stuff he had standing outside that I had tasted and approved. Why was he so insistent? There had to be a trick. When he went inside to get the honey I drove away rather than face another ripping-off.

The truck driver, appeased by such high-level begging, agreed to leave sometime after midnight. He would arrive by 6 a.m. Mohamed suggested we get some men to help the next morning. It was now past one o'clock; the streets of Maadi were empty, apart from roving packs of cowardly dogs and taxis with men sleeping inside. Mohamed drove down to the poorer area of El Arab. Two men in rags slept on the kerb. They were from Upper Egypt and eager to work. Very, very eager. They wanted to come right now, even though there was nothing for them to do. Roused from their Ramadan slumbers they just wanted to work anywhere, for anyone, anytime. They had a childlike enthusiasm that was infectious. You never see that enthusiasm in the better-dressed, more worldly-wise workers. It was something good and human that gets pounded out of you by the ordinary urban grind. They agreed to find two more and be at the flat at six. They wanted to bring five others but I said four would be fine. And at the same time I knew they would probably be unable to find our flat despite the easy directions and it being so near. The most excited one was wall-eyed and saluted the car repeatedly as we roared away into the fume-laden night.

Mohamed arrived on time as always at five, his face crumpled and lined yet full of knowing cheer, his breath smelling of cigarette smoke. Being utterly dependent on him reminded me of boyhood missions with my father – fishing without licences or stealing unused runner-bean canes from a market garden.

Dawn at the rendezvous point. Beautiful polluted orange skies layered beneath grey on the darkened stretch of the motorway. This was the closest legal point to our apartment an eighteen-wheel lorry could approach. It seemed foolish to be waiting for something so big to happen in Egypt, of all places. Little things might be expected with humility in Egypt – but surely not one's life's possessions? The driver had answered a phone call at 4 a.m. saying he was almost in Cairo. I took this to be another lie. At 5.45 he was at the pyramids. 'Ask him to describe them,' I told Samia, 'as a test.' It was now past dawn and Mohamed could no longer smoke. He flicked through his vinyl covered zip-up pocket edition of the Koran, possibly for my benefit, I thought uncharitably. Something with English writing on pulled up alongside. A salt- and dust-stained lorry with the container chained to its middle. From England with English writing. Things were verging on the unbelievable, the undeserved, the miraculous.

Mohamed now exhibited the kind of knowledge that all good Egyptian drivers hoard. The secret route off the motorway? Reverse four hundred metres in a wobbly high-pitched scream then turn left behind a Caltex garage towards that enormous pile of empty crisp packets surmounted by grey-shouldered crows. Drive through them, scattering black flapping wings, into a deep inky puddle that smells unnaturally of the sea. Emerge invigorated and descend a gravel bank, making sure the bottom of the car is thoroughly scoured by stones and broken glass. The truck hesitates but follows. Then, through a tunnel under the motorway, breaking down a mini-*barchan* dune of litter and cardboard boxes. Lost? Go straight on past unlit, unwindowed twelve-storey blocks along an unmade road submerged beneath great oily puddles of sewage water. This is the moment of greatest tension – will the sewage water wash through the bottom of the doors? Barely a dribble. Now plain sailing along a road as potholed as a First World War battlefield and over a giant, well-nicked concrete kerb on to a minor road I actually recognize. By a route both clever and circuitous we enter our street without passing a single checkpoint, cop or even police conscript with a sweaty notebook.

The men recruited the night before were not there. It seemed an immense desire to work was not enough; you needed to turn up too. Mohamed set off on another crazy quest, and in the time it takes to smoke a king-size cigarette (no lie) he was back with six more raggedy-looking workers from Upper Egypt in white plastic wellies. I was plagued with wondering why the men from the night before hadn't turned up.

A Fiat car blocked the lorry's ability to park. Cars leaving for work were already honking in a queue behind it. The six workers were eager to demonstrate their worth. They ignored the Fiat's handbrake and bounced and skidded the car out of the way. Enough room was left for cars to squeak by the lorry with minimal hornwork.

We all stared at the back of the container, which was pad-locked. The driver did not have the key. It was quite a big padlock and of course no one had a saw. I had once had a key but had long ago lost it. A key had seemed irrelevant then, but now it was, well, key. With the impatience of born vandals two of our workers set to with a half-brick but it was no good. Then the driver, who was rather well spoken and sported a natty trimmed moustache, produced an iron bar from his cab – most drivers have them in Egypt for roadside displays of machismo. In what I suspected was his party piece he hit the padlock with two strikes. Miraculously it broke in two.

The doors swung open and I observed my life upside-down. Customs must have gone through everything. The unloading began.

One pot, one picture and the decoration on a lamp were broken. A box of books was mysteriously damp. A few tools were rusty. Everything else was unchanged. Even my antique Chinese desk that had reputedly once · belonged to the celebrated cult leader and mystic J. G. Bennett seemed no worse for wear.

Then the problems. The two eager men of the night before plus five others (we'd said *four*, hadn't we, though that was now academic) had at long last found our street. They appealed to me for justice but in a brutal Darwinian struggle, the current movers sensed a dilution of wages and drove the sad-eyed eager useless ones away. Then the driver of the now empty container (everything unloaded and a bit too much *on show* all along the street for my liking) wanted Mohamed to lead him *back* to the motorway. Without prompting Mohamed refused to leave his supervisory position. He was upstairs and I was downstairs, and the Upper Egyptians ferrying boxes were between us. It is well known that movers will steal what they can prise free of any container. Well known by Mohamed and Samia, at least. Our men had shamelessly poked around in some of the boxes and I had told them off but they were hardly to be trusted. I gave away some English coins and some Australian Scout badges that miraculously fell to hand when souvenirs were demanded.

The driver moaned and groaned and pleaded, but we were firm. Mohamed gave him directions but I could tell they were crap. In this country you only got guided in; it was up to you to make your own escape. I gave him a tip, feeling guilty but resolute (the bigger picture etc.), and left him mumbling about how he was certain to be caught. I knew he would be caught. So did Mohamed. The traffic police would skin him for baksheesh, but they wouldn't hold him – as long as he paid.

Sensing a momentary weakness, the workers turned on us in a rehearsed show of indignation at our wage offer. They had removed their wellies to work, the wellies merely being a badge of office that poorer workers lacked. Now they made a theatre of reaching for their white boots, about to storm off. I relented, after suitable indignation at the high price they demanded – £3.50 per man. One of the workers spoke good English, 'My name is Mohamed and I am a graduate of

Sohag college in Arabic literature.' He had a scholar's care with books, was a gentle fellow but no hard worker. As I had always observed, there was one chap, their leader in the negotiations, who worked with the methodical speed and restless activity of real workers the world over. The rest were simply plodders plucked from the fields, but given that the lift was broken (of course) and everything was carted up six flights of stairs they kept going at a pyramid-building rate. Two months to load by one weeping Englishman. Three hours to unload by six workers in white wellingtons, two iron-willed overseers and several wellwishers and assorted helping hands.

The contents had arrived. My Naga spears (at least the handle parts). My rug from Isfahan. My eleventh edition of the *Encyclopedia Britannica* printed on onionskin paper. My son's plastic helicopter. My wife's print of Klee's 'The Kiss'. Our old oak chest that we'd bought in an auction years ago when we felt rich. The desk. It didn't look like much. It was all grubby and walked on – you could see the footprints in improbable places all over the sofa – but it was our stuff.

I had been resigned to never seeing it again. But, unlike in England, here in Egypt I had never felt particularly *worried*. Maybe anxiety lessens as you learn to live in the Orient. Or maybe success seems just too improbable to be worth investing any belief in.

The industrial modern world demands belief. It works so well you expect miracles daily, and the slightest screw-up drives your blood pressure skyward. Here I'd learnt that mostly things didn't happen. And they always took longer. And just when they couldn't ever possibly happen a miracle made everything work faster than in the clunky Western world I had escaped. But you couldn't rely on it. That was the catch. The only thing you could rely on was that life would never turn out as you planned, imagined, hoped or feared; it was indeed, again, an adventure.